P9-BYS-656

PLEASE CHECK FOR
ACCOMPANYING MATERIALS:
1 DVD
(inside back cover)

DIGITAL FILMMAKING FOR TEENS

J/YA/778.59
Shaner
12/09

Pete Shaner and Gerald Everett Jones

DISCARD

THOMSON
COURSE TECHNOLOGY
Professional ■ Technical ■ Reference

Childrens Room
Cheshire Public Library
104 Main Street
Cheshire, CT 06410

DIGITAL FILMMAKING FOR TEENS

SVP, Thomson Course Technology PTR: Andy Shafran
Publisher: Stacy L. Hiquet
Senior Marketing Manager: Sarah O'Donnell
Marketing Manager: Heather Hurley
Manager of Editorial Services: Heather Talbot
Senior Acquisitions Editor: Kevin Harreld
Senior Editor: Mark Garvey
Associate Marketing Manager: Kristin Eisenzopf
Marketing Coordinator: Jordan Casey
Project Editor and Copy Editor: Marta Justak
Technical Reviewer: Christopher Llewellyn Reed
Teen Reviewer: Andrew Martin
PTR Editorial Services Coordinator: Elizabeth Furbish
Interior Layout Tech: Susan Honeywell
Cover Designer and Illustrator: Mike Tanamachi
DVD Producer: Pete Shaner
Indexer: Kevin Broccoli
Proofreader: Tonya Cupp

© 2005 by Pete Shaner and Gerald Everett Jones. All rights reserved. No part of this book may be reproduced or transmitted in any form or by any means, electronic or mechanical, including photocopying, recording, or by any information storage or retrieval system without written permission from Thomson Course Technology PTR, except for the inclusion of brief quotations in a review.

The Thomson Course Technology PTR logo and related trade dress are trademarks of Thomson Course Technology PTR and may not be used without written permission.

iMovie, iPod, iLife, iDVD, iPhoto, iTunes, FireWire, QuickTime, and Final Cut Pro are all registered trademarks of Apple Computer, Inc., registered in the U.S. and other countries. Canon is a registered trademark of Canon, Inc. Gee Three and Slick are trademarks of Gee Three.com. Final Draft is a registered trademark of Final Draft, Inc. Sonicfire and SmartSound are registered trademarks of SmartSound Software, Inc. All other trademarks are the property of their respective owners.

Important: Thomson Course Technology PTR cannot provide software support. Please contact the appropriate software manufacturer's technical support line or Web site for assistance.

Thomson Course Technology PTR and the author have attempted throughout this book to distinguish proprietary trademarks from descriptive terms by following the capitalization style used by the manufacturer.

Information contained in this book has been obtained by Thomson Course Technology PTR from sources believed to be reliable. However, because of the possibility of human or mechanical error by our sources, Thomson Course Technology PTR, or others, the Publisher does not guarantee the accuracy, adequacy, or completeness of any information and is not responsible for any errors or omissions or the results obtained from use of such information. Readers should be particularly aware of the fact that the Internet is an ever-changing entity. Some facts may have changed since this book went to press.

Educational facilities, companies, and organizations interested in multiple copies or licensing of this book should contact the publisher for quantity discount information. Training manuals, CD-ROMs, and portions of this book are also available individually or can be tailored for specific needs.

ISBN: 1-59200-603-5
Library of Congress Catalog Card Number: 2004114416
Printed in Canada
06 07 08 WC 10 9 8 7 6 5 4 3

THOMSON
COURSE TECHNOLOGY
Professional ■ Technical ■ Reference

Thomson Course Technology PTR,
a division of
Thomson Course Technology
25 Thomson Place
Boston, MA 02210

http://www.courseptr.com

Acknowledgments

There are a lot of talented people behind this little book. We want to thank Kevin Harreld, acquisitions editor, for suggesting this title and for enthusiastically believing we were the team to deliver it. (And thanks, as well, to Steve Foldvari of Sony Pictures Digital for introducing us to Kevin.) Marta Justak, editor, provided a light but firm touch at the author-ego control panel and added professionalism to every page of the manuscript. We also value the stellar contributions of cover artist Mike Tanamachi, proofreader Tonya Cupp, layout tech Susan Honeywell, and indexer Kevin Broccoli. We want to give a special mention to Richie Adams, who did the stunning title design for the DVD.

Christopher Llewellyn Reed gave us a solid reality check as technical editor. As both a high-school teacher and a film instructor, his advice was invaluable. He's currently director, Media Arts, at LREI (Little Red School House and Elisabeth Irwin High School) in New York, NY. He's also one of the founding faculty, and Assistant Director, of the School of Cinema and Performing Arts (www.socapa.com). Chris and some of his SOCAPA students brought us a wealth of short films to look at and enjoy, many of which you'll find in the Student Film Festival menu on the DVD. Profuse thanks and sincere wishes for success to the SOCAPA students who contributed their work, including videos, director's commentaries, and/or photos: Kendall Anlian, Camila Fernandez, Nicole Katz, Blake Lewis, David Marcus, Alexa Matz, Jonathan Schwob, Adam Weissman, and David Yeomans. We'd also like to acknowledge and thank the actors in the student movies, some of whom also appear in photos in this book: Derek Abbott, Atraue Brown, Vawnshekia Brown, Ray Chandler, Megan Driscoll, Justin Goldring, Bonnie Jonas, Richard Molson, Chris Overton, Ophélie Poncet, Nick Rosser, Will Sullivan, and Marina White.

Heartfelt personal thanks for their professionalism and enthusiastic participation to our photo models and video production cast and crew: Richie Adams, Joshua Carter, Caleb Cindano, Gordie Germaine, John C. Graas, Elizabeth Hughes, Libby Lavella, Peter Meech, Eve Miller, Bill Pitcher, Traci Shiraishi, and Georja Umano, and the canny comedians of *Friday Night Live* and the faithful supporters of Unleash the Beach.org.

Thanks to our colleagues at the software companies that provided demo applications for the DVD: Frank Colin, vice president, product development, Final Draft, Inc.; Bruce Gee, CEO, Gee Three.com; and Brian Dickman, vice president, marketing and Richard Manfredi, director of public relations, SmartSound, Inc.

Reassuring hugs and kisses to Georja Umano, whose joy of living is contagious, as well as to Matt Wagner of Waterside Productions, who always makes good things happen.

About the Authors

Pete Shaner is a motion-picture writer-director who has written and directed two independent features: *Lover's Knot* (starring Billy Campbell, Jennifer Grey, and Tim Curry) and *Nicolas*, a supernatural thriller (the first independent feature ever shot in 24P HD). In addition, he co-wrote and directed the second unit for the action movies *Shootfighter* and *Shootfighter II*. He also has written for the TV series *JAG* and worked as the on-set technical advisor for *A Few Good Men*. He teaches DV production and techniques at UCLA Extension.

Gerald Everett Jones has written more than 20 books on computer and business subjects, including *Easy Photoshop Elements* and *How to Lie with Charts*. His screenplay *Ballpoint*, a comedy about the outrageous huckster who promoted the ballpoint pen in 1945, was among ten projects to be accepted into the Screenwriter's Lab of the Independent Feature Project/West. He is a past director of the Independent Writers of Southern California (IWOSC) and is a member of the Dramatists Guild and the Writers Guild of America. He has professional expertise in computer graphics, industrial video, and website development and served as writer and executive producer of the InnRoom Shopping Network, a private TV channel in luxury hotels.

Pete and Gerald also coauthored *Real World Digital Video*.

Contents At a Glance

TABLE OF Contents

Introduction: Now Anyone Can Make a Hollywood Movie

As a technology, moviemaking has been around about as long as the automobile—for about a hundred years. And in that century or so, cameras have evolved from hand-cranked film spoolers into the *high-definition (HD)* digital kind filmmakers are just starting to use today. Although early popular movies were silent, flickering, black-and-white, pie-in-your-face comedies, the movies of today are more likely to be super-realistic widescreen extravaganzas with bone-rattling surround sound.

NOTE

When a movie or a computer term first appears in the text, we'll highlight it in italics. That also means you'll find its definition in the glossary in the back of the book. (Sometimes, we also use italics for emphasis and those words will not be in the glossary, but you should be able to tell the difference.)

A century ago, the tools for making color movies with sound simply didn't exist. But just 50 years ago, about the same time the first V8 engines appeared in cars, movie gear had become very sophisticated (although none of it was computerized yet). Back then, movie tycoons had to invest a small fortune to buy this complicated gear. And they needed to hire lots of highly trained technicians to operate and maintain it. What's more, every movie consumed thousands of feet of film. The film was not only expensive to buy, but it also had to be developed in special-purpose chemical laboratories before anyone could see the results. (Some people still make movies this way, but they are about to retire!)

Today, you can make a very respectable movie with tools that will fit in your backpack. In this little book, we're going to show you how to do just that. And the emphasis will be on *showing*, not telling, because, well, it'll be lots more fun that way. In fact, you can learn a lot just from screening the DVD we've included at the back of this book. But if you read the book, too, you'll understand better *why* we advise you to do a thing in a particular way. It's also easier to remember how to do something when you know and appreciate why you're doing it.

We will emphasize Hollywood-style moviemaking, the way the pros do it. (But on a teen-affordable budget.) We'll often use feature film techniques as examples, partly because lots of you share our love of movies. And we'll even encourage you to recreate a favorite scene or two. But remember that the advice and suggestions we give can apply to many other kinds of video projects. You might be just as interested in shooting a music video—now there's a hot project!—or a documentary of your camping trip or a video webzine with school news. We'll offer tips on doing all those things and more.

Quite frankly, in all the history of moviemaking, now is the very best time to be starting out. For one thing, all the tools you need are about as expensive as buying a couple of home computers. (And if you can't buy it, we'll suggest where you can borrow it.) These tools aren't difficult to operate, especially if you know some of the pro's tricks, which we will shamelessly confess.

But best of all, you're living at a time when worldwide video communication is about to explode. The Internet has been around less than 40 years, and, like you, it has yet to realize its full potential. It's already changed the way people all over the globe communicate, and even bigger changes lie ahead.

Consider the fact that you are living at a time when anyone who knows the stuff in this book can distribute her movie to anyone on the planet. . .

. . . at the press of a button (or click of a mouse). . .

. . . and almost for free.

Oh, there's another difference between the old days of film production and now. It's a big difference, and maybe the biggest one of all. Back when it took megabucks to make a movie, the people who owned and managed the studios had a lot of influence over the *ideas* in movies. Today, millions of people can afford to own—and many more can borrow or rent—the relatively inexpensive tools of digital video production. So now, more than ever, moviemakers everywhere on Earth, in rich countries and poor ones alike, should know:

If you don't need their money, they can't tell you what to make.

We don't mean you shouldn't value the opinions and suggestions of your parents and teachers—that's a whole other story! We're just saying that yours is the first generation in the history of moviemaking that doesn't have to go begging for big bucks just to put your stories on the screen.

You Don't Even Need to Go to Film School (Maybe)

Until fairly recently, there were only two ways to learn the art and craft of moviemaking: You could learn on the job, if you were lucky enough to talk your way onto a movie set or into a TV studio. Or you could go to film school. Fifty years ago, colleges and universities didn't even offer courses in film or television. People who worked in the mass media had to get most of their training on the job. Since then, colleges started to offer degrees in subjects like media studies, visual studies, entertainment studies, mass communication, and so on. Today, if you apply for a job at a movie studio or a television network, they might expect you to have majored in one of these areas.

But with the invention of digital video, most of the traditional reasons for going to film school went away. Here are the main benefits for a film-school education, as well as the reasons they needn't apply to you:

Access to equipment. As we just said, you don't need millions or even thousands of dollars of specialized hardware. Sure, the kinds of lights and cameras and sound gear they use to make big-budget movies are still incredibly expensive. But expensive gear is no longer essential for hands-on learning of the basics of visual storytelling. There are still reasons to use the expensive gear to achieve the very best quality. However, some movies made with inexpensive DV equipment have been good enough to be shown in commercial theaters.

Access to directors and guest lecturers. Film schools invite big-name moviemakers to visit classes to share their knowledge. But with the advent of the DVD, you have the same opportunity—for nothing more than the cost of a trip to the corner video store. Switch on the "Director's Commentary" track to any movie that has one. You'll get shot-by-shot descriptions, and probably more information than you'd get in a live seminar. So think of the DVD of any feature film you admire as your personal "film school in a box."

Access to classic movies. What did we just say about DVDs? If your local video store doesn't have it, might we suggest www.netflix.com? Also, some public libraries are beginning to stock classic films
on DVD.

Networking. Film-school students can help create career opportunities for each other after graduation. And influential alumni who are already in the business are sometimes (but not always) able to help. This is the one factor that hasn't changed. And, yes, big media companies and movie studios may still expect to see a film-school degree on your resume—with one exception...

...if you've already made a movie that knocks their socks off.

So, to recap: You don't need a lot of expensive gear, and you can probably borrow what you can't buy (or don't already own). You don't need to wait until film school—and, practically speaking—you can get much the same training by watching DVDs closely, particularly if you pay close attention to the commentaries.

What you *will* need is a small group of motivated friends who also want to get into this stuff. Making movies successfully takes a team. In fact, building a team and learning how to be an effective member of a team are among the most important skills a moviemaker can ever learn. We'll show you who should be on your team, and we'll tell you why.

And along the way, you'll find out why it takes a team to make a movie.

How to Use This Book

One way to use this book is simply to read it from cover to cover (duh). Its chapters and topics follow the sequence of producing a video. You start with an idea, write a script or an outline, plan for production, shoot, edit, and finish. Then you show it proudly to friends, family, and everyone in the great wide world.

But there are other ways of approaching the task. For example:

- You should find a DVD tucked into the back of this book. Load it into a DVD player or a computer with a DVD drive and screen some of the clips. We made some of them, and you'll also find some student productions. By the way, there's nothing here you can't shoot in an afternoon.
- For any clip that interests you, after you've screened it once, rerun it with the Director's Commentary turned on.
- Pick a clip you'd like to imitate. It might be one from our DVD, or it might be a scene from one of your favorite movies.
- Decide what your role will be—writer, producer, director, camera operator, sound technician, lighting technician, musician, narrator, actor, or editor. If you're in doubt, read Chapter 4 to help you decide. (Even if you're recreating a scene, the "writer" may create a shooting script for you to follow.) Don't try to do it all yourself—remember, you need to build a team. To keep the team small and tight, you'll need to double up on some of the roles. The director might also be the camera operator, for example. Or the producer might be the writer or one of the actors.
- Before you shoot, read the parts of the book you know you need help with. For example, writers and producers should read the chapters on scripting (Chapter 2) and preproduction planning (Chapter 4). Camera operators and lighting techs should read up on camera controls (Chapter 3) and the basic principles of three-point lighting (also in Chapter 3). Directors should read it all!
- Also on the DVD, you'll find examples of movie production forms, script format, and demonstration versions of software applications.

NOTE

VERY IMPORTANT: IF YOU PLAN TO SHOOT ANY ACTION SCENES—INCLUDING FIGHTS OR STUNTS—PLEASE READ THE SAFETY INSTRUCTIONS IN CHAPTERS 5 AND 7 BEFORE YOU SHOOT OR EVEN REHEARSE.

You'll also find some general safety pointers in Chapters 5 and 7 that apply to all kinds of shooting situations. For example, whenever you're working with lights—even ordinary household lights—there can be a risk of fire. And whenever you're stringing electrical cords, there's always a risk that an overeager actor or crewmember will trip over one of them. (We'll tell you how it's possible to capture wild action and still be safe.)

You're probably impatient to point a camcorder at something, and we understand.

Go right ahead. Point and shoot. Then come back to Chapter 3 and read how the image quality will be disappointing if you don't turn off some of the camcorder's Auto controls!

The Biggest Hollywood Secret

Okay, we said we were going to confess the secrets of the Hollywood movie pros. We'll start with the biggest one of all.

We envy you.

Let's repeat: It's the best possible time in the history of the world to be starting out as a moviemaker.

So, let's make your movie!

1 What's Your Project?

When you write an essay for school, your instructor expects your ideas to be original. Copying someone else's work will probably get you expelled. Certainly, thinking on your own is an important and essential skill for any educated person. But when you're learning techniques of visual storytelling, don't be too worried about being original. In fact, knocking off scenes from your favorite movies can be a great way to start—maybe it's the best way.

Don't Think Outside the Box—Blow It Open!

As you start out, we recommend you deliberately try to recreate and imitate scenes from your favorite movies. Why? Here are four reasons:

- You will begin with a ready-made enthusiasm for the material.
- A typical movie scene is just 1–2 minutes long. No matter what your level of skill, that's an achievable goal. (In Chapter 2, we'll show you what a *scene* is and how it helps tell a screen story.)
- You don't have to worry about writing a story. The essential drama (or what an audience wants to see) is already built-in. (Drama always involves *conflict,* including conflicts of ideas, but we'll get to that, too.)
- Imitating a Hollywood production will give you an opportunity to pick a scene that contains some *movie magic*. For example, knowing how to make someone disappear, as if by magic, is a valuable trick of the trade. (For more information on dissolving evil witches, see Chapter 7.)

As every honest magician will say, "There are tricks to every trade, and my trade is all tricks." Movie magic also relies heavily on playfully deceiving the audience. For example, actors and stunt people in fight scenes rarely even touch one another, much less exchange physical blows. We'll show you how to make it *look* real—even how one actor can appear to strangle another very realistically while applying no pressure at all to the victim's neck.

But whatever you do, don't attempt to recreate your favorite scene without reading our advice on safety first. (See "Things to Think About on the Set" in Chapter 5.) Professional movie people always put safety first. As you might guess, part of their artistry is making the audience *think* the actors are at risk when they're not.

Even when professionals are incredibly careful, accidents can happen. There can be physical danger to cast and crew even when you're faking an action or simply trying to follow the real thing, such as a fast-moving bicycle. Wherever we can, we will tell you how to be safe. But, it should go without saying, that you should *not* attempt any scene that involves the slightest foreseeable physical danger to anyone. Moviemaking involves careful planning, and we'll show you how to plan shots and actions in detail. At the same time, we'll advise you how to always think about safety first—*before* you attempt the shot.

So, you might guess we're not going to show you how to actually blow anything up. (If those are the scenes you love the most, forget about it.) But we give you full permission to create an explosion on the screen, by way of video editing and digital effects. Pros know that physical explosions are not only extremely dangerous to cast and crew, but they're also *very* expensive. So even pros fake these things whenever possible, and we strongly advise you to do the same.

So, what's all this about thinking outside the box? You said don't bother with being original.

And blowing it open? What's up with that?

By thinking outside the box, we mean you can innovate by doing it the same, yet different. Start by imitating scenes you admire. You'll learn more, and faster, about movie-magic tricks that way. But then, mix it up. Put your own spin on it. Think how you wish it *had* been done. A Hollywood joke is that every producer wants "a new idea that's stood the test of time." In other words, figure out how to tell a familiar story in a fresh, unfamiliar way.

Movie audiences are like little children this way. They want to hear their favorite story—again. But they want the thrill of hearing and seeing it for the very first time. If you can find a way to do that, someday you may capture the hearts and minds of millions of viewers. And you will be a very popular moviemaker, indeed.

So—with apologies to any of you budding pyromaniacs—*that's* what we mean by "blowing the lid off the box."

It's All About DV

This book talks about and uses DV tools and techniques. DV means *digital video*, but not all digital video is DV. Technically speaking, DV is the name of a videotape recording format, such as VHS or Hi-8. But unlike DV, VHS and Hi-8 are older-generation analog formats. They won't work with computer editing software—unless you go through the hassle of converting them to digital. (Don't go there. It's better to borrow a DV camcorder than to make do with the Hi-8 you have at home.)

We recommend that you do all your work in DV because it's inexpensive, it gives high-quality results, and it's designed to plug right into your computer.

The particular type of DV camcorder cassette you will be using is called *Mini DV* (see Figure 1.1). These cassettes are about the size of a small box of wooden matches. A Mini DV cassette that will hold a full hour of recorded video costs about five bucks. Buy a few, just in case you ruin one or just want to experiment.

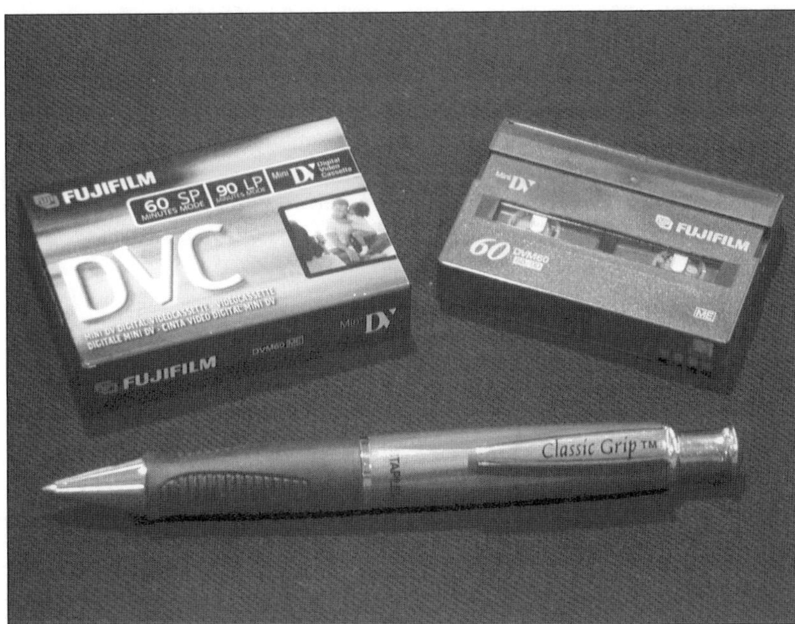

Figure 1.1

Buy the cassettes labeled *Mini DV* or *DVC* and 60-min *Standard Play (SP)*. We don't advise using the 90-min *Long Play (LP)* tapes. The tape stock is thinner, and they can lose data from tape wear and jam in the camcorder more easily.

> **TIP**
>
> We recommend using your DV cassettes just once. Don't reshoot and tape over scenes. That way, you'll always have a backup of your video data. And you can use the least expensive tape because the brand doesn't matter. You also don't need the more expensive tapes (costing about $10 more) with the *IC* feature.

You don't need to go on a big shopping spree to get started making videos. In fact, you can make your first video from a few digital snapshots (or scanned photos) on just about any newer-model computer you can get time on, either at home or at school.

But we're all for preproduction planning, so here's an advance look at the gear you'll need for the projects we'll describe.

The Two (or Three) Big-Ticket Items

There are two essential pieces of gear: a DV camcorder and a computer with video editing software. And we can offer some good reasons to also buy an external FireWire hard drive on which to store your video clips.

> **NOTE**
>
> *FireWire* is Apple's brand name for a high-speed data connection between video hardware devices, such as camcorders, digital tape machines, computers, and external hard drives. The computer industry name for it is *IEEE 1394*, and Sony calls its product *iLINK*. All three names refer to the same thing. Different types of connection, such as USB and Ethernet, generally don't handle video as reliably as FireWire does.

We'll provide more information in later chapters, but here's what you need to know about the gear before starting out.

DV Camcorder

The camcorder we will use in our examples is the Canon ZR40 (see Figure 1.2). We chose it because the Canon ZR series is very popular, it's fairly easy to use, and it gives good results. Its list price at the time this book was printed was $399. (We'll tell you how to shop for a used camcorder in Chapter 3. Before you buy, read the sidebar "You Don't Need to Own a Camcorder.")

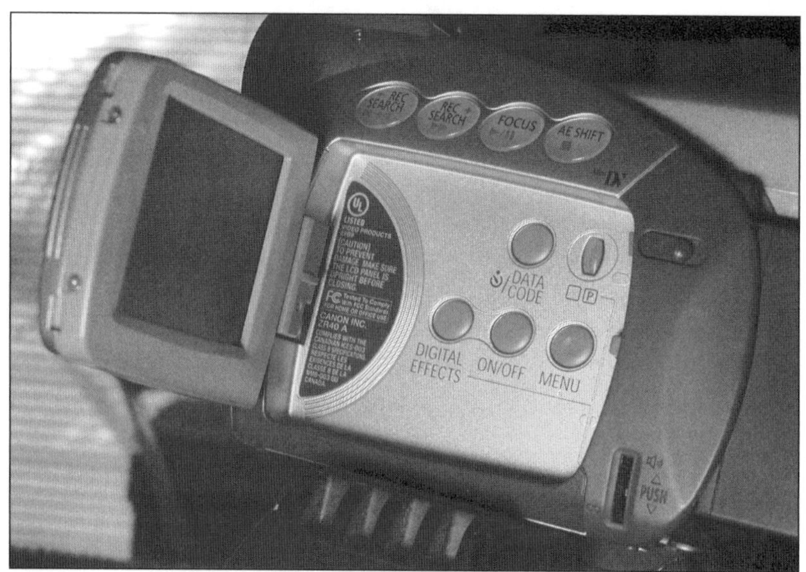

Figure 1.2

Most consumer camcorders have a flip-out LCD screen so you can cradle the camera in your hands, away from your body as you shoot. If you look through the viewfinder eyepiece instead, the bobbing of your head as you walk will cause the camera—and the shot—to bob up and down. A drawback is that this Canon ZR series camcorder loads cassettes from the bottom, which can be inconvenient when the camera is mounted on a tripod and you need to change cassettes.

YOU DON'T NEED TO OWN A CAMCORDER

Before you go rushing out to buy a camcorder (or plead for one as a gift), consider that you don't actually need to *own* one. You'll need it during shooting, which for the types of projects we'll discuss will take you the better part of just one day. And you'll also need it for the time it will take to *upload* your video clips to the computer. Once your clips are stored on the computer's hard drive, you won't need the camcorder anymore until you're done editing. You might want it then for recording output– possibly for less than an hour.

Just because we use the Canon ZR40 camcorder as an example doesn't mean that we recommend you go out and buy that particular one. There are many, many makes and models of low-cost consumer DV camcorders. And they all give good results. Others you might also consider are the Sony Handycam DCR-HC series, Panasonic PV and NV series, JVC GZ and GR series, and the Canon Elura or Optura series. Among the Canon ZR models, we *don't* recommend the ZR80 or any model that doesn't have jacks for an external microphone or S-Video output. However, in other respects it's just as useful as the other ZR models. You can also use any Digital-8 camcorder, provided you shoot in digital mode. (These camcorders use the larger Hi-8 cassettes rather than Mini DV, but the clips upload to your computer as DV.) If you can avoid it, don't use a camcorder that records directly on DVD instead of tape, such as the Sony DCR-DVD series, because the video files it records are MPEG2, which are lower in quality than DV.

NOTE

Throughout this book, we'll use the terms *camcorder* and *camera* to mean the same thing. Technically speaking, a camcorder is a video camera that has a videotape recorder built-in.

Most of the time you spend producing a short video will be involved in editing at the computer. To edit a 1–2-minute show could easily take you a week of your spare time, or more. So, it's perfectly reasonable to borrow a camera for an afternoon's shooting. Also, you don't need to use the same camera for shooting and for uploading, as long as they are both DV. So, to produce one short, you'll typically need the use of a camcorder for two days—one when you're shooting, one when you're uploading to the computer.

If you borrow a camcorder, be sure to handle it with care, because these little electronic marvels are fragile. There are three easy ways to break one: dropping it, spilling any kind of liquid on it, or jamming a cassette in with force. So, if you're going to borrow a camcorder, don't try to use it until you've read our operation tips in Chapter 3.

When you're starting out, we don't recommend using a *prosumer* or professional model camcorder. Examples would be the Canon XL series, any Sony DVCAM camcorder (including the PD series), the JVC GY series, or the Panasonic DVX series (see Figure 1.3). These camcorders cost upwards of

$2,000, and beginners will find them harder to use. We're not steering you away from them because they're expensive to buy. You can probably borrow one from a school program or rent one from a camera store. No, it's more a matter of where you should put your attention. If you use a camera that has professional controls, you'll be more apt to become immersed in the details of camera operation.

Figure 1.3
The Panasonic AG-DVX-100 is a good example of a prosumer camcorder that's popular among independent filmmakers. Even though these are wonderful cameras, we recommend you start out with a simpler, consumer-level camcorder that has fewer manual controls.

We'd prefer you concentrate on storytelling, instead.

After you've shot and edited a couple of short projects, we'd encourage you to try a more sophisticated camera. And, if you take a course in DV production, you'll get your hands on one sooner or later. At that point, the skills you developed with the little ZR will come in handy. And you'll better appreciate why the controls on professional cameras can be so complex.

Personal Computer

The computer we purchased to produce the examples for this book is an Apple iBook G4 (see Figure 1.4), which had a list price of $1,099 when this book was printed. This computer comes with iLife 4 application software, which includes iMovie 4 for video editing. (To support editing, we recommend adding 256MB of memory for a total of 512MB, which costs $100 more, at list price.)

TIP

The iLife suite runs only on Macs. If you have an older Mac (OS 9), you can purchase iLife for $49 (for details, see www.apple.com).

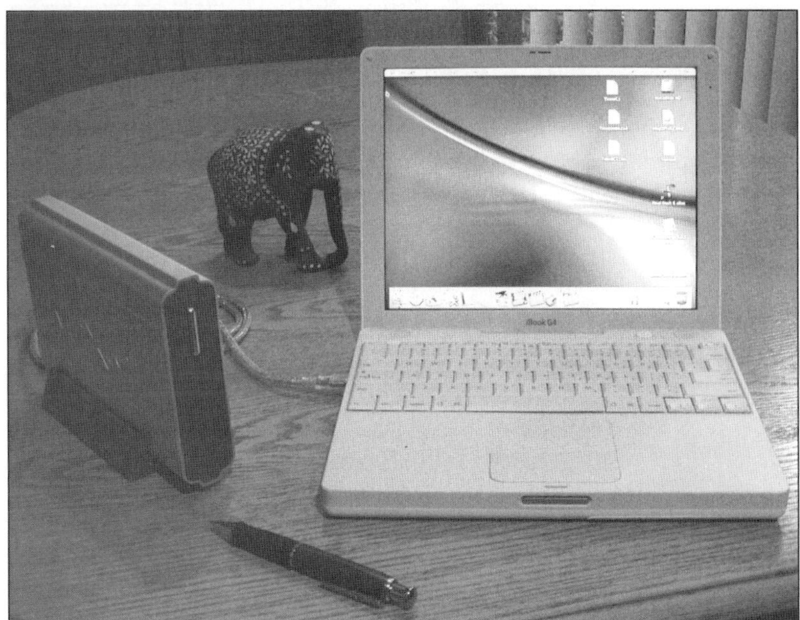

Figure 1.4

The Apple iBook G4 makes an excellent computer-based editing system. It comes with iMovie application software, and it's also powerful enough to run Final Cut Pro. It's shown here with a Maxtor 160GB external hard drive, which plugs into the computer's FireWire port and improves editing performance by storing video clips on a separate drive.

Although we use iMovie for the book's examples, you can do a perfectly acceptable job of editing with Windows applications such as Microsoft Movie Maker, Pinnacle Studio, Sony Vaio Suite, ArcSoft ShowBiz, or Ulead VideoStudio—and there are many others.

As with our camcorder choice, we chose iMovie because it's popular, inexpensive, and easy to use. And, as we did for camcorders, we'd advise against starting out with professional-level editing software. Sure, you want to learn Apple Final Cut Pro eventually. Or, if you're using a Windows computer, you'd consider Adobe Premiere Pro, Avid Xpress DV, Pinnacle Edition, Sony Vegas, or Ulead MediaStudio Pro (and there are others, including a Mac version of Xpress).

But like getting your hands on an XL2 camera, it's too easy to get lost in learning a complex set of controls. Good editing—at any level, beginner or pro—is always about storytelling. An entry-level editor like iMovie is so easy to learn that you can concentrate on telling your story without getting distracted by technical details.

External FireWire Drive

For technical reasons, it's best not to store your uploaded video clips on the same computer drive that holds the editing program itself. Oh, yes, you can do it. But you might experience the annoying phenomenon of *dropped frames*—video hiccups. To avoid this, you can buy an external FireWire drive for about $1 per gigabyte (GB). For this book, we bought a 160GB Maxtor drive for about $200 (refer back to Figure 1.4). It connects easily by way of a supplied cable to the built-in FireWire port on the iBook. (For more information on configuring hard drives for video editing, see the Appendix.)

Another excellent reason to invest in an external FireWire drive is if you plan to do your editing on borrowed computer time. When you are moving around between computers, you can take your FireWire drive and your video and project files with you.

TIP

If you plan to move from one editing computer to another, as in a school media lab, leave your FireWire drive formatted the way it probably comes, as FAT32. This is the only disk format that is compatible with both Mac and Windows. Also, if the drive can use both FireWire and USB 2, stick with FireWire for video editing.

Output Hardware

The iBook we bought doesn't come with a DVD burner. However, it can burn a CD, which can hold a short video CD-R or VCD file. (We'll say more about that in Chapter 9.)

If you want to publish your video show on DVD, you'll need DVD authoring software and a DVD burner. (The iLife suite includes iDVD, which works only with the Apple SuperDrive burner.)

As an alternative, you can output your show to VHS videotape. You start by outputting from the computer to the camcorder through FireWire to record a fresh DV cassette. Then you plug the camcorder's analog Video Out into any VCR and make a VHS copy of the DV cassette. In a similar way, you can also use a TiVo as a video recording device.

Other Gear

If you want to start scoring the other gear you'll need for your video shoot, we've listed most of it in Table 1.1. None of this stuff should be expensive. You can find these items, or close substitutes, around the house. Most of it is lighting gear, which we'll show you how to *rig* and use in Chapters 3 and 5.

Even if you plan to do most of your shooting handheld, you should have a tripod. To hold a little camera like the ZR, you don't need to spend more than $30–50 on a collapsible tripod small enough to fit in your backpack (see Figure 1.5).

Table 1.1 Other Gear You May Need

Item	Used for
Mini DV cassettes	Buy several—camcorders can jam and *eat* a tape
Photographer's tripod	Stationary camera mount
Extra camcorder battery pack(s) and charger	Keeping camera powered outdoors
Camcorder carrying case (or backpack with padding material)	Transporting and protecting the camera
Lavaliere microphone	External sound for closeups and interviews
Microphone (dynamic type)	Sound source external to camera
6-12 ft mic cable with adapter	Rigging the mic
Broom handle	*Boom pole* for the mic
Large sheet(s) foam-core art board	Sunlight reflector (soft)
Aluminum foil	For making a hard sunlight reflector (*shiny board*)
Duct tape	Start calling it *gaffers' tape*
Wooden clothespins	Start calling them *C-47s*—don't ask why!
Photoflood lamps	Interior movie lights
Photoflood reflectors (clamp-on type)	Interior movie lights
Ladders and/or chairs	Interior movie light stands
Extension cords	Power for interior movie lights and camera
Electrical plug-in strips	Power for interior movie lights
Music stands	Cheap substitute for *C-stands*
White handkerchiefs	Start calling them *silks*
Dark-colored bath towels	Start calling them *flags*
Clothes hanger wire	For rigging silks and flags on your C-stands

The gear shown in Table 1.1 is optional, depending on how you plan to shoot. If you were to buy (or borrow) just one item in the list, let it be an external microphone (a *mic*). You can buy one for less than $50. There's more about mics in Chapter 5, where we tell you how to rig an inexpensive mic at the end of a broomstick. It won't give professional-quality sound, but it'll be a whole lot better than relying on the camcorder's built-in mic, for reasons we'll carefully explain.

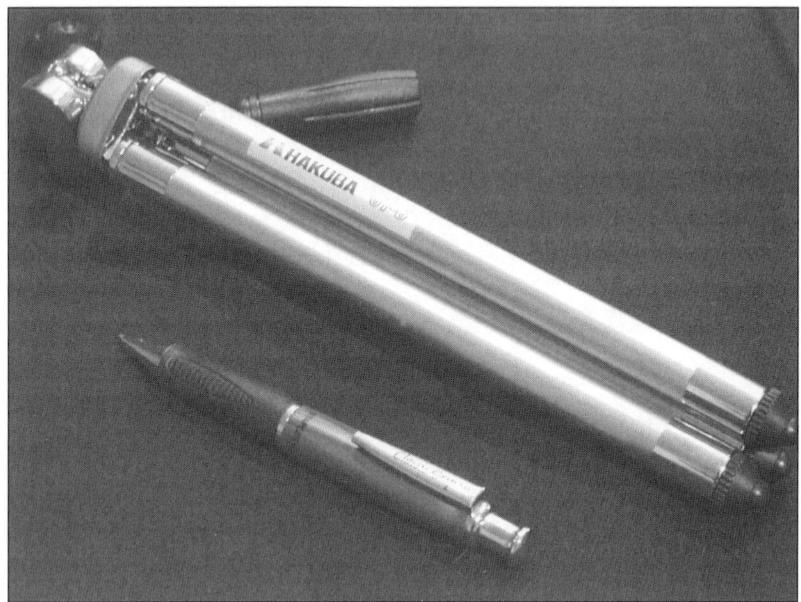

Figure 1.5

This Hakuba tripod is so small you can carry it anywhere. When collapsed, it's less than a foot long—small enough to fit in your backpack along with your camcorder—but it extends to a maximum height of 42 inches. This tripod is designed mainly for static shots. If you need to swivel the camcorder during a shot, you'll need a larger, sturdier model.

Where to Borrow It

Now, you *can* rent all kinds of professional movie gear from some photo outlets and camera stores. But, depending on the store's policy, someone over 18 who has a credit card will probably have to be responsible for it.

However, there are several places in your town where you can borrow the stuff (by paying a small course fee):

- **Schools.** Some high schools have media labs, and many that don't will have after-hours camera and video clubs. Ask around, and you might be able to borrow a camcorder, lights, microphone, and computer editing system.
- **Cable TV stations.** The operators of cable stations are required by law to offer *public access programming,* a way for ordinary folks to put their shows on the air free of charge. To achieve this, many stations offer inexpensive courses in video production, equipment included. Okay, the equipment might be antiquated and not DV, but it doesn't hurt to find out. Call the station, ask for the public access department, and ask what's available. You might need an adult sponsor, but it's worth a try.

- **Community college extension classes.** Many community colleges offer low-cost video production courses, usually during evening hours. Depending on the policy, you might not have to be college age to take the courses. If you're enrolled, you'll probably have access to the media lab and its computer editing systems, and possibly to other equipment, as well.

You Can Start Right Now

So, if you haven't picked up on it by now, we'll spell it out: There's no excuse *not* to start making your own videos right now. You don't need a rich relative to buy you the gear—it's fairly inexpensive. But if you don't already have it and can't afford to buy it, you can probably borrow what you need. Or you can become a familiar face in the media lab, if your school has one.

And you don't need professional-level stuff. Coping with its complexities will only get in the way of thinking about your story.

Remember—no matter how skilled you become, now or ever—it's always all about storytelling.

In the next chapter, we'll talk about what a story is and, most of all, what a *screen story* should be.

FROM THE DIRECTOR'S CHAIR

Director Francis Ford Coppola (*Apocalypse Now, The Godfather*) once commented that directing a big-budget movie is like running down the tracks trying to keep ahead of a speeding train. If you trip, you're dead meat. One thing no director can afford to do on the set is hesitate. Time is money, cast and crew are waiting for instructions, and the sun keeps moving and the light keeps changing. You have to work fast, work smart, and always know what you want (or act like you do).

A lot of the work of making a feature film goes into detailed planning long before the camera rolls. Now, planning might sound like boring stuff that business executives do, but it's absolutely essential. You need to think carefully ahead of time about every important detail you want to see on the screen and in the soundtrack. Because if you don't plan for it, it won't be there for your camera to see.

This is why we emphasize *thinking* about your project in the early chapters of this book. Some of it's creative—what shots will tell the story? And a lot of it is technical—how will we light the scene?

And in the real world, when you're spending other people's money, they always want to know ahead of time exactly what realizing your grand creative vision will cost.

Let me put it this way: Planners get to make their movies. Dreamers don't.

Even if you're not spending big bucks, planning has its benefits. We shot "Neo's Ring" in a day with a few friends who got nothing for their trouble but cold pizza for lunch. If we hadn't planned our shooting day very carefully, they'd have sat idly by for long periods of time while we fretted about what to do next. Your volunteer cast and crew can't ever think that you're wasting their time. Otherwise, if you ask them back—whether it's for an extra shooting day or for the next project—they'll tell you they have better things to do.

2 Pick a Story

It's every moviemaker's goal to create an experience that will satisfy an audience. You must make something that people will want to watch.

Every movie worth watching tells a story. It's true for blockbuster action-adventure films. It's true for TV commercials that try to sell you something. And it's true for music videos—even if there isn't a story in the song lyric. It's even true for abstract video art, which seeks to transform the way you think or feel in the moment you're watching it (see Figure 2.1).

Figure 2.1

All visual presentations, whether film or video, aim to change the way the audience thinks or feels. Abstract video art dazzles with its imagery, but it doesn't usually tell a story. However, it does evoke emotions, perhaps strong ones. This blurred image of a salsa dance floor conveys the soul of the music and the frenzy of the dancers.

So, start out by understanding the story you want to tell. Do that before you pick up your camcorder and call your actors to the set. In particular, understand the *drama* in your story and how you plan to put it on the screen in a way that will excite and entertain the people who watch it.

In the first chapter, we suggested that your first video project might be to recreate a scene from a movie you like. Even if you're borrowing someone else's story, you should understand the story it tells—and why that story works as screen drama.

Wait, you might say. Lots of videos don't tell stories. Instructional videos, for example, teach the audience how to do something—cosmetic makeovers, for example. But even a video that offers an explanation or delivers a message must also tell a "story." The story covers all the steps required to do the thing, presented in a logical sequence.

So, your story can be a message, but it still needs all the elements that make stories interesting to watch.

Your Three Main Choices

There are many, many types of screen stories and messages, but let's consider three main ones:

- Narrative
- Documentary
- Performance

Narrative

Narrative movies tell what we all think of as traditional stories—for example, knights and dragons, star troopers and aliens, or a boy and the girl next door. Feature films fall into this category. The stories may be fiction, such as improbable sci-fi fantasies. Or, they may be based on real events—the life story of a famous person, for example.

In a classic narrative, a hero does battle with an opponent to achieve a worthy goal. There are, of course, many variations. But even a tender love story is a kind of "battle," a contest of wills between opponents (the lovers) to reach a goal (usually, deciding to stay together, despite their differences).

Some movies—particularly the made-for-TV kind—say "based on a true story" or "inspired by real events" under the title. This means that at least some of the characters in the movie actually lived, and some of the events actually happened. But it's also a sort of warning that some elements of the story are made up. That's often done to make a real story more dramatic and more compelling to an audience.

Real life, just the way it happens, isn't always dramatic. Let's face it—life can be downright boring at times. So just turning your camera on and pointing it at reality won't necessarily capture an interesting story.

Remember this notion that good stories must be dramatic and compelling. Drama makes a story interesting and exciting to watch. (We'll explore the idea of what makes a story dramatic shortly.)

NOTE

Speaking of drama and conflict, Harry Potter's educational adventures at the Hogwarts School are much more thrilling because the audience knows a single fact—the evil Voldemort wants to kill him. Harry is the son of two powerful wizards, whom the villain has already killed. Harry is always in mortal danger because Voldemort wants to do away with him before the boy develops his mature supernatural powers. The audience cares more about Harry because he's always literally fighting for his life.

Documentary

An example of a documentary video is any clip on the TV evening news. A news clip aims to capture a real event; it's not a fanciful story at all. The clip might show the event as it unfolds—for example, a surveillance camera's record of an armed robbery. Or a reporter might visit the scene soon after the crime and interview witnesses, who appear on camera and describe what they saw. In this case, a documentary is called a "slice of life" because it *documents,* or makes a record of, real life.

TIP

An on-camera interview is a type of documentary that's fairly easy to shoot. You don't necessarily need a crew, and it can be an excellent first project. We've included several examples on the DVD, including "Selling the Punch" about safe stunt-fighting techniques.

Now, we said that life, just the way it happens, can be boring. And that popular movies often play with the truth to make it more interesting. In a narrative movie, the main goal is to entertain. So, studio executives figure that it's not so terrible to make stuff up as long as it makes a better story.

TIP

"Reality TV" shows like *The Apprentice* are documentaries. But the circumstances are contrived, and the results are not exactly accidental. For example, players in this game with Donald Trump are cast and teams are picked to emphasize the clash of personalities. Notice how much the audience *cares* about the outcomes! These shows are realistic situations that are altered by using Hollywood story techniques to make them more dramatic.

Most people regard documentaries as a form of news. They assume that documentaries try to show the truth, with no distortions. Indeed, documentary moviemakers try to show the truth—or what they consider to be the truth. They don't—and shouldn't—alter the facts, but they can be guilty of selecting only those facts that support their opinions. Experienced filmmakers know that, if a documentary doesn't have a unique point of view, audiences will find it much less interesting to watch.

In fact, the goal of documentarians is usually to persuade as well as to entertain. The producers not only want to show what happened but also to have the audience form an opinion about it. Of course, they want the audience to buy *their* opinion. That's not the same as trying to tell an entertaining, fanciful story, even a story that teaches some kind of moral lesson.

You may have seen feature-length documentaries by Michael Moore, which include *Roger & Me, Bowling for Columbine,* and *Fahrenheit 9/11*. He claims that the things he shows in his movies are facts. But he admits that the things he says—as a narrator—are his opinions about what those facts mean.

NOTE

Many documentaries don't appear to be controversial and don't try so hard to persuade. But it's not exaggerating to say that all documentaries have a point of view. For example, you might think that a show about the history of the dinosaurs on PBS or The Discovery Channel has a neutral point of view—but you'd be wrong. The entire presentation is based on the assumption that scientific study is valid and valuable. And it implies—perhaps without specifically raising the issue—that Darwin's Theory of Evolution is also valid. However, if you step outside this scientific point of view, you'll find many people who argue vehemently that the whole notion of evolution contradicts religious teachings about the creation of life and must therefore be incorrect. Controversy? You bet!

Moore's comments describe pretty accurately what all documentaries do. Yes, they show real events. But real events, by themselves, aren't necessarily interesting or meaningful to an audience. That's why a standard technique of documentaries is to link the events with *voiceover* narration. The audience hears the narrator talking on the soundtrack but doesn't see her. Instead, scenes appear on the screen that illustrate what she's talking about. The narrator not only helps the audience understand what they are seeing but also suggests what they should think about it. The narrator's commentary also adds interest—overcoming, in a different way than fiction does, the problem that real life sometimes just doesn't make sense.

All documentaries have—and should have—a point of view. And skillful documentarians can be influential makers of public opinion. Now, we could advise you not to abuse this power. We won't. Go ahead. Shake up the world. Some people say that DV really means the "Democratization of Video." Through desktop video and the Internet, millions of people now have access to the tools of mass media—for the first time in human history. That's real power. Don't let anyone take it away!

NOTE

Okay, it may be confusing that narrative movies tell fictional stories and documentaries almost always have narration. But, think about it this way: By providing a *story line*, or thread of events, narration puts the narrative into documentaries. It's always all about the "story!"

Performance

By *performance video,* we mean a record of an artistic performance. A rock band number. A stand-up comic's routine. An actor's audition tape.

NOTE

There's a special category of theater called *performance art,* and we're not necessarily talking about that. We mean a taped record of any kind of performance, such as musical, theatrical, or comedic.

These videos must also tell stories that are interesting to watch. For example, a music video that simply captures an on-stage performance may succeed as music, but it may be deadly dull visually (see Figure 2.2). That's why the slick music videos you see on TV add visual stories to accompany the music. The lyrics of the song may suggest the visual story. Or, if there's no story in the song, the video makers will build one, usually around either the fantasies the song evokes or the star's persona and lifestyle.

Figure 2.2

No matter how much energy a musician shows on-stage, it might not interest an audience enough to carry a whole music video. Instead, you can add a visual story to the music track that illustrates the story in the song lyric, a fantasy suggested by the song's mood, or a revelation about the singer's lifestyle.

Stand-up comedy doesn't usually rely on a separate visual story line. After all, the audience wants to see the comedians' gestures and body language as they deliver their jokes. You might well ask how a joke—especially a snappy one-liner—can be a story. It's usually not. Instead, it's an illustration of the comedian's overall story. Like some music videos, the comic star's story centers on his lifestyle or reputation. The lifestyle is often fictional or exaggerated, to emphasize its humor (see Figure 2.3).

Figure 2.3

Some comedians do *skits*—acted-out stories—that involve fictional personalities they create. Here's Los Angeles comedienne Georja Umano displaying a whole lot of feminist attitude in her skit, "Pick Up the Phone and Call Angry Housewives Moving and Storage."

For example, Chris Rock has built a comic reputation as a person who is easily pissed off. Stupidity, in all its forms, infuriates him. All his jokes build on that story.

When an actor does an audition tape, a scene for a demo reel, he won't get any calls if he picks an uninteresting story. What makes a scene interesting? Drama—ah, we keep coming back to that!

What Makes a Good Screen Story?

A good story has a beginning, a middle, and an end. It takes the audience on a ride from here to there. In fact, movie executives often refer to great stories as "rollercoaster rides." When they find a story they like, they've been known to say, "That's a ride I'd like to take."

But just the idea of a rollercoaster ride is not a story. Footage of you and your friends screaming and holding fast as you plunge up and down the rails could be a gigantic bore for anyone who wasn't there. No, a good story about a rollercoaster ride would have a beginning, a middle, and an end. If your story doesn't have these three steps, the audience won't be satisfied. Your show will seem incomplete. It will play like a single scene that makes a point, perhaps, but "goes nowhere." Your ride should take the audience from a starting point where they believe something, through a series of events that leads to a discovery, and finishes by changing how they think or feel about the thing you focused on at the start. Here's how a story should get from here to there:

- In the beginning, we see you trying to convince a friend to go with you to the theme park. Your friend might be afraid to go on the ride. You have to convince him it'll be fun.
- In the middle, we see you getting on the ride, still debating about whether it's a good idea. Then you take the dizzy ride, and we, as the audience, participate in all its twists and turns, all your gasps and yells.
- Then at the end, we see you and your friend looking back on the experience. We find out what your friend thought of it, whether he's still your friend, and we form some idea about whether we'd consider doing it ourselves!

Again, the ride by itself is not a story. It's a situation. And the idea of a guy who's scared to go on a ride isn't a story, either. That's a type of character. But the idea of two characters that decide to go on a ride that tests their friendship—now, that's an interesting story.

We've already used the term *scene* a few times, but we haven't explained it in movie terms. Here goes: In any movie, a scene does one of two things (or both):

- Gives the audience new information about a character.
- Shows an *action* that advances the story. (An action is anything that we see a character do on the screen.)

A good screen story can be shown visually as a series of scenes. A comic strip is an example of a series of visual scenes that follow a story line. A series of scenes that shows a major event in a movie is called a *sequence*. One test of whether your story is visual can be whether it works as a *story-board*, which resembles a series of comic-strip-style panels.

TIP

Another way to tell whether your story works visually is to imagine how it would play as a silent movie. Would the audience get the story if there were no dialogue at all? At some film schools, first-year students are required to shoot their projects as silent movies, which forces them to think more visually. You might want to consider a silent movie as your first project. Take a look at "Sweet Reward" on the DVD (see Figure 2.4).

Conflict: The Essence of Drama

Drama is what makes a story interesting to watch. Quite simply, drama is conflict—in all its forms—over something that matters to the audience. That's why action-adventure movies are full of fight scenes. Every audience in any country in any language can understand the drama of a physical struggle.

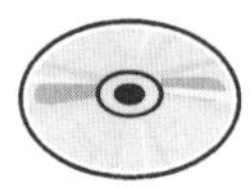

Figure 2.4
Making a silent film is a wonderful way to develop your visual storytelling skills. "Sweet Reward" is a silent short by student Kendall Anlian. It tells the story of a practical joke that backfires. (Photo courtesy Kendall Anlian, SOCAPA)

But fight scenes, in themselves, aren't necessarily any more interesting than that rollercoaster footage. The audience wants to know the story behind the fight. They want to know what the hero is fighting for—what's her goal? And what does her opponent want? What's at stake for both of them? What is each putting at risk? His life, certainly. But possibly, his way of life, his ideals, his beliefs.

The bigger the stakes, the higher the drama. So it should come as no surprise that the typical action hero's goal is to prevent the destruction of the world as we know it!

But conflict doesn't always involve physical violence. That's just as true in our daily lives as it is on the screen. Arguments, debates, court trials, or differences of opinion, are all forms of conflict. And they can all be the stuff of compelling drama.

Thinking Visually: Avoiding the Dreaded Talking Head

Audiences would much rather see an action take place than hear a character describe what is happening off-screen. One of the most common mistakes of the rookie moviemaker is the dreaded "talking head"—having characters talk about what they have done or are going to do, rather than showing them doing it (see Figure 2.5).

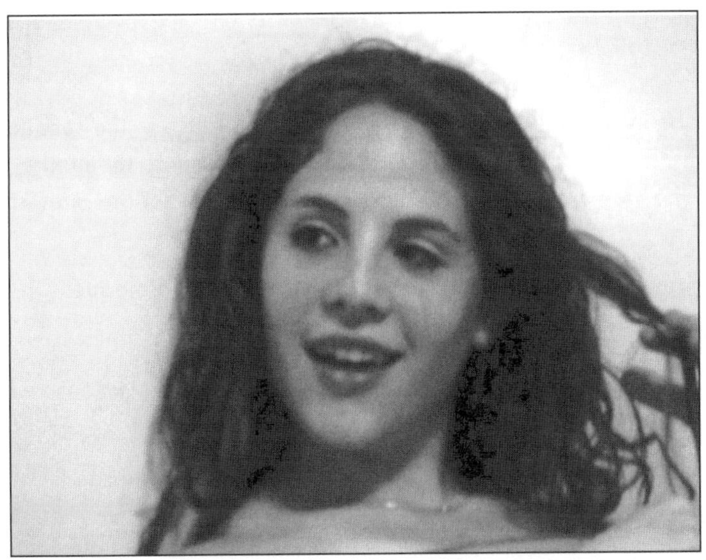

Figure 2.5
For talking-head scenes to be effective and interesting, the dialogue must carry the drama. In a love story, the drama is often from the lovers' disagreement, with perhaps an emotional element of longing or betrayal. (Photo courtesy Adam Weissman, SOCAPA)

For example, here's the script for a talking-head scene:

```
OUTSIDE MUTT'S HOUSE, HE AND JEFF STAND TALKING

MUTT: What do you say we get a video, grab a pizza, and invite Pookie and Mookie over to my house?

JEFF: Yeah, sounds like a plan.
```

Here's the same story, told visually:

```
OUTSIDE MUTT'S HOUSE, HE AND JEFF CLIMB INTO HIS CAR

MUTT (as he gets behind the wheel): Here's my plan...

IN THE VIDEO STORE, JEFF AND MUTT HOLD DIFFERENT DVDs, CAN'T SEEM TO DECIDE WHICH TO RENT

AT THE VIDEO CHECKOUT COUNTER, MUTT PAYS FOR A DVD WHILE JEFF LOOKS ON APPROVINGLY

IN MUTT'S CAR, HE SPEAKS ON HIS CELL PHONE

IN POOKIE'S CAR, SHE SPEAKS ON HER CELL PHONE, SEEMS TO NEED CONVINCING, THEN GETS A NOD OF ENCOURAGEMENT FROM HER PASSENGER, MOOKIE

AT THE PIZZA PARLOR, MUTT AND JEFF HAGGLE OVER THE MENU

OUTSIDE THE PIZZA PARLOR, MUTT EMERGES WITH A STEAMING CARDBOARD BOX; JEFF FOLLOWS DUTIFULLY
```

```
IN MUTT'S LIVING ROOM, HE LIFTS THE LID ON THE PIZZA, OFFERING SLICES TO COMELY GUESTS POOKIE AND
MOOKIE, AS JEFF SMILES BROADLY AND POPS THE DVD IN THE PLAYER
```

So, one way to solve the talking-head problem is simply to show rather than tell. Notice in the second example that Mutt doesn't explain his plan. He just says, "Here's my plan," and we cut to the next scene. Telling the story this way engages the viewers' curiosity. If they want to know what the plan is, they'll have to pay attention and watch.

Notice also that none of the scenes that show the unfolding of Mutt's plan contain any dialogue. Oh, you could have some. But you don't need it to explain what's happening.

Emotion: The Prize at the Bottom of the Box

Another way to relieve the boredom of talking heads is to keep the dialogue but also to charge it with emotion.

And the best way to engage the viewers' emotion is—you guessed it—to start an argument.

In the story of Mutt and Jeff, it's a snore to listen to Mutt talk about his plans. But if he and Jeff disagree about what to do, that's more interesting. And you can end up giving the audience the same information.

Notice in the second, more visual example, we don't just show the boys running errands. They disagree about making choices—about DVDs and pizza toppings. And through this disagreement, we get a sense of the characters' personalities: Mutt is the instigator. Jeff always gives him a hard time, probably to make him think he's not just a follower. But he ends up going along, anyway.

In fact, turning up the emotion makes any scene work better. That's why the audience wants to know what the hero has at stake when he picks up his light saber to do battle. They want to—they need to—*care* a lot about who wins.

The most thrilling ups and downs in any movie rollercoaster ride are emotional. And you engage emotions by showing a conflict in which something valuable is at stake. If you can figure out how to take an audience on a rollercoaster ride of emotion, you'll deserve your own star on the Hollywood Walk of Fame.

Your Screen Story Checklist

Okay, here's a recap of the advice in this chapter. Refer to this list as you think about what to shoot for your video project:

1. Decide whether your project is narrative, documentary, or performance. Then think about how you'll show and tell it as a story that an audience will want to watch.
2. How does your story unfold? What are its beginning, middle, and end?
3. How can you show your story as a sequence of visual scenes?
4. If you're shooting a documentary, what facts do you want to show? What is your opinion or your point of view about those facts?
5. Pick a scene to shoot. How does it show more information about a character or advance the action of the story?
6. Is the scene dramatic? What is its conflict?
7. Who are the characters in the scene, what does each want, and what's at stake for them? (See Figure 2.6.)
8. How will you make the audience care about what happens in the scene?
9. Is the scene visual? Does it rely on action more than on dialogue?
10. When the scene (or movie) is over, what do you want the audience to do? To think? To feel?

Figure 2.6

A chase scene can be exciting, but it helps to know what's at stake. Who are these men and why are they chasing this fellow? What do they want? Is it something in the briefcase? What will be the consequences if whatever they're after falls into the wrong hands? (Photo courtesy David Yeomans, SOCAPA)

Get It in Writing

For a lot of good reasons, it's good to have your scene on paper. You needn't be too worried at this point whether it's in the form of an outline, a storyboard, or a script. (We've included a sample script on the DVD.)

We'll call it a "script" even if it's just some notes or a few sketches. You'll need it for planning your shoot, as well as for discussing what you're going to do with your cast and crew. In fact, having a script promotes teamwork because it's a written agreement about what you're going to shoot. And if you'll be recreating a scene from a movie, make yourself a script to go by.

We encourage you to pick a short scene rather than a longer project. We don't want you to wait too long before you get something on tape. But after you've shot and edited a few of these shorts, you might want to try writing a longer screen story. By all means, come here to review the advice on what makes good stories. But this brief chapter can't begin to describe what's involved in actually writing a screenplay. For that, we can recommend two of the many excellent books on the subject:

- *The Art of Dramatic Writing* by Lajos Egri (a book for playwrights that has become a bible for screenwriters, too)
- *Screenwriting 434* by Lew Hunter (a case study in how to write a script, following an actual film-school course)

For now, once you've picked a scene and you're confident it will work on the screen, go ahead and read Chapter 3 to prepare for the shoot.

FROM THE DIRECTOR'S CHAIR

Professor Lew Hunter of UCLA, who wrote the book on screenwriting we recommend so highly, has over the years been a personal friend, a mentor, and a colleague of ours. Lew has taught some of the most successful screenwriters in Hollywood. Notable among them is Shane Black, who broke into the business with a screenplay called *Lethal Weapon.*

Lethal Weapon has become a classic in the genre of action movies. And there's no question that its chase scenes, fights, and explosions are thrilling. But they're all the more thrilling because of the underlying emotion in Black's screenplay. It's something Lew preaches—that an action story always works better when it has "heart." In the case of *Lethal Weapon,* it's the close bond between the two main characters. Sgt. Murtaugh (Danny Glover) is a mild-mannered veteran cop, a family man who's looking forward to retirement. Sgt. Riggs (Mel Gibson) is a suicidal rogue with a death wish. Murtaugh thinks Riggs is reckless and foolish, but the brash younger man never hesitates to risk his own life in seemingly impossible situations to save his partner.

The brotherly bond between the two officers is the emotional heart of the story, the element that makes the audience care all the more about the outcome of every fight with the bad guys.

And, it's also what screenwriters call an *engine of comedy.* The clash between the two personalities is always entertaining and often funny. As Riggs dashes back impetuously into yet another life-threatening situation, all Murtaugh has to do to make the audience laugh is shake his head in bewilderment.

On our DVD, "Neo's Ring" is primarily an action story involving a frenzied chase, but notice that it kicks off with the beginnings of a love story. If Traci doesn't make it back from that alternate universe she's trapped in, there's a guy waiting on a park bench who will be devastated.

3 Getting the Basics

Okay, you've picked a scene from your favorite movie that you want to shoot. Or, if it's not your first time out, you have a story of your own you want to tell, an event you want to capture, or a message you want to deliver.

It's time to gather up your gear, take it out of the box, and find out how it all works.

You might wonder whether you really need to know these kinds of technical details. Maybe you don't think of yourself as a technician. Perhaps you don't expect to actually operate the camera, the lights, or the sound equipment.

Even if you think of yourself mainly as a writer or an actor and you never intend to touch a camera, it's still a very good idea to know how this stuff works. After all, how else will you know what's possible? Also, the basics of movie production will become a common language for your cast and crew. This language will help you share your ideas about what you want to create—and you don't want to be left out of that discussion.

Again, on any movie set, it's all about teamwork!

Get to Know Your Camcorder

As we said in Chapter 1, we're going to use the Canon ZR40 consumer camcorder in our examples. It's fairly typical of the low-cost DV models from various manufacturers.

For example, all camcorders have the same basic controls and functions. But the exact ways you operate them—starting with the types and locations of the switches on the camera—can vary considerably from one make or model to another. So, keep the user's manual for your camcorder handy. You may need to refer to it as you read this chapter to see how the controls on *your* camcorder work.

TIP

You don't necessarily need to buy a camcorder. It's perfectly okay to borrow one. Just treat it with respect by learning how to use it correctly and handling it with care.

Before you shoot your scene, set aside at least a couple of days to familiarize yourself with the camcorder's controls. Start by shooting a *test roll.* Point the camcorder at your dog or your baby sister and try to get an acceptable image on tape. And remember, test rolls aren't just for newbies. Professional cinematographers often use rented cameras they've never seen before, and none of them would think of shooting an actual scene without shooting a few test rolls first.

SHOPPING FOR A USED CAMCORDER

An alternative to buying a new camcorder or borrowing one is to buy a used one. However, these are delicate instruments that are easily damaged. Handle your camcorder with care. Keep it away from moisture, dirt, and sand. And, you'll be truly sorry if you drop it.

We don't advise buying a used camcorder on the Internet or through the mail, unless you're dealing with a reputable store or outlet that offers a warranty. Preferably, inspect the unit before you buy it. Take along your own DV cassette, load the camera, and shoot some footage on the spot. Play it back on the camcorder and see what you get. Use the Fast Forward and Rewind controls to shuttle the tape back and forth several times. You're trying to see whether it will eat tape, getting it tangled and snarled in the tape-drive mechanism, which is a common problem with defective camcorders. (Jamming the seller's camcorder might be embarrassing, but it's not as bad as taking the problem home with you!)

You can shop for used camcorders on eBay, but our favorite site for this stuff is www.craigslist.org, which runs free classified ads. There you may be able to find one for sale in your local area—so you can pay a visit to the seller and try before you buy.

How Camcorders Work

Film cameras record images on chemical coatings that are sensitive to the color and brightness of light. By contrast, DV camcorders—in fact, all types of video cameras—use photocells instead of film. The photocell generates electrical signals, responding to the brightness and color of light that it receives. Electrical circuitry in the camcorder converts those signals into digital data and records it on the magnetic tape of the DV cassette.

NOTE

The type of photocell chip in most DV camcorders is called *CCD*, or *charge-coupled device*. A CCD is a matrix of *pixels*, or individual light-sensitive picture elements (see Figure 3.1). A pixel responds to one primary color of light—either red (R), green (G), or blue (B). Consumer camcorders typically have a single CCD that arranges R, G, and B pixels side by side on the same chip. Prosumer and professional camcorders give sharper images by using three separate CCDs, one for each RGB color. This type of camera is designated *3CCD*. In general, three chips are better than one, but more advanced single-chip technologies are on the way.

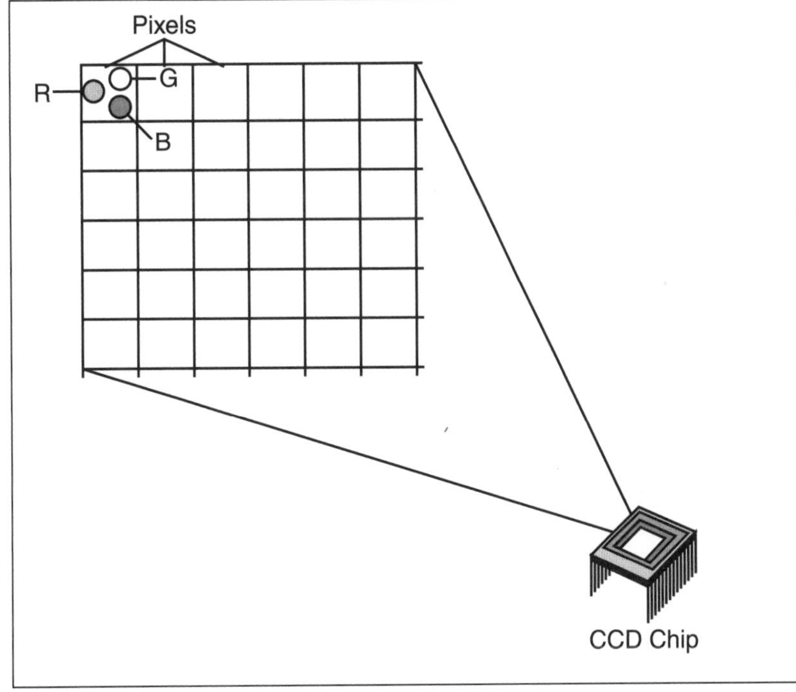

Figure 3.1

In a camcorder with a single-chip CCD, such as the Canon ZR, red (R), green (G), and blue (B) light-sensitive photocells are arranged side by side in a matrix.

When it comes to capturing images, all camcorders have three basic controls:

- Exposure
- Focus
- Zoom

Exposure

The camcorder's exposure setting controls how much light reaches the CCD. It works much like the iris of your eye—opening wider to admit more light, smaller to admit less. And it has the same purpose, which is to make the scene appear neither too bright nor too dark.

The camera's variable opening works much like the iris of your eye. It's called the *aperture.* (It's also correct to call it the *iris.*) The precise amount of opening is called the *f-stop* (just as it is on photographic cameras). When the aperture is open wide, the f-stop number is small. A setting of f/1.6 is as wide as you can get most camcorders, for example. When the aperture is small (called *stopped down*), the f-stop number is larger. A setting of f/11 or f/16 is stopped down all the way, depending on the camcorder.

So, for practical purposes, when you're talking with your crew about adjusting the camcorder's sensitivity to light—the exposure, the aperture setting, and the f-stop all mean the same thing. (Technically, they mean the function, the mechanism used to set it, and the numeric index that tells you by how much.)

The camcorder's current f-stop setting may appear in its viewfinder or LCD display so you can monitor it during shooting. (The Canon ZR series does not have this feature.)

Focus

The lens of the camcorder serves the same purpose as the lens of your eye, which is to gather light and concentrate it on a small, light-sensitive area. In your eye, the area is the retina. In a video camera, it's the CCD.

The muscles that control your eye adjust the thickness of its flexible lens so that the edges of images appear sharp and not blurry. An image is in focus if it appears sharp. By contrast, the glass lens of the camcorder isn't flexible. The focus control on the camcorder varies the *distance* of the lens from the CCD, which has the same effect.

It shouldn't be difficult to tell whether you're in focus during shooting. If your subject looks blurred in the camcorder display, then adjust the focus.

Zoom

Zoom is related to focus, but it's not the same thing. Zoom controls how much the lens magnifies the image and how close your subject appears to the camera. The least magnification corresponds to the Wide (W) zoom setting (see Figure 3.2). The greatest magnification is the Telephoto (T) setting (see Figure 3.3). Notice also that the greater the zoom setting, the narrower the field of view. That is, the farthest W setting is literally the widest shot the camera can see.

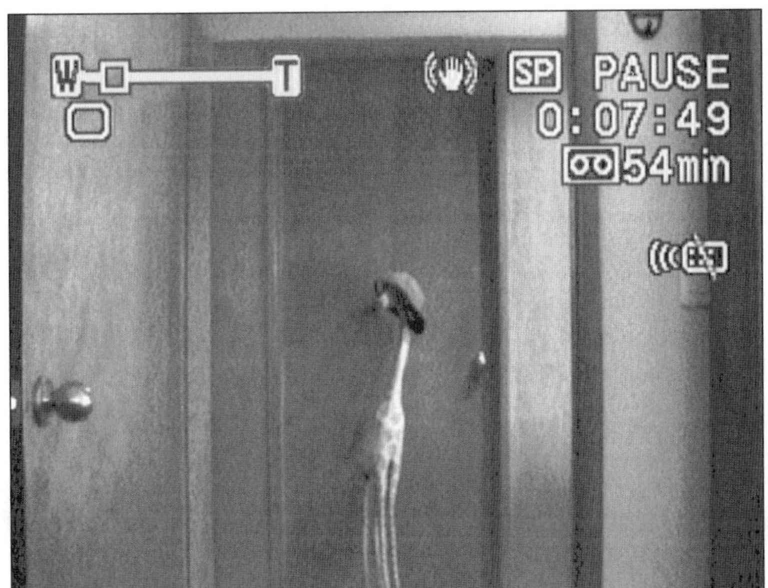

Figure 3.2

When the camcorder is zoomed out all the way (farthest W setting), the result is a wide shot.

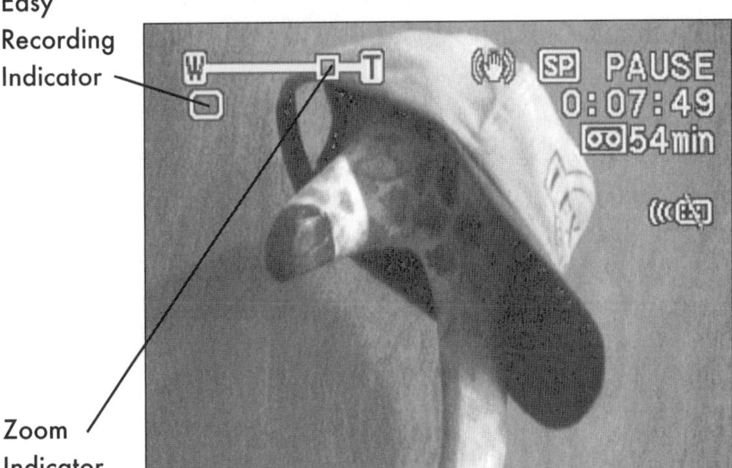

Figure 3.3

Zooming in moves the Zoom Indicator (top left of the display) toward the Telephoto (T) setting. The result is a close shot.

If the camcorder has a zoom control (as most do), the setting should be continuously adjustable from W to T. The adjustment may be a collar-like ring on the lens that you turn with a twist of the wrist. Or, as on the ZR, it may be a rocker switch that you press in one direction or the other, holding it down until you want the zooming to stop.

When you activate the camcorder's zoom control, its current setting should appear in the camcorder display (refer again to Figure 3.3).

Depth of Field

An artistic effect used by Hollywood cinematographers is selective focus, or shallow *depth of field.* In a typical example, the star's face would be in focus in the foreground, and the background would be soft and blurry (see Figure 3.4).

Figure 3.4

Selective focus, or shallow depth of field, is desirable because the viewer's eye will seek out areas of the image that appear sharpest. This is one of the ways a director can control your attention. In this shot, the subject is in focus and the background is blurry, achieved by shooting the subject from a distance with the camera zoomed all the way in (Telephoto setting).

PRO TIP

You might admire shots with selective focus in your favorite movies, but it might not be possible to create exactly the same look with a video camera. For technical reasons, it's more difficult to achieve selective focus in video unless your Telephoto setting is zoomed in all the way and your camcorder provides 12× optical zoom or greater. (That is, the highest magnification of the zoom makes objects appear 12 times larger.) Otherwise, when you focus, both the subject and background will be sharp.

Hands-On Camcorder Tips

All digital camcorders have various automatic, or *auto,* modes. Manufacturers include them because most people just want to point and shoot and not fret with manual adjustments.

Auto modes *are* amazing, when you think about the digital wizardry involved. But if you were a film-school instructor grading cinematography students, an expert human would get an A+, and the highest-priced camera would range between F and C-, depending on which of its functions you were evaluating.

Cameras vary in the ways you turn these settings off. Here's where you'll need to consult the owner's manual for your model. Less expensive consumer models like the Canon ZRs require you to go through the menu to change settings (which isn't as easy as it should be). Prosumer and professional cameras have their auto modes, but they are designed with manual operation in mind. They usually have buttons or switches so that it's quicker and easier to change settings, as well as to inspect them between shots.

Here are the typical built-in smarts that most camcorders have—and the ways to work around them.

> **TIP**
>
> On many camcorders, including the ZR, the unit will retain the last settings you used (provided a little watch battery inside it isn't dead). However, recheck them each time you turn the camcorder back on, confirming auto controls are off by inspecting the readouts in the display.

Full Auto is totally automatic. If it's on, none of the other manual controls will work. Its purpose is to let you point and shoot, and forget about your settings. The Canon ZR's fully automatic mode is called *Easy Recording*.

Easy enough. However, the Canon ZR uses the term Auto somewhat differently. To use some manual controls, you actually must switch to its Auto mode, which can be rather confusing. You see, on this camcorder, Full Auto isn't Auto. It's Easy Recording, as we just said. The Auto mode isn't fully automatic. It lets you select which controls you want to use, and which you want the camcorder's smarts to set for you.

To switch to Auto mode on the ZR:

1. Move the Program Selector switch to the right, which selects Program AE (P) mode (see Figure 3.5). (There are actually several program modes available, but Auto is the default setting, so you don't have to do anything else.)
2. To return to Easy Recording (Full Auto) mode, move the Program Selector switch to the left.

To follow the camcorder instructions in this chapter, you want to be in Auto mode all of the time. So just slide the switch to the P setting and leave it there.

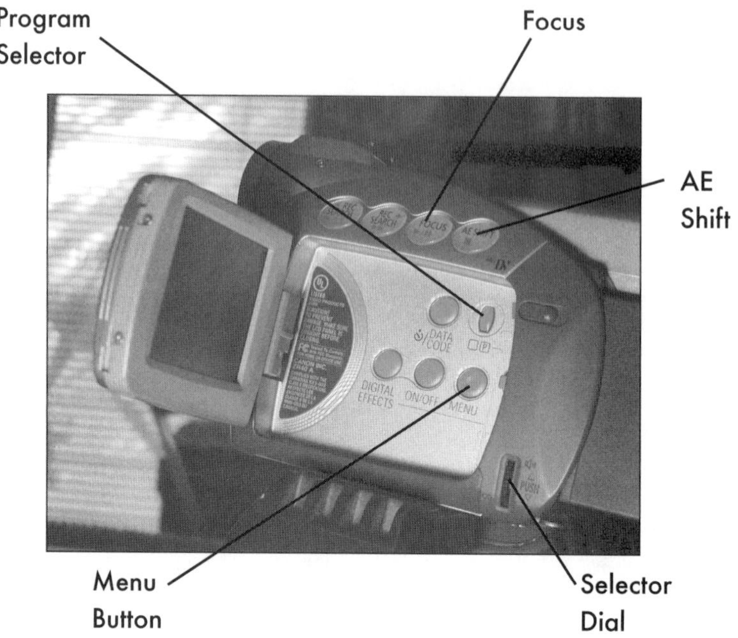

Figure 3.5

Familiarize yourself with these controls on the Canon ZR. You'll need to flip open the LCD to reach some of them. Note that the Selector Dial works two ways: *Turn* the dial to scroll through menus and *press* the dial into the camera (like pressing a button) to make a selection.

Automatic Focus (AF) tries to keep edges sharp in the center of the picture. It won't work if your subject isn't centered. And if it moves, AF can't find the edges fast enough, so your subject keeps going in and out of focus.

As a matter of good practice, leave AF off while you're shooting.

To turn AF off on the Canon ZR and focus manually:

1. Make sure the Program Selector is in the P position. Refer again to Figure 3.5 for the location of these controls on the camcorder.
2. Zoom in on your subject all the way until the indicator points to T.
3. Press the Focus button. The indicator M. FOCUS will appear in the display.
4. Adjust focus by turning the Selector Dial.
5. To turn AF back on, press the Focus button.

Manual focusing can be difficult on nonpro cameras. You have to find the setting where the subject doesn't appear blurred in the display. But the display is awfully small, whether you're looking through the viewfinder or at the LCD.

A quicker and more reliable method is to control both focus and zoom. On camcorders like the ZR, you can do this by switching on AF briefly before each shot.

To control both focus and zoom:

1. Start with AF off in Program mode, as described earlier. This will be your normal setting.
2. Zoom in on your subject all the way.
3. Press the Focus button to engage AF. It will take a moment to find the focus. Wait until the image in the display appears to settle.
4. Press the Focus button to disengage AF.
5. You can now adjust the zoom anywhere within the W→T range, and the subject will remain in focus.

However, if the subject moves or you change your shot, you may have to readjust—starting again by zooming in all the way and then focusing.

NOTE

You might think that setting focus manually is a pain, and, yes, it can be. But if you shoot a scene with AF on—particularly if it has moving subjects—you'll quickly find out why you should turn it off. With AF on, anything that crosses between the camcorder and your subject will cause the focus to be "kicked out." And if action is breaking fast, the focus will keep moving in and out, as the camcorder's digital smarts try to figure out just what it should be focusing on.

Automatic Exposure (AE) looks for a medium-average light level, giving most weight to the center of the frame. It often guesses wrong, particularly when you move quickly to a brighter or darker area while the camera is rolling. You can fix slightly underexposed scenes when you're editing, but you can't ever do anything about totally overexposed (*blown-out*) areas that have gone pure white.

The Canon ZR40 doesn't permit you to turn AE off entirely. Instead, it has a mode called AE Shift. When this mode is on, you can turn the Selector Dial to adjust the exposure as much as two f-stops above or below the setting that AE calculates.

To adjust exposure manually:

1. Make sure the Program Selector is in the P position.
2. Press the AE Shift button. The AE indicator will appear in the display (see Figure 3.6).
3. Adjust exposure up or down by turning the Selector Dial. The number in the AE display indicates how far you're adjusting above (+) or below (-) the AE setting in quarter-stop (0.25) increments.

NOTE

F-stops on a manual camera are marked on a numeric scale from 1–16. (The highest value depends on the capabilities of the particular lens.) A quarter-stop above the 1 setting would be written f/1.25, for example.

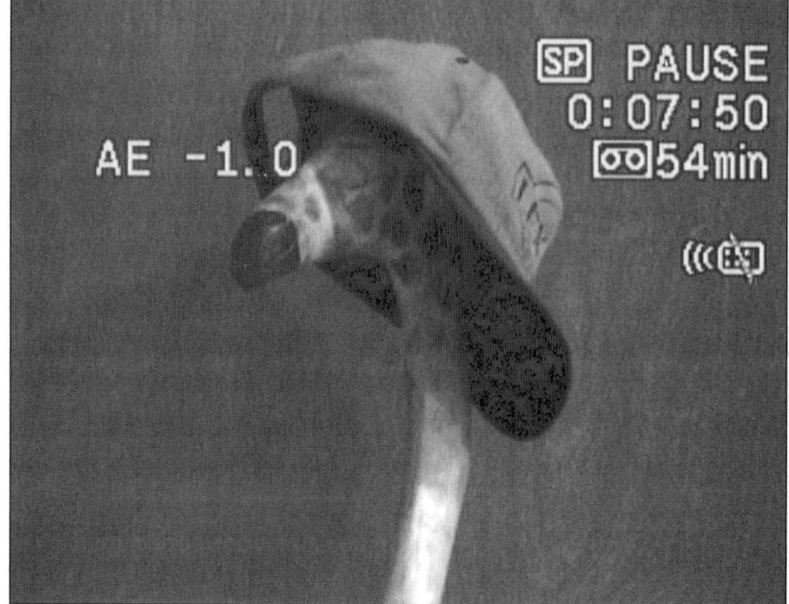

Figure 3.6

The display indicates that AE Shift is on, and the current adjustment on the Selector Dial is one full stop below the calculated exposure (-1.0).

PRO TIP

On pro cameras, use the *zebra* function to adjust exposure. This function fills overexposed areas in the display with distinctive stripes. When you expose correctly, the stripes disappear.

Automatic Image Stabilization (the digital kind) tries to remove jiggle. But it sacrifices resolution (picture detail) because it needs to reserve a broad border around the picture as a buffer. You might try leaving it on if you're working handheld and following action. Pro cameras use electro-optical stabilization, which cushions the shot mechanically. It adjusts a movable prism inside the camera to compensate for jiggling.

When Image Stabilization is on in the ZR, a "shaky hand" symbol appears in the display (see Figure 3.7).

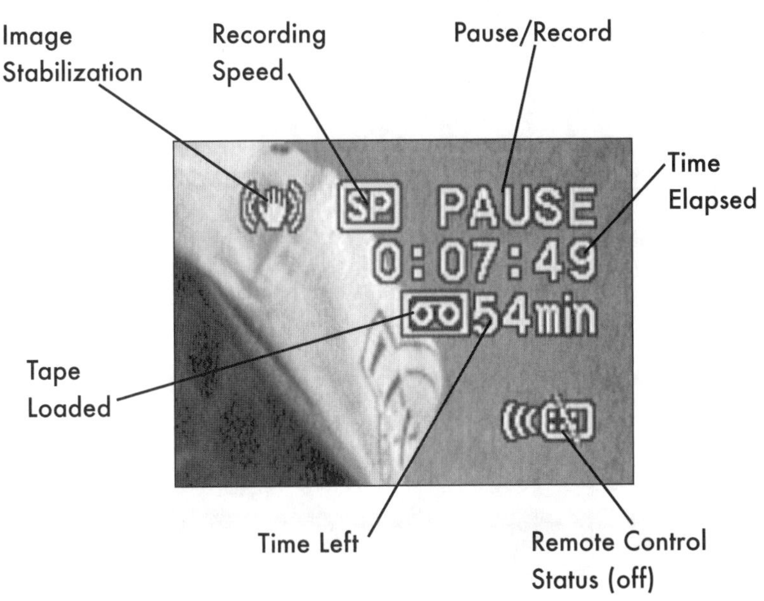

Figure 3.7

The "shaky hand" symbol in the upper left of the display indicates that Image Stabilization is on. Other indicators are recording speed Standard Play (SP), PAUSE (which will show RECORD when recording), and amount of tape used in hours, minutes, and seconds (HH:MM:SS). The cassette symbol indicates that a tape is currently loaded in the machine. The readout 54min indicates the amount of time left on the tape. The symbol at the bottom shows that the camera's remote-control sensor is currently turned off.

Turning Image Stabilization off in the ZR requires stepping through a series of menu selections. We'll show each of the steps here, both to demonstrate how this function works, as well as to familiarize you with the camcorder's menu system.

To turn image stabilization off in the ZR:

1. Make sure the Program Selector is in the P position.
2. Press the Menu button. A list of choices will appear in the display, with CAM. SET UP highlighted (see Figure 3.8). Press—don't turn—the Selector Dial into the camcorder to make the selection (refer again to Figure 3.5 for its location on the camcorder).
3. Turn the Selector Dial to move the menu highlight to the IMAGE S. selection (see Figure 3.9). Then *press* the Selector Dial to select it.
4. Turn the Selector Dial to move the menu highlight to OFF (see Figure 3.10). Then press the Selector Dial to select it.
5. Turn the Selector Dial to move the menu highlight to RETURN (see Figure 3.11); then press the Selector Dial.
6. Once again, turn the Selector Dial to move the menu highlight to RETURN (see Figure 3.12); then press the Selector Dial.

Figures 3.8–3.12

Turning Image Stabilization off involves a sequence of menu selections. They work much the same for various camcorder functions: After you press the Menu button, move the highlight up or down in the display with the Selector Dial; then *press* the dial into the camcorder to make the selection.

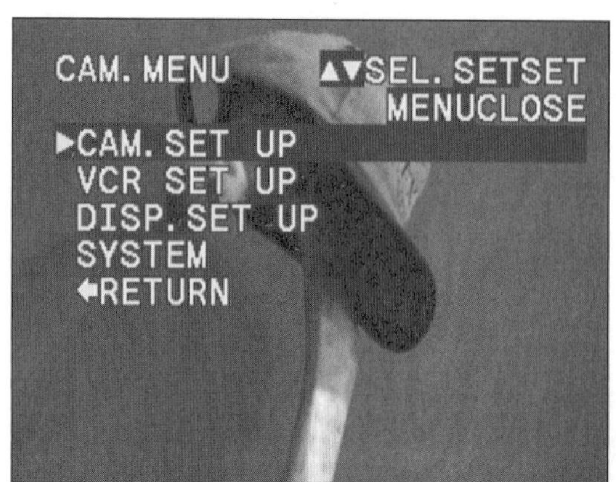

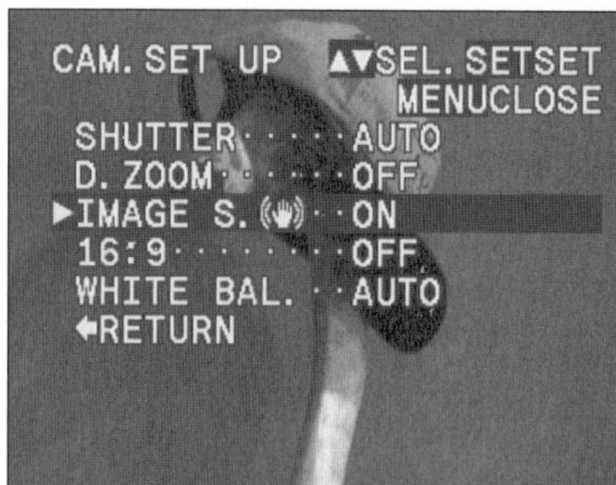

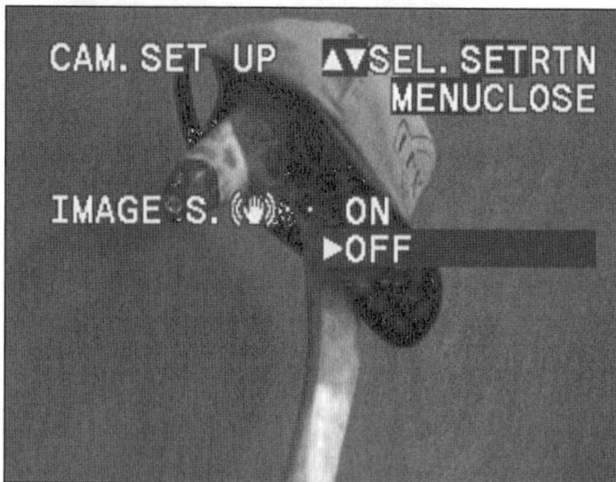

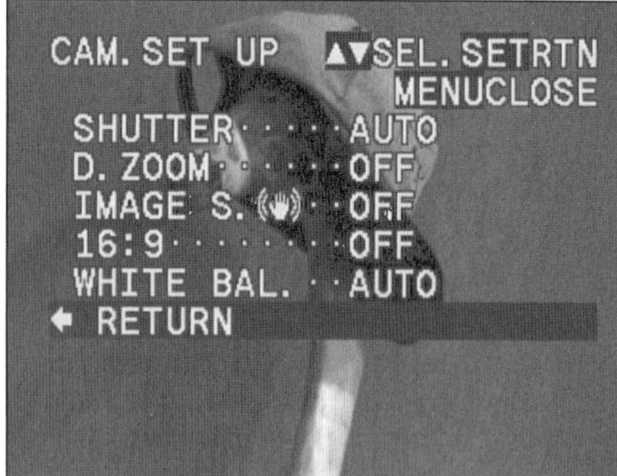

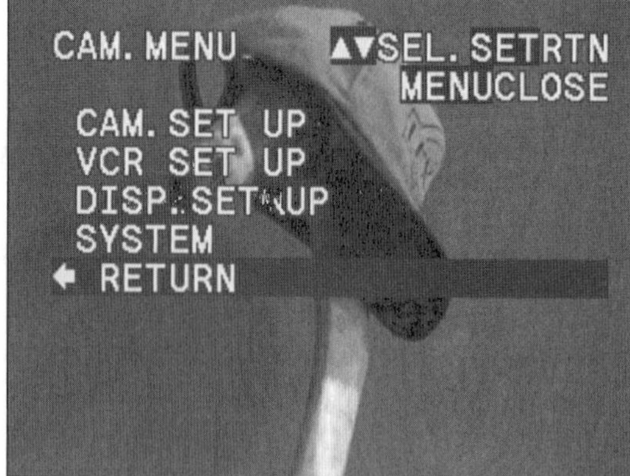

Auto White Balance (AWB) assumes the brightest area in your shot is white, and it sets all other colors accordingly. The purpose is to achieve the best color balance for a particular shot and lighting setup. It's better to set white balance manually, focusing on a white card or wall each time you change lighting, change your setup, or turn the camcorder on. (If *white balance* isn't set, or is set incorrectly, your images may have an overall blue, orange, or green tint, depending on how you lit the scene.)

To set white balance manually:

1. Make sure the Program Selector is in the P position.
2. Press the Menu button. A list of choices will appear in the display with CAM. SET UP highlighted. Press—don't turn—the Selector Dial into the camcorder to select it.
3. Turn the Selector Dial to move the menu highlight to the WHITE BAL. selection (which is set to AUTO by default). Then *press* the Selector Dial to select it.
4. Point the camcorder to fill the frame with a brightly lit white card or sheet (or the brightest white thing on the set). Turn the Selector Dial to move the menu highlight to SET. Then press the Selector Dial. When the SET indicator stops flashing, the white balance is set.
5. Turn the Selector Dial to move the menu highlight to RETURN; then press the Selector Dial.
6. Once again, turn the Selector Dial to move the menu highlight to RETURN; then press the Selector Dial.

Automatic Video Gain (Low Light) applies extra electrical voltage to the camera's CCD, making it more sensitive. But "turning up the volume" on the image shows up as video noise, which gives a grainy look. A better approach would be to throw some light on the scene, if you can. Or tell yourself the grain lends a pleasing artistic softness to your imagery.

The ZR's Easy Recording mode switches to Low Light automatically in dim light. Its Low Light and Night modes are separate from Auto, and you have to turn one or the other of them on through the Program Menu. In other words, as long as you're in Auto mode, the camcorder will not switch automatically to Low Light.

Special Modes for Special Circumstances

Relying on an auto mode can be useful if the action or the light is changing so fast you'd otherwise miss the shot. For example, you might try turning automatic image stabilization on when you can't avoid taking the camera on a bumpy ride.

Camcorders can have some other auto modes that you'll either use less often or should forget altogether.

These include:

- LP recording speed
- Spotlight mode
- Sand & snow
- Digital zoom
- Variable shutter speed
- Semi-auto modes
- Alternate frame rates and scanning modes
- Widescreen aspect ratio
- Digital effects

LP Recording Speed

The usual camcorder setting is Standard Play (SP). Don't switch to Long Play (LP) or use LP tape. Doing so is for amateurs who care more about convenience than the quality of their recordings.

Spotlight Mode

Use Spotlight mode with a camera-mounted photoflood. It tones down the overly bright area in the center of the frame. It works best outdoors when you keep the sun in back of the subject. (See "Tactic Three: Cheat the Sun" later in this chapter.)

Sand & Snow

This mode does the opposite of Low Light and tones down bright backgrounds. You can guess from its name where it might come in handy. (The ZR also has a Portrait mode for closeups, but it's better to stay in Auto and make your own adjustments.)

Digital Zoom

Many camcorders can use two types of magnification, optical and digital. Optical zooming is done by way of the camera lens. Digital zooming extends the zoom range by enlarging pixels. For most types of shooting, turn Digital Zoom mode off. If it's on, your images can lack sharpness, and extreme zooming will also greatly magnify any jarring of the camera.

Variable Shutter Speed

You won't find this control on some camcorders. Related to exposure, shutter speed controls how long light shines on the CCD each time it records a frame. (It does not control how many frames the camera records each second.)

The Canon ZR40 permits manual adjustment of shutter speed from 1/60–1/8000. The main reason to adjust Shutter Speed is to control how much blurring occurs in an action scene. If you're just trying to adjust exposure, don't fool with this.

The ZR also has a Sports mode, which adjusts shutter speed for fast action. However, you'll have more control if you stay in Auto mode and adjust Shutter Speed yourself.

PRO TIP

Whenever you see erratic action in the movies, you can bet the filmmaker is varying the shutter speed for effect. You'll find examples in *28 Days Later, Gladiator,* and *Gangs of New York,* to name a few. One particularly effective use is to increase the shutter speed as a fighter pulls away from an opponent. The jerky moment *away* from the clash emphasizes how devastating and horrific the blow was.

Semi-Auto Modes

Expensive pro cameras are more apt to have these semi-automatic modes: You can use Shutter Priority (you set shutter speed, camera selects exposure) with fast action. Or use Aperture Priority (camera sets shutter, you set exposure) in low light.

Alternate Frame Rates and Scanning Modes

Different regions of the world have their own broadcast television standards. DV camcorders intended for use in North America capture 30 frames per second (fps) using an *interlaced* scanning mode. The frame rate and scanning mode are written this way: 30I. Interlacing divides the frame into two successive fields to reduce flicker—actually capturing 60 still images each second.

Some prosumer and most professional camcorders offer alternate frame rates and scanning modes. For example, the Panasonic DVX-100 offers 24P—a frame rate of 24 fps and progressive scanning mode, which captures an entire frame at a time, with no interlacing. Many people think 24P looks more like motion-picture imagery.

For now, don't worry about shooting in 24P. Most consumer camcorders don't offer this mode, and there are other ways to achieve much the same *film look* when you're editing.

Widescreen Aspect Ratio

The ratio of the width of a TV screen (or video frame) to its height is the *aspect ratio.* Standard DV has an aspect ratio of 4:3. High-definition television (HDTV) uses the 16:9 widescreen format. If your camcorder has the option of shooting in 16:9, you'll make your life more complicated if you use it. An easier option is to convert to *letterbox* framing when you're editing.

TIP

Who needs aspect-ratio numbers? To imagine 4:3, think of the screen of any television that has a picture tube. To imagine 16:9, think of a new plasma flat-screen set.

Digital Effects

Some camcorders, including the ZR, offer transition effects such as fades and dissolves. Leave these alone. You can do all of these effects and more when you're editing.

TIP

A good overall rule of camcorder operation is to shoot "plain vanilla," avoiding special settings and effects. You can then add whatever effects you like when you're editing. If instead you make such a choice in-camera, you're pretty much stuck with it. For example, if you decide to shoot in Sepia (tinted monochrome) mode, you won't be able to restore the scene's original colors.

How to Hold Your Camcorder

To get steady, stable shots, we recommend mounting your camcorder on a tripod whenever possible. But there will be times when you want to take off and follow the action and shoot handheld.

Learn to shoot handheld the right way: Avoid holding the viewfinder to your eye, which will pick up the bobbing of your head as camera jiggle. If the camera has a flip-out LCD viewfinder (as the ZR does), look at that instead, and cradle the camera away from your body. Your elbows will work as shock absorbers.

As you begin to master the camcorder controls, shoot some test rolls in the kinds of situations you'll encounter when you're actually shooting your selected scene. When the conditions are challenging—for example, low light or fast action—learn some dexterity with the manual controls so you won't miss the shot.

And if you do have to resort to one or more auto modes, find out which combination of them gives you the best images.

Where's the Light?

As you're deciding what gear you need for the shoot, you can't avoid thinking about how you're going to light your shots. Decisions about lighting affect how much and what kind of equipment you need. And, the more equipment you need to take, the bigger crew you'll need to transport and rig it all.

In this book, we concentrate on shooting guerilla style on an ultra-low budget with a small crew. So that means keeping lighting gear to a minimum and finding ways to use available light sources as much as possible.

Good movie lighting has two basic purposes—one technical, the other artistic:

- Control contrast in the image
- Show the audience where to look

Controlling Contrast

If you've ever used a film camera (whether still or movie), you'll find that video is more difficult to light correctly. The problem is the limited contrast range of the CCDs in video cameras. Too much light on the subject, and the lighter areas will all register as blown-out (100 percent) white. Not enough light, and darker areas will be muddy, lacking detail. In a video image, no matter how good your camcorder is, you'll never be able to show detail in *both* the light and dark areas of the image in the same frame. So you go for lighting that's either bright or dim overall.

PRO TIP

In video, the range between the lightest and the darkest pixels values can't be much more than five f-stops.

Available light often does an acceptable job of illuminating your subject—meaning, if you can see it, you can probably shoot it. But the problem is that there's often just one light source—say, the sun—and the brighter it is, the deeper the shadows it casts. Shadows create deep contrast, and, as we just said, that's a technical problem in video. (It's also a problem because dark shadows on people's faces can make them look ugly, which is not a good thing unless you're shooting a horror movie.)

Showing the Audience Where to Look

The artistic goal of movie lighting is to direct the viewer's eye. We've already mentioned selective focus as one technique for achieving this. But another effective way of drawing attention is to highlight (throw more light on) the area of interest. For example, an old Hollywood trick is to shine some extra light in the star's eyes so they appear to sparkle with personality.

However, every highlight you add also creates a shadow. The brighter the highlight, the deeper and darker the shadow. So, when you're chasing the artistic goal of lighting up your actor, you run smack up against the technical problem of staying within video's narrow contrast range: You can have bright or you can have dark, but you can't go for both in the same shot.

The Principle of Three-Point Lighting

The ideal solution to the challenges of lighting your subject attractively is called three-point lighting. The technique is at least as old as the movies themselves. And in any situation—whether you've got no equipment or truckloads of it—you should try to light every scene from at least three directions.

Here are the elements of any three-point lighting scheme (see Figure 3.13):

1. **Key light** is the main highlight on the subject. It's usually hard (casts sharp shadows) and comes from above and in front of the subject.
2. **Fill** is area lighting on the opposite front side of the subject, usually a soft light that fills in shadows cast by the key light (thereby reducing overall contrast range and flattering the subject).
3. **Backlight** comes from behind the subject and helps separate it from the background, giving the illusion of depth.

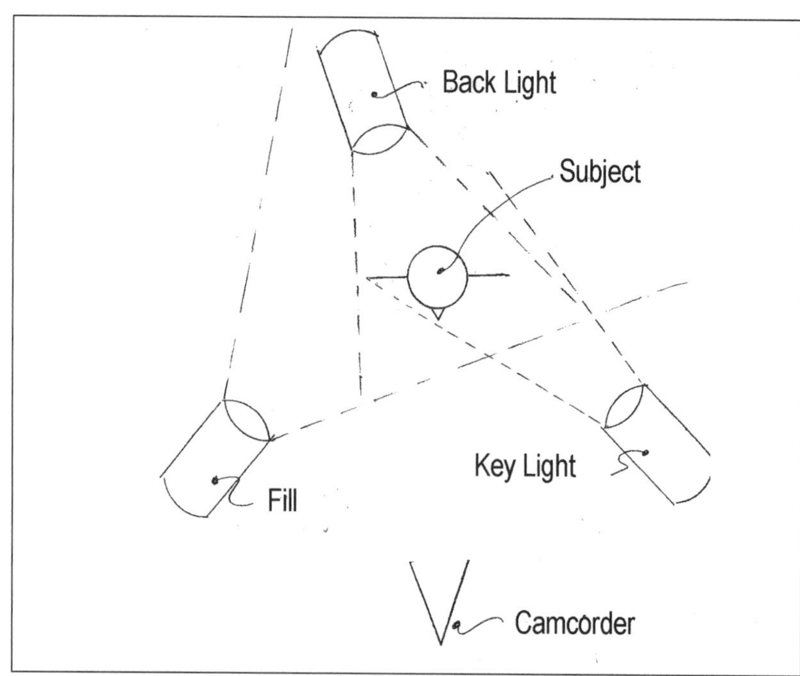

Figure 3.13

An ideal lighting setup casts light on the subject from three different directions. Key light is the main source that draws attention to the subject. Fill softens shadows made by the key. Backlight separates the subject from the background.

Hard or Soft Light?

Besides the amount of light falling on your subject, you want to pay attention to whether its quality is hard or soft. *Hard light* is bright and harsh and produces deep, sharp shadows. Sunlight is the ultimate hard light. *Soft light* produces a glow, with subtler shadows. The light is soft on an overcast day. The clouds serve as *diffusion,* scattering and softening the hard light of the sun. A *silk* is a lighting technician's tool for diffusing a hard light source, such as the sun.

We'll talk more about lighting in Chapter 5. For example, we'll describe additional light sources besides these three that you can use to flatter or highlight your subject.

Color Balance

If a scene has correct *color balance*, skin tones look warm, trees are green, and the sky is blue.

Camcorder images can have weird and undesirable tints in different types of light. Sunlight (*daylight*) appears blue. Indoor light from *tungsten* (wire-filament) lamps appears orange. *Fluorescent* lighting (from tubes of glowing gas) varies from blue to green, depending on the tube's type.

In general, you don't want to intermix lighting—daylight and tungsten, for example—in the same shot. In fact, you want to keep lighting consistent throughout the entire scene, or series of shots. If you're shooting indoors, cover windows with dark material to keep the sunlight out. Or turn all the lamps off and use sunlight exclusively. Outdoors, try to use reflected sunlight, rather than lamps, to fill in shadows.

Another tool for controlling color is the camcorder's white balance control, which we'll discuss in greater depth shortly.

PRO TIP

Movie lighting technicians sometimes intermix light sources by using gels, or tinted sheets, to color-correct light sources. For example, they mount CTO (Color Temperature Orange) gel over windows to remove the blue cast from incoming sunlight. Or they put CTB (Color Temperature Blue) in front of tungsten movie lights to match the sun's tint when shooting outdoors.

Lighting Tips

Shooting outdoors in bright sunlight is a worst-case scenario. If you stop down (decrease the exposure) so faces and highlights don't blow out, you'll lose all the detail in the shadow areas, and even medium-toned clothing can go way too dark.

Besides the sun, your lighting tools of choice outdoors should be:

- **Bounce board**. Large white card (such as foam-core) to reflect soft light—for soft key and fill.
- **Shiny board.** Bounce board with aluminum-foil surface to reflect hard light or key light. (Pro boards are two-sided—shiny and dull.) See Figure 3.14.
- **Flag.** Opaque panel, usually black felt, for masking light.
- **Silk.** Panel of translucent white cloth or plastic, used to filter and soften a hard-light source (usually, the sun).

Figure 3.14

As an alternative to carrying a bulky shiny board, you can buy circular, collapsible shiny disks called *photo reflectors* at any pro camera store. These reflectors are particularly easy to transport and to set up. The rectangular reflector shown is an even cheaper alternative. It's an automobile windshild screen.

A crewmember can hold and position a bounce board during a shot, or you can mount a reflector or flag on a *C-stand* (see Figure 3.15).

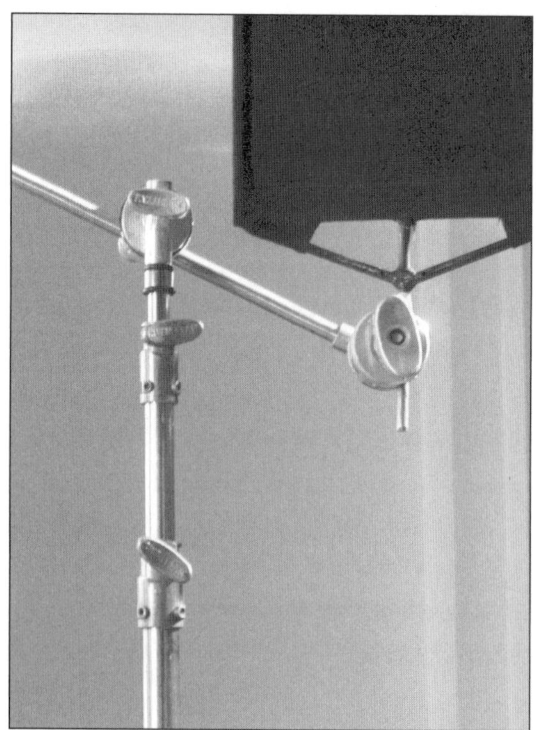

Figure 3.15

A C-stand is a heavy-duty, all-purpose, hold-everything tripod used by movie crews. Here it's used to hold a flag of black felt.

But we don't expect you to have any of this pro gear. You can use handkerchiefs or thin bed sheets for silks, dark bath towels for flags, aluminum foil taped to poster board for shiny boards, and music stands to serve as C-stands. Figure 3.16 shows this kind of inexpensive setup.

Figure 3.16

As a light-duty alternative to a silk on a C-stand, fasten a white handkerchief to a music stand with clothespins. The handkerchief serves as a silk, softening the light source, which in this case is an ordinary gooseneck reading lamp.

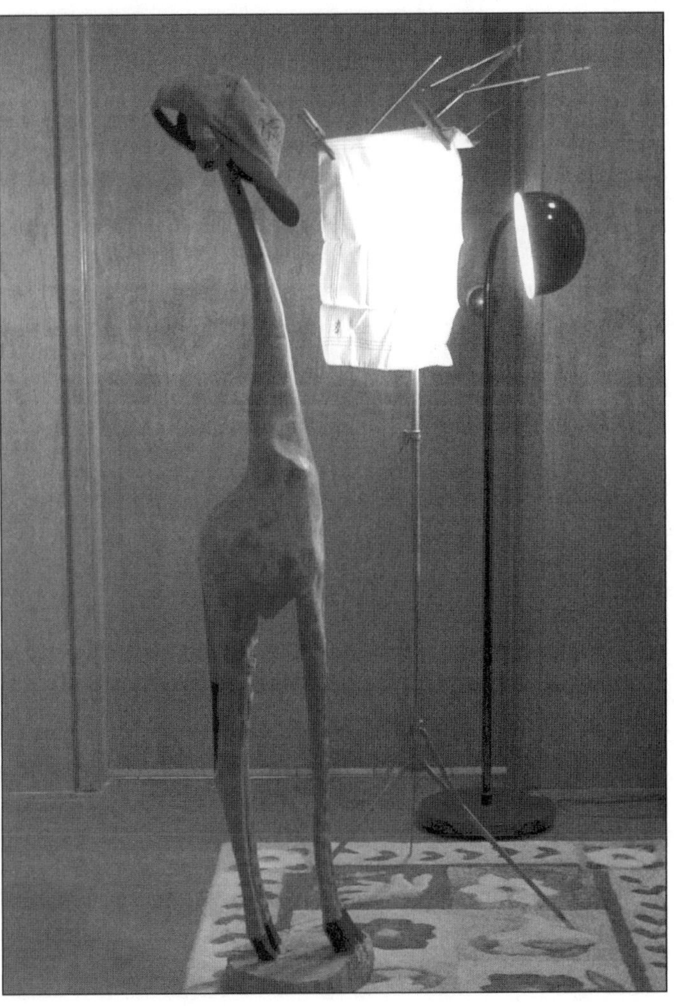

NOTE

To avoid risk of fire, don't let a silk or flag actually touch any lamp. Even household lamps can get very hot, and the halogen kind is particularly dangerous. Also, never drape a lamp with any kind of material—instead, rig a stand and position it at least a foot away.

Follow the Guerilla's Code—Improvise!

In general, do whatever you can (safely) to selectively reflect, block, or filter available light and affect the quality of the image. Here are some other ways to light a scene using the materials at hand.

- String a rope between two trees and hang a white sheet on it with clothespins to act as a big silk to make bright sunlight softer.
- Hold a bounce board over an actor's head (but out of the shot) to create shade and soften shadows.
- Use a shiny auto windshield screen as a reflector.
- Rearrange furniture to 1) position actors so the main light source falls on them as key light, and 2) block unwanted light from window areas.

Despite the lighting challenges involved in shooting outdoors, we expect you'll want to go there. Let's be real—for reasons of both safety and freedom of movement, you don't want to go shooting action scenes indoors.

So here are some tactics for outdoor shooting.

Tactic One: Shoot on Overcast Days

You'll need the least amount of equipment if you take the easy way out and shoot only when the sky is overcast. The cloud cover acts like a giant silk stretched over the sky, and the resulting light is soft and flattering. Even on a cloudy day, a bounce board held next to an actor's face will create a highlight. (But it will only be visible in closeups.)

Tactic Two: Move into the Shade

If it's a bright, sunny day, move cast and crew into the shade. It will take a bit more rigging than shooting on an overcast day. Reflect the sun back at the subject as key light, possibly using a shiny board and perhaps masked by a flag for greater control. Use a bounce board from another angle to provide fill. Face your subjects away from the sun, using it, in effect, as backlight.

Tactic Three: Cheat the Sun

If you want to venture into the bright sun, mount a spotlight on the camcorder and use that for the key light. Face subjects away from the sun, using it as backlight. Provide fill with a bounce board. If the camera has a Spotlight mode, turn it on to tone down the spot and avoid blowing out the highlights.

You can see a good example of this technique in *Star Wars Episode II: Attack of the Clones* when Anakin returns to Tatooine. Even though this big-budget HD production no doubt had the luxury of all the movie lights they needed to provide fill, notice that the sun is always at the actors' backs when they are in the bright afternoon sun on desert sand.

TIP

Another useful technique is to avoid dressing your subjects in dark-colored clothing. This also helps narrow the contrast range. In many of *Episode II*'s scenes, notice that most of the costumes have about the same medium-toned grayscale value. Distinctions between characters are made instead with color—dressing the stars in the warmer tones so your eye is drawn to them.

Getting Good Production Sound

The goal of the sound crew on the set is to capture clean, intelligible dialogue. Period. Music and sound effects should be added in postproduction.

There are three basic problem areas in production sound:

- Audio perspective
- Audio levels
- Noise

You can deal with the first two effectively by setting up properly. Noise will be a bother no matter what you do, but there are some steps you can take even if the thunder gods have it in for you on shoot day.

Audio Perspective

Most, if not all, camcorders have a built-in microphone. But using it causes a big problem. It's almost always too far away from the actors for the soundtrack to seem realistic. That is, the *audio perspective* is wrong.

Actually, there's one situation where the built-in mic works well—when you're doing a very close shot on a subject who is just 1–2 feet from the camera (see Figure 3.17).

Figure 3.17

Shooting zoomed out all the way (W setting) with the subject close to the camcorder, the audio perspective of the built-in mic is just right—but that's the only time! (To get this close, a special wide-angle adapter is shown mounted on the end of the Canon ZR40 camcorder.)

Some pros who are working without a crew mount so-called shotgun mics on top of their camcorders. The highly directional shotgun will give a closer perspective wherever you point the camera. However, it will not only get the actor's speech but also the sound of the busy highway in back of her.

The best professional solution is to use a shotgun mic mounted on a boom pole (see Figure 3.18). This requires a member of the crew to hold the pole above the heads of the actors as they say their lines during a take.

Figure 3.18

It requires a skilled operator to hold a boom pole and its shotgun mic above the actors during a take. The boom's shotgun mic is especially sensitive wherever you point it. So the operator has to pay close attention to keep pointing the mic toward whoever is speaking.

However, shotgun mics are expensive. What's more, their electrical signals generally need amplification and special adapters to work with consumer camcorders.

You can rig an inexpensive mic as a boom by simply taping it to the end of a broomstick. Fasten it so that it dangles downward when the tip of the pole is held above the actors. This type of mic isn't as sensitive or as directional as a shotgun, but it'll do a much better job than the one in the camcorder.

TIP

A boom mic focuses on a particular spot much like a camera lens does. The correct way to hold a boom mic is to point it down, directly at the chest of the person who is talking. Even though speech comes out the mouth, you also want to get the full, rich tones that resonate from the chest.

One type of inexpensive mic is a lavaliere, or lav (see Figure 3.19). There are several ways to use one or more lavs:

- Tape a lav to a broomstick, as just described, so it dangles about a foot from the end.
- Use it as a plant mic, so-called because you hide it somewhere on the set– for example, inside a plant on the table where the actors are sitting.
- Clip the lav to the actor's clothing. (This is the lav's intended use, but if you have more than one actor, you'll need a lav on each. And then you'll need to combine the separate audio signals by running them though a mixer to create a single-line input for the camcorder.)

Figure 3.19

A lav is a tiny battery-powered mic that actors can wear pinned to their clothing or tucked in their hair. You can also "plant" a mic in an inconspicuous place on the set or even tape it to the end of a broomstick as an improvised boom.

> **TIP**
>
> Be sure that the small watch battery that powers the lav mic is fresh, and carry at least one spare battery with you on shoot day.

Whatever the type of external mic, it plugs into the camcorder's auxiliary audio input. The jack is labeled MIC on the ZR, but on some models it might be called Ext Mic, Aux Mic, Audio Line In, and so on.

Like most consumer camcorders, the ZR's external mic jack accepts a mini plug (see Figure 3.20). However, some mics, including all pro types, use XLR-type plugs and jacks (see Figure 3.21). You'll need an adapter like the one shown in Figure 3.22 to convert XLR to mini. However, mics that use XLR plugs operate at voltages that might be too low for consumer camcorders. So, if you're lucky enough to have a pro mic, shoot a test roll with it plugged into your camcorder. Or you may end up with no sound at all!

Figure 3.20

The cables of most consumer-type mics end in this type of mini plug. You insert it in the MIC input of the ZR (located next to the DC IN power jack on the right side as you point the camcorder away from you). Plugging in the external mic automatically switches off the camcorder's internal mic.

Figure 3.21

Professional mics use three-prong XLR plugs. This type of mic might not work well—or even work at all—with a consumer camcorder without amplification.

Figure 3.22

To use a professional mic with a consumer camcorder, you'll need an adapter cable that connects XLR output to a mini plug.

Audio Levels

On some camcorders like the ZR40, you can't adjust the audio level, or input mic volume. The camcorder relies on its Automatic Gain Control (AGC). This feature monitors the audio track and boosts the gain (volume) when sound is faint, doing the opposite when it's loud.

Loud noise can produce distorted sound. But most inexperienced crews have the opposite problem—speeches they record are too faint to be understood. Using an external mic and aiming it properly during a take is the main cure for that.

Low-level sound is also very difficult to fix when you're editing. If you try to make it louder, the dialogue can be distorted, and you'll also be increasing the volume of background noise, such as traffic. Again, the best solution is to record audible sound in the first place.

By the way, one mic that is close to the subject and properly aimed is usually all you'll need. Don't worry about capturing true stereo on the set. Like music and effects, stereo (or surround sound) can and should be created artificially when you edit.

PRO TIP

Pro camcorders let you turn off AGC and adjust audio gain manually. However, you'll have better control over levels if you use a portable audio mixer. The best setup is to run the boom mic output through a mixer and into an external DAT recorder. This is called *dual system* sound (even if you don't record or use the camcorder's mic track).

Noise

The ways to prevent or at least minimize noise are pretty straightforward:

- Pick locations keeping in mind whether buses or aircraft will be roaring by on shoot day.
- Put windscreens on mics (see Figure 3.23).
- Listen to the audio track through headphones carefully during takes, signaling the director silently in case of a glitch.
- Pay attention during takes for any noise that occurs while an actor is speaking—a door slam, dog bark, or car horn. When in doubt, retake the shot. Noise that occurs during pauses can be removed when you're editing.

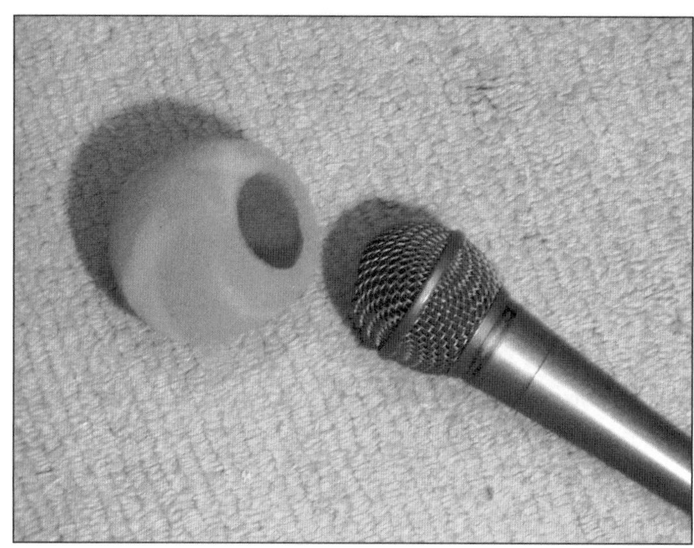

Figure 3.23

A windscreen is a foam-rubber shield that fits over the end of a mic. The microphone shown here is a dynamic type. These tend to be less expensive than shotgun models, and they are less precise, picking up sound from all directions. Singers and interviewers use dynamic mics.

We've got more tips on how to capture good production sound, but we'll save those until you're on the set in Chapter 5.

Plan, Then Shoot

Now that you have the basics of camera operation, lighting, and sound—are you ready to shoot?

In a word, no.

Yes, you've decided what to shoot, and this chapter gave you a good overview of the tools you'll need and how to use them. And, especially if you intend to be the camera operator, you now know you'll need some hands-on practice shooting test rolls before you have to do it for real.

The next chapter is all about what the pros call preproduction planning. You'll decide which of the tools we've described here you'll actually need on shoot day. You'll also break down your scene into a sequence of shots, and you'll begin to think in terms of the setups you'll need to capture each shot.

FROM THE DIRECTOR'S CHAIR

You could read a ton of books about moviemaking, but you won't learn as much as you would by picking up a camcorder, shooting some footage, and then studying the results. Do that a few times, and a lot of the advice we give you in this chapter will start to make practical sense.

Admittedly, the Canon ZR40 camcorder we use in our examples is a long way from a pro camera that might cost as much as $50,000. But the technology behind all the inexpensive DV camcorders is truly amazing. And the imagery is really pretty good.

How good is it? See for yourself. We shot "Neo's Ring" with a Canon XL1. That's a so-called prosumer camcorder, meaning it has some professional features but sells for a consumer-level price. It's a very popular camera among indie filmmakers and costs about $3,000. Compare the quality of those images with the behind-the-scenes videos that show the making of "Neo's Ring." We shot all of those with the ZR40.

4 Planning Your Movie

Experienced filmmakers think before they shoot. The pros call it *preproduction planning,* and it's the focus of this chapter.

If you're burning to shoot your first scene, you might wonder what all the fuss is about. So, if you're in a hurry, then go ahead. It won't cost you more than a few hours of your time and some inexpensive DV tape. But you'll quickly discover that the results can be disappointing unless you plan in advance.

TIP

If you intend to stage a fight scene but you're impatient to shoot, at least take a few minutes to screen our short "Selling the Punch." You'll find it on the DVD, and it'll show you how the pros take swipes at each other without getting hurt.

Quite simply, thinking ahead saves time and money. On a large-scale movie, preproduction planning is crucial. Salaries of cast and crew, cost of equipment, and expenses to transport it and keep people fed all add up to big bucks. Even on low-budget projects, millions of dollars may be at stake.

But—even more important—planning helps assure that you'll get all the shots you need. You always want to be thinking ahead to what shots you'll need to assemble a story in the edit. If you think it through in detail, you'll know who needs to be in the cast and crew. You'll know what equipment and supplies to take. And you'll know what tasks each person must do, and in what sequence.

You must think ahead because if you miss a shot or forget a prop, you might not have a chance to reshoot. Or, if you do go back, the conditions won't be the same.

The magic of the movies comes from capturing fleeting moments—and when they're gone, they're gone.

Making Choices

Making a movie is all about making choices. Some of these choices are creative—*what's the story?* Others are technical—*what's the f-stop setting?* Traditionally, there is one and only one person responsible for all these choices—the director. However, the director doesn't necessarily make every decision. For example, on a fully staffed Hollywood crew, the *director of photography (DP)*—not the director—determines how to set up lights and adjust the camera. The director doesn't need to understand the technicalities involved (although the best of them do). But he or she must ultimately decide whether those technical choices achieve the desired creative result. Bottom line, the director must decide where to put the camera, when, and why.

While you might not aspire to be the director on your shoot, you should learn to think like one. It will help you understand how a movie crew works together to achieve the director's vision (see Figure 4.1).

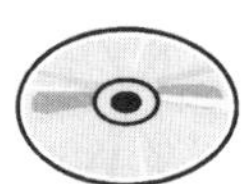

Figure 4.1
As every director must do, student filmmaker Jonathan Schwob must be responsible for every creative and technical decision involved in making "The Sword and the Gun." In this shot, the choices of wardrobe, props, placement of actors on the set, and camera angle all contribute to an intended dramatic effect. He was possibly imitating the work of John Woo. That's not a bad thing. So did another young director named Quentin Tarantino. (Photo courtesy Jonathan Schwob, SOCAPA)

Even though many of these choices are technical, moviemaking is, after all, an art. Choices aren't necessarily right or wrong. They just work to achieve an effect you want on the screen, or they don't.

If you're the director, there's really only one hard and fast rule: *Have a reason for every choice you make.*

What Are the Basic Decisions?

Here are the basic decisions you need to make before you set out to get the first shot:

- What does the story need?
- Where can we shoot?
- What shots do we want?
- How long will it take?
- How will we get it all?
- Do we need to rehearse?

What Does the Story Need?

Start with a script (see Figure 4.2). The motion picture script format has become a standard in the industry. It is set up to make production planning easier. However, you don't need to worry about formatting your script. But, at a minimum, be sure you get the following three elements down on paper for each scene:

```
EXT. MUTT'S HOUSE - DAY

MUTT (17) is a linebacker type with a smart mouth. JEFF (16),
one of the scrawnier ones who reads mostly action comics,
hangs on his friend's every word. They're headed for Mutt's
car, a battered Metro, which is parked in the drive.

                    MUTT
          (getting behind the wheel)
          Here's my plan...

                                              DISSOLVE TO:

INT. VIDEO STORE - IN THE SHELVES - DAY

Standing in the Action/Adventure section, Jeff an Mutt hold
different DVDs and can't seem to decide which to rent.

                                                   CUT TO:

INT. VIDEO STORE (CONTINUOUS) - DAY

At the checkout counter, Mutt pays for a DVD while Jeff looks
on approvingly.

                                                   CUT TO:

INT. MUTT'S CAR - MOVING ON HIGHWAY - DAY

Mutt speaks intently on his cell phone.

                                                   CUT TO:

INT. POOKIE'S CAR - MOVING ON CITY STREET - DAY

POOKIE (16) drives as she talks excitedly on her cell. She
dresses what she thinks is upscale but nothing matches. Her
passenger MOOKIE (16) isn't totally present. Pookie turns to
Mookie, who nods her head in encouragement.

                                                   CUT TO:

INT. PIZZA PARLOR - DAY

Mutt and Jeff haggle over the menu.

                                                   CUT TO:
```

Figure 4.2

Motion picture scripts follow a strict format that aids production planning. But you don't have to follow this format for your first project. Just be sure your script describes the setting, location, action, and dialogue. Here's how the scene between Mutt and Jeff we discussed in Chapter 2 would look on the page in this professional format. Notice how much more information the screenwriter must provide in a professionally formatted script. (A demonstration version of Final Draft screenwriting software is provided on the DVD.)

- **Setting and location.** Where does the scene take place? Where in the great wide world must the audience think the characters are?
- **Action.** What does each character do?
- **Dialogue.** What does each character say?

Professionals create scripts even for unrehearsed shows, such as interviews and documentaries. Even though it's impossible to know exactly what the subjects will do or say, the script serves as a preproduction guide. And in any production, the script is a basis for discussion and agreement. It's vitally important for your crew to understand what shots you need before you set out to get them.

PRO TIP

There are two basic formats used for professional scripts. In general, feature films use *motion picture format,* and commercials use the two-column *audiovisual format.* We've included examples of each on the DVD. Feature filmmakers prefer movie format because it roughly translates into one page of script for each minute of running time. This is a helpful rule of thumb in preproduction planning.

You'll also need to pay attention to other specifics, such as props, but concentrate on just these three elements first. (We'll get to the rest shortly.)

Of the three elements, the setting and location are the least important to the story you're trying to tell. The story unfolds in action and dialogue.

We're not saying that location is totally unimportant. When you're selecting a location, ask yourself whether it adds or detracts from the story you're trying to tell. For example, what mood does its lighting evoke? If you're shooting a dark thriller, it will be more effective to stage it indoors in dim light rather than outdoors in the bright sun.

You want to understand how to make the story work on the screen. Even if you're recreating a scene from a movie, ask yourself:

What does each character want? An actor calls her ultimate desire in a scene her *objective.* As the director, you must know specifically what each character is trying to achieve in each scene. And you must encourage acting performances that let the audience know, as well. For dramatic reasons, sometimes you don't always want the audience to know *why,* but there's rarely a good reason for them not to know *what.* In a screen story, a physical objective will be the most visually interesting (see Figure 4.3). For example, each character wants to gain possession of the same thing, and they fight over it. If the objective isn't to win a thing, it's usually to win an argument. One character wants to persuade the other to take some physical action in a later scene.

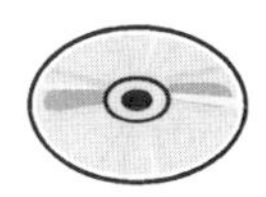

Figure 4.3

The actors' objective in Nicole Katz's "Sweet Obsession" is to gain possession of a candy bar they spy on the floor. (Photo courtesy Nicole Katz, SOCAPA)

What's the action? An action is anything the audience sees a character do on screen. Talking about an action that happens off-screen is not an action. Movie action is the most important element of storytelling. The audience will remember—and will believe—what characters do much more than what they say. In fact, a good definition of character in movies as in life is the sum total of a person's actions. In terms of the story, the sequence of actions by all characters is its *plot.*

What's at stake? You must understand—and your scene must make the audience understand—the possible consequences of each character's actions. What does the hero stand to gain by winning? By losing? In movies, the hero and his opponent often want the same thing. And usually—unlike the hero—the opponent is willing to fight dirty to get it. The higher the stakes, the greater the excitement for the audience.

What's the mood? A creative decision that affects a lot of later technical choices is mood. Is the scene (or the story itself) horrific and dark? Comedic and sunny? Mysterious and murky? Bottom line, what's the quality of the emotion you want the audience to feel during the scene? The answer will affect the location you pick to stage the scene, how you light it, and how you coach the actors' performances.

Breaking Down the Script

At this point, a professional producer does a meticulous script *breakdown.* That is, she identifies and lists each physical element that must appear on the screen or in the soundtrack. From the list of elements, the producer develops a schedule, specifying which elements will be needed on each day of shooting. When the schedule is completed, she knows which people, what equipment, and what supplies she needs—and how many days for each. Only at that point can she determine how much it will cost to shoot the movie. A budget follows from knowing what you need (whether it's an actor or a truck) and how many days you need to pay for it.

An easy and effective way to break down your script is to use a set of markers, highlighting each element in a different color:

Cast. What are the characters? What are the physical descriptions and apparent ages of each? Do they need any special talents, such as the ability to ride a skateboard or do a handstand? For more ambitious projects, you'd hold auditions and select the actors who best fit the parts. But for your short scenes, you might very well work with a small circle of friends, who can do double duty as crew when they're not on camera. But, obviously, you can't count on your lead actor to hold a boom mic if he's also supposed to be in the shot!

Extras. In a movie breakdown, *extras* are on-screen actors who don't have lines to say. Use this category for people you might recruit on location to fill in a crowd. But any character who does some significant action in the script—even if he has no lines—should be on your list of actors instead. As a general rule, all actors are involved in any rehearsals you do, but extras might not be.

Wardrobe. What will the actors wear? Does the action of the scene depend on any specific item of clothing? For example, does the script call for an actor to doff his hat? Also, will any clothing become soiled or torn during shooting? For example, will the splatter of fake blood spoil a shirt? If so, you must have a few clean, identical shirts available—enough to retake the shot several times, if necessary.

Props. If the plot hinges on a briefcase or backpack, you'd better have one when you need it. If you're doing a fight scene, make sure you have the right kind of fake weaponry. (For more information on staging fights, including choice of harmless weapons, see Chapter 7.)

Makeup and Hair. If actors must look just so on-screen, you'll need someone paying attention to makeup and hair on the set. And they'll need supplies. For example, hairspray and hairpins can keep hair from falling into an actor's face during her closeup, especially in a breeze. You might want some foundation cream or dusting powder to take down the shine on sweaty brows and noses. And a selection of makeup crayons comes in handy for creating fake scars and bruises. (In Chapter 7, we'll describe how to mix very realistic stage blood from everyday kitchen food items!)

Sound Effects. In general, your main goal on the set is to record clear dialogue. Music and sound effects can and should be added later when you're editing. But your script breakdown should identify any sound you might need to capture when you're on location. For example, if the script calls for the sound of a car door slamming, you can roll the camcorder and shoot it *wild*—shot separately with no dialogue over it so it can be added to the soundtrack in the edit.

Vehicles and Animals. Items in this category can require special handling, especially regarding safety. We strongly advise not shooting in traffic, and even a scene involving a moving bicycle or a skateboard can be challenging to shoot safely. But it might serve the story to shoot it in or around a parked car—say, a convertible. And, although the family dog is a charming and probably a willing subject, you'll find that even the best-trained animals can be unpredictable in front of a camera.

Where Can We Shoot?

In movie terms, a location is a place, such as a castle, and a setting is a specific spot within it, such as the entry hall. When thinking about your scene or script, the first consideration about setting is where you want the audience to think they are. But from a practical standpoint, it will depend mostly on where and when you have access and permission to shoot. That means that the choice might come down to a backyard or basement, whether it's supposed to be a castle or a cave.

Here's how to think about location and setting, no matter how narrow your list of options:

Interior or Exterior? A screenwriter will indicate in the scene heading whether it takes place indoors (INT. for interior) or outdoors (EXT. for exterior). However, the choice might not make a difference to the logic of the scene. For example, it might not matter whether we see the lovers seated on a park bench or at a table in a restaurant. However, your choice will have both creative and technical consequences.

From a creative viewpoint, choice of location is probably the most important factor affecting the mood of a scene (see Figure 4.4). Indoor locations can seem narrow and confining, enhancing a sense of drama, or even intimacy. Outdoor locations can convey a sense of freedom and openness. Following on this decision are all the technical choices you must make about lighting, which further affect the overall mood. Remember, for good color balance, you don't want to intermix daylight (sun) and tungsten (lamp) sources of light. So when you're shooting interiors, you want to block any sun coming in the windows and use light from lamps. Or, open the shades wide, let the sunlight pour in, turn off all the lamps, and use reflected light for fill. When you're shooting exteriors, stay in the shade for technical reasons of reducing contrast, but perhaps show some sunlit areas in the background to brighten the mood.

As with so many of your other choices, safety must also be a factor. For example, don't stage fight scenes indoors. The actors will have much less freedom of movement, which increases the risk that someone will get hurt.

Day or Night? Scene headings also show the screenwriter's preference for time of day. This distinction has two purposes: 1) It helps the audience follow the logic of the story. If the preceding scene showed the main character getting into bed at night, her following scene at the breakfast table should be in daylight. 2) When shooting interiors, you need to know whether it will make sense to the audience to see light coming through the windows. Certainly, if the logic of your story requires a scene to be set at night, it will be easier to shoot it as an interior. Even if you shoot it during the day, you can either set up in a windowless room or tape dark construction paper over the windows.

Figure 4.4
Notice how the choice of location affects the mood of a story. In the scene on top, the confining space of the dark hallway increases the tension among the players in the scene. The director of the scene on the bottom chose to shoot a lovers' spat outdoors, which lends an airy mood to an otherwise bitter disagreement. Consider how each type of story would play differently if it were set in the other's location. (Photos courtesy Nicole Katz and Alexa Matz, SOCAPA)

PRO TIP

In practice, most movie production is done during the day. It's difficult and costly to shoot exteriors at night, both because you need lots of artificial lighting gear and labor rates are expensive after normal working hours. Instead, night scenes are shot in partial sunlight with a special filter over the camera lens. The pros call this shooting *day-for-night*.

Location Scouting. Inspecting places to shoot is called *location scouting,* and a producer or producer's assistant usually takes still photos to discuss later with the director. Of course, your first consideration is how appropriate the look of the place is to the story. That's a creative decision. But choice of location also involves two major technical considerations involving lighting and sound.

As to lighting outdoors, take into account not only where the sun is but also where it will be in the sky at the times you plan to shoot. Where can you place reflectors to create fill? Is there a place where you can move into the shade to help control contrast? (It's also smart to have a place to go for shelter if it starts to rain.)

If you're shooting interiors, whether you're using household lamps or movie lights, find out where the electrical outlets are (and remember to bring extension cords and plug-in strips). Also, know where the *breaker panel* is if you overload a circuit and all the lights go out! (And, plan to bring a flashlight.)

As to sound, avoid noisy locations. You don't want to shoot near a busy street where the roar of motorcycles or the rumble of buses will ruin your soundtrack. Also, to minimize unwanted noise, avoid shooting in or near buildings that have loud ventilation systems or electrical equipment.

What Shots Do We Want?

The purpose of creating a storyboard is to see in advance how your story will look on the screen as a sequence of images. But to create a storyboard, or just to visualize your story in your imagination, you should understand all the options you have for composing your shots (see Figure 4.5).

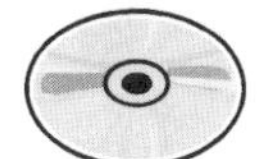

Figure 4.5

In a sense, a director composes each shot in much the same way a painter or a still photographer arranges her subjects within the frame. In "Click" by David Marcus, he poses his actors for a still shot that will be taken by another character—a photographer. (Photo courtesy David Marcus, SOCAPA)

Types of Shots

Anyone who has watched movies or television already has an intuitive sense of *shot design.* A moviemaker will vary the composition of his shots to keep the audience interested, as well as to show them where to focus their attention.

Variations on shot design include:

- Framing
- Focal length
- Camera angle
- Camera movement

Framing

Framing determines which subjects—and how much of them—you include within an image. The basic choices for framing are:

Long Shot. A *long shot* (abbreviated *LS* in scripts) shows the whole body of an actor, as well as some of his surroundings (see Figure 4.6). Directors sometimes use long shots at the beginning of a scene to place the actors in a particular setting. A long shot might also show the front of a building in which the following scene will take place. A long shot that visually orients the audience in this way is called an *establishing shot.* A long shot taken from far away—showing an entire building from across the street, for example—is called an *extreme long shot (ELS).*

Figure 4.6
In this scene, a pair of lovers is introduced in a long shot as they stroll into the park where the rest of the action will take place. (Photo courtesy Alexa Matz, SOCAPA)

PRO TIP

An establishing shot need not be a long shot. For example, a closeup of a hand putting coins in a fare meter could establish that the following scene will take place on a bus.

Medium Shot. A *medium shot (MS)* frames the actor or actors from the waist up (sometimes, from the knees up). It's good for showing gestures and body language between characters. A commonly used type of medium shot shows two actors in conversation (see Figure 4.7). It's fittingly called a *two-shot.*

Figure 4.7

A two-shot frames both lovers. It can set the stage for the conversation that follows. (Photo courtesy Alexa Matz, SOCAPA)

Closeup. A *closeup (CU)* usually features just one actor, framing her head and shoulders. It's the right choice for showing facial expressions and emotions. Another term for closeup is *single,* and a closeup that includes a portion of the other actor's body is called a *dirty single* (see Figure 4.8). A dirty single is useful for showing both the featured actor's speech and the partially framed actor's reactions to it.

Figure 4.8

A variation of the closeup, a dirty single, frames the featured actor as well as some of the other actor's body. The audience can see not only the featured actor's face, but also some of the other actor's body language. In the reverse shot, the camera looks back at the other actor. In editing, the shots are intercut to create a continuous conversation. (Photo courtesy Alexa Matz, SOCAPA)

Dialogue between two actors is often shown as a series of *intercut,* or sequentially alternating, closeups. The camera focuses on one actor and then on the other. Turning the camera in the opposite direction to frame the other actor is called a *reverse angle.*

A variation on the closeup is the extreme closeup (ECU), which can be used to show intense emotion (see Figure 4.9). Extreme closeups are sometimes so close that they frame only the actor's eyes.

Figure 4.9

An extreme closeup (ECU) can emphasize the actor's emotional reaction. ECUs will have more emotional impact on an audience if you use them sparingly, especially at significant pauses in the dialogue. (Photo courtesy Alexa Matz, SOCAPA)

An ECU on a meaningful object—a closeup of a weapon in an actor's hand, for example—is called an *insert.*

Focal Length

Recall from our description of camcorder controls in Chapter 3 that you can vary a zoom lens anywhere between its wide and telephoto settings. (Refer again to Figures 3.2 and 3.3.) In technical terms, this varies the *focal length* of the lens. Wide shots take in a broad view of a scene, and telephoto shots narrow in on objects at a distance.

PRO TIP

Professional cameras offer a variety of interchangeable lenses of different focal lengths. These give the DP a high degree of control over focusing and depth of field. Some of these lenses also have zoom capability (variable focal length). If you have an inexpensive camcorder, you can't change the built-in lens. The way you vary its focal length is with the zoom control. However, you can buy adapters that fit over the lens. One type affects focal length at the wide end, and another type extends the telephoto end of the camcorder's zoom range.

You can use focal length in combination with framing to vary the appearance of any shot. A closeup shot with a telephoto lens, for example, can be very flattering to the subject. It can also use the shallow depth of the telephoto field to blur objects in the background (see Figure 4.10). By contrast, a closeup shot with a wide-angle lens tends to distort the face, giving it a comical look (see Figure 4.11).

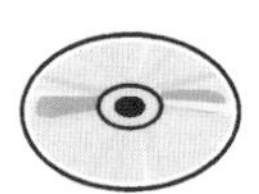

Figure 4.10

In this telephoto closeup from "The Sword and the Gun," the shallow depth of field puts the character in the foreground in focus, while his partner in the background appears *soft*, or out of focus. (Photo courtesy Jonathan Schwob, SOCAPA)

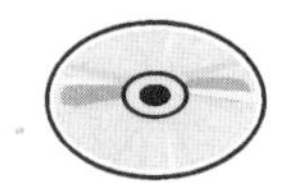

Figure 4.11

This closeup from "Bad Boy" by Camila Fernandez is not only wide—comically distorting the actor's face—but also at a low angle, corresponding to the *point of view (POV)* of the title character, a little boy. (Photo courtesy Camila Fernandez, SOCAPA)

Camera Angle

When the camcorder is roughly on the same level as the subject, the camera angle is said to be *neutral.* Variations are *low* (see Figure 4.12), below and looking up at the subject, and *high* (see Figure 4.13), above and looking down. A low angle lends power to the subject, and a high angle takes it away.

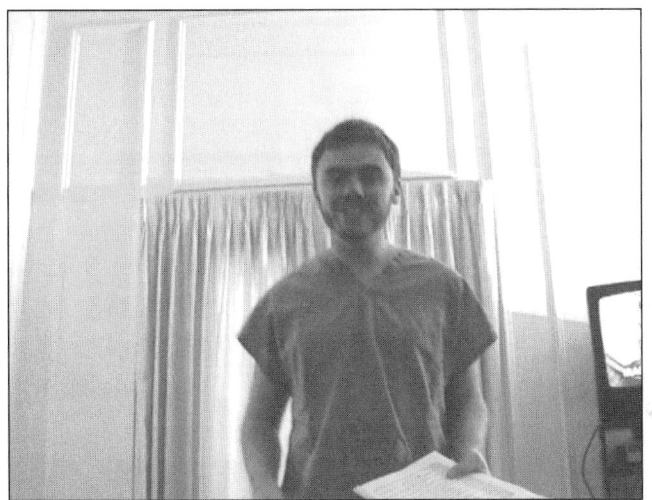

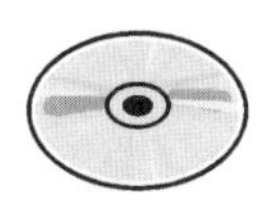

Figure 4.12

In this shot from "Bad Boy," the low angle on the patient aide emphasizes his dominance over the little boy. Notice also how it matches the angle of the closeup of the receptionist in Figure 4.11, helping to create the illusion that the entire movie is seen from the boy's POV. (Photo courtesy Alexa Matz, SOCAPA)

Figure 4.13

In this shot a high angle on the characters tends to diminish them in the eyes of the audience. The impression is belittling. In a drama, such a shot could help alienate the audience from the characters. In a comedy, it could help you poke fun at them. (Photo courtesy Blake Lewis, SOCAPA)

Camera Movement

A whole range of other choices opens up when you consider moving the camcorder during a shot. Zooming *during the shot* is one of them. Two other types of movement are *panning* (moving horizontally, from side to side) and *tilting* (moving vertically, up and down; see Figure 4.14). The most common reason to pan or tilt is to follow the subject as it moves. And you can do either type of move easily, whether the camcorder is on a tripod or handheld.

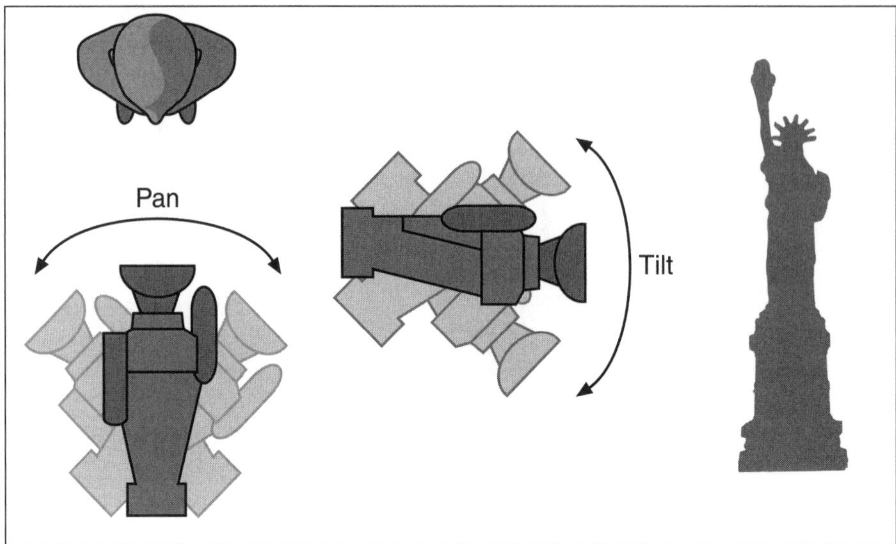

Figure 4.14
Panning the camera from side to side can follow a moving subject horizontally. Tilting up and down can follow it vertically. Most tripods are equipped with swivel heads for this purpose, or you can cradle the camcorder in your hands and turn it smoothly by angling your wrists or by turning your body.

There are quite a few other ways to perform camera movement—each with its own technical term—but we'll save that discussion for Chapter 5 when you're actually on the set.

To recap briefly, you have a variety of ways to design each shot of your movie. You can vary framing, focal length (by adjusting zoom), camera angle, or camera movement. For any size of framing, you can use any or all of the other techniques in combination. It all depends on how you want the audience to view the scene. And it's another one of those creative decisions that brings a lot of technical choices along with it.

Your Goal—Get Coverage

Movie crews generally don't shoot in chronological sequence (also called *story sequence*). To save time, they tend to go after the most essential or the most difficult shots first. They also get all the shots they'll need in a particular *setup* at the same time—regardless of where they go in the story—before they change the placement of the lights and camera.

WHAT ABOUT MULTIPLE CAMERAS?

Traditional Hollywood movie production style is shot with a *single camera,* one angle and lighting setup at a time. While it's possible to shoot with multiple cameras on a scene, especially with inexpensive digital camcorders, that's not how the pros generally do it. Remember, an important goal is to light the scene carefully so that the audience knows where to look. If this is done properly, the lighting will be right from only one angle and that's where you must put the camera. Movie crews do use multiple cameras, however, to record events that will only happen once, such as crowd scenes and special-effects explosions.

If the producer has broken down the script properly, she can leave it to the editor to assemble the story by following the script. But the assembly will be very difficult, if not impossible, if the director doesn't manage to get all the required shots.

In a sense, everyone in the cast and crew—including the director—is working for the editor. The purpose of shooting is to deliver adequate *coverage* to the editor of all required shots, and several choices (takes) of each.

Over the years, the movie industry developed a kind of formula for getting reliable coverage. It's designed around the common situation of shooting two actors—Ramon and Raquel, say—in a dialogue scene. Here's what to shoot, and in what sequence:

1. The entire scene with both actors in a medium two-shot (less commonly, as a long shot). Keep the camera rolling from beginning to end, without pause. This take is called the *master scene* because the editor can cut back to it at any time, if necessary.
2. The entire scene, closeup on Raquel, whether she is speaking or not.
3. Extreme closeup on Raquel.
4. The entire scene, closeup on Ramon, whether he is speaking or not.
5. Extreme closeup on Ramon.
6. Inserts.
7. Wild sound effects and *room tone* (see following information).
8. Establishing shots.

When you're shooting closeups, you might be tempted to save time by shooting only that actor's speeches. That's usually a mistake, however. The actor's reactions make some of the best editing choices, perhaps staying close on his face when he's listening to the other actor.

As an aid to production planning, as well as for reference on the set, some directors compile a *shot list* for each setup. It looks much like the numbered list above, with notations for any variations in focal length, camera angle, or camera movement.

How Long Will It Take?

As a general rule, a crew that has some experience working together can shoot about four to eight minutes of running time per day. If your script is in standard movie format, that's four to six script pages. (It'll be less if there's a lot of action or any unusual requirements.)

Now, understand we're talking about running time. From the list of coverage we just presented, you'll see that you need to shoot the scene several times at a minimum. In practice, you'll need at least several takes of each shot, maybe more. An actor might blow (misread) a line or fumble an action, or a car horn might interrupt his speech.

To estimate the amount of time you need on the set, figure you'll have to retake each shot at least three times to get it right. So, to get just five minutes of finished movie, you could easily fill up a 60-minute DV cassette. (Take several with you!)

Besides the time when the camcorder is actually rolling, you need time to set up when you arrive and to pack up when you leave. Allow at least a half-hour on each end, more if you bring your own lights.

You'll also need time between takes to fix makeup and hair, repair or replace props, make wardrobe adjustments, and travel to and from the location—if it's not in your own backyard.

If you shoot on someone else's property, allow plenty of time to clean it up. Leave the place in as good a condition as you found it—or better.

And occasionally, you should let cast and crew take a break and have a snack. Everyone will be happier, and they'll do better work.

So, for even the shortest scenes of one or two minutes, shooting will likely take an entire day.

When you're planning your shooting days, it's best to overestimate the time you'll need. It's a pitfall to get behind in your schedule and throw the crew into a panic. The last thing you want to do is hurry, for two good reasons: The quality of the work will suffer, and it's unsafe. Even on professional crews, most accidents on the set happen when people hurry and try to cut corners.

How Will We Get It All?

Remember that if you don't get what you need on shoot day, it might be difficult or impossible to go back. For this reason, think about how you'll get some of the essential stuff that inexperienced crews often overlook:

Establishing shots and inserts. Do these last, but do them. A five-second take of the front of a building or the sign on a street corner might be all you need. (You *can* come back later for these, especially if no actors are in the shots.)

Title backgrounds. When you're creating storyboards and shot lists, think about how the titles and credits will look (see Figure 4.15). Get some establishing shots or some extreme closeups that use the location to reinforce the theme of your story.

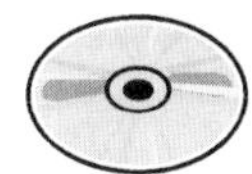

Figure 4.15

Title shots for Nicole Katz's "Lava Mi Gato" help establish the fact that the plot centers on the main character's distress over her lost cat. (Photo courtesy Nicole Katz, SOCAPA)

Special effects. Read Chapter 8 on polishing your movie and work backward to the extra shots you'll need for special effects (see Figure 4.16). While you can do some tricks through clever editing, others won't be possible at all unless you know how to provide the raw material.

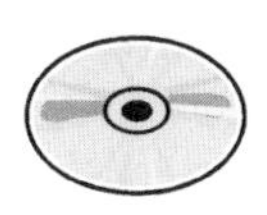

Figure 4.16

The shooting of "Lava Mi Gato" anticipated the need to get this special effects insert in which a piece of fur is tossed into an open washing machine. A shocking red tint added during editing enhances the nightmarish impact of the shot. (Photo courtesy Nicole Katz, SOCAPA)

Presence. Also called room tone, *presence* is the sound on the set when no one is talking and nothing else is happening. The director calls for quiet from the cast and crew and lets the camcorder run for a minute or so. The editor will use this recording to fill in pauses in the dialogue.

Wild sound. Your script breakdown should have included any sound effects you need. Record them wild—never during dialogue—so the editor can add them anywhere in the soundtrack.

Do We Need to Rehearse?

Yes and no. Experienced actors like to rehearse because they want to understand their characters and how they interact. That's a good thing. If you can't do a rehearsal at the location, you can hold it at your house. Try to arrange the room to match the playing area of the set, including tables and chairs.

But be cautious about over-rehearsing. Shooting video isn't like doing theater, where a performance is perfected during rehearsal and then repeated night after night. The best moviemaking is spontaneous—catching surprises during performance on-camera. If the actors rehearse too much, their decisions about their characters can get locked in well before shoot day. Avoid that.

If they want, you can rehearse a couple of times right before you shoot the scene when you're on location. But even then, you might just as well roll camera. All it will cost you is some tape, and you might capture a special moment you can use in the editing process.

An exception to this advice is stunts, which should always be rehearsed carefully, and in slow motion, before you ever do it for real.

Always, always, always: Safety first.

That said, let's make your movie!

FROM THE DIRECTOR'S CHAIR

One last word of advice before you pack up your gear and head for the rising sun.

Keep in mind, no matter how carefully you plan, something—maybe a lot of things—won't go right.

Work with it. Use it. Keep the camera rolling, and don't look back.

And remember that you can't make a mistake. Unless a studio is bankrolling you, or unless someone on your crew gets seriously hurt—you can't make any mistake that will matter at all to anyone but you.

What if someone asks you about something you did that they think looks like a mistake?

There's an all-purpose answer. Remember what we said at the beginning of this chapter about the director being responsible for every moviemaking choice.

If, after it's all cut together and you exhibit your work for anyone who cares to see—if someone remarks about some choice you made—whether it was an accident or something you planned carefully....

Smile, and just say,

"Did you like that?"

Now it's time to let you in on a secret. If you've watched "Neo's Ring" already, you may have guessed it. When we were shooting the chase scenes, Traci forgot her backpack. And no one, including the director, caught it. We had an emergency meeting on the set. We realized we didn't have time to reshoot it all. Should we ignore it, insert some dialogue to excuse it, or show her shoving something in her pocket before the chase?

You be the judge of whether our little ploy worked.

Did you like that?

5 Shoot It!

Okay, it's time to issue the call to cast and crew, set up, roll tape, and call "Action!"

The previous chapter recapped lots of things you should think about before you get to the set. This chapter walks you through what a movie crew does when it gets there—all of which you should think about *before* you get to the set.

We've already covered the basics of camera work, lighting, and sound. We'll now concentrate on how you keep these and other factors under control as you're shooting—and pretty much all at the same time.

Things You Must Control

As the job title implies, a director is the person in control of the set. Even if you're not the director on your project, you should still learn to think the way a director thinks. Because everyone on the set must serve the director. If you know the basics, when the director asks you to do something, you won't have to ask why, you'll just do it.

If you're the director, you shouldn't make a habit of explaining why. There isn't time. A movie crew is always working against some kind of time pressure. For example:

- How much tape do we have?
- How long will the camcorder battery last?
- When will the sun set?
- When will the janitor want to leave and chase us out?
- How much longer will we have the star before her shift starts at the bookstore?

So the objective is to keep moving and to think ahead. The crew should be asking themselves:

- Where will the sun be at 11 o'clock?
- Where will the next *setup* be?
- How will we get our gear from here to there?
- Can we get one more shot before we break for lunch?

On a professional movie set, the *first assistant director* is responsible for staying on schedule. At any point, if the crew is waiting, she must know what they're waiting for and how long it will take. At the same time, she's figuring ways of making whatever it is happen sooner. Whether you actually have someone assisting the director like this, that's the mindset you all need when you're shooting.

NOTE

On a full-scale production, the director has at least two assistants. The first AD (often just called "the AD") is in charge of getting things done. The second assistant director, or second AD, is primarily responsible for making sure the cast goes through makeup, hair, and wardrobe, as well as for escorting them to and from the set. The director's staff also includes all-around helpers called production assistants, or PAs. (The slang term for a PA is *gofer,* as in "go for this" and "go for that.")

Neither, as a rule, should a director explain how to do anything. Movies are creative collaborations. Relying on people to know how to apply their talents can encourage their creativity. It also promotes the spirit of teamwork. For example, long before shooting starts, the writer, the producer, and the director usually collaborate on the story and its visualization. But shooting can be just as collaborative. Remember, the director probably isn't—and shouldn't be—an expert in every creative department (see Figure 5.1). Rather, it's his job to make decisions about suggestions from the cast and crew, for example:

- Is the camera angle too low? The shot too wide?
- Do you like her hair?
- What about his costume?
- Should the shadows on her face be softer?
- Should that actor exit quicker?
- Can you hear her line above the traffic noise?
- Should we do another take?

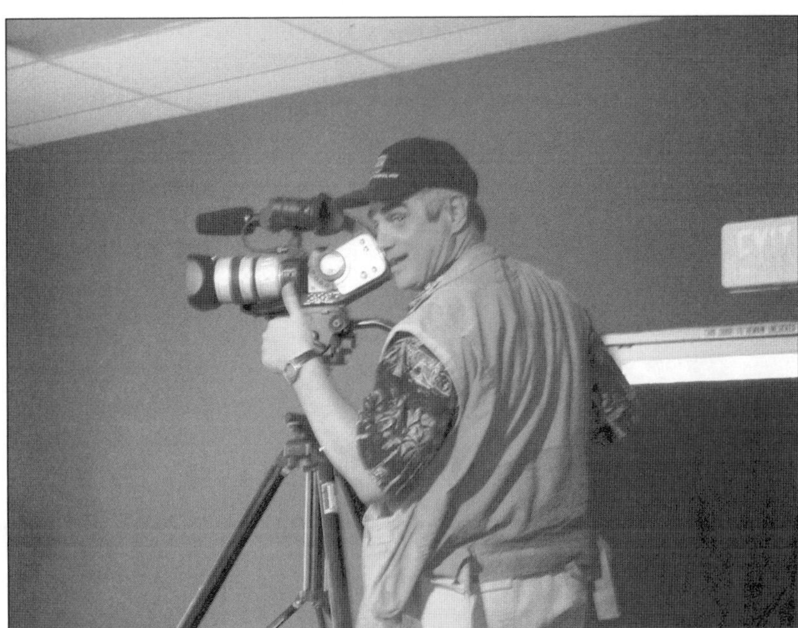

Figure 5.1

On a movie set, everyone in the cast and crew must agree that the director makes all the decisions. The director doesn't necessarily have to be an expert at everything. But he must have strong opinions about what he likes, and must state them clearly.

There's another reason for not becoming immersed in the details of any particular craft. It's too easy to get distracted. The director has to keep his eye on the big picture, bringing all aspects of production under control at the same time:

- Light
- Sound
- Actors and performances
- Crew

Controlling Light

Lighting is a complex topic. We've already talked about the basic principles of three-point lighting. And there is much, much more you can learn about what the pros call *lighting theory.*

But let's keep it simple and real. No matter how much you know about lighting or how much gear you can afford, your main goal is to show the audience where to look. Their eyes will be drawn to the brightest object in the shot, to the brightest colors, and to things that move. So, always look for ways of using light, positioning actors, and composing your shots that will draw attention to the subject of the scene.

No matter how much planning or scouting you've done, the location will look different on shoot day. If you were hoping for a sunny sky, it'll be overcast—or vice versa. If you planned to shoot outdoors, it'll rain and you'll have to go indoors. And even when you're all set up (especially outdoors), you'll have to make continual adjustments as the sun and the clouds move and the light changes.

The key to controlling light successfully is to learn how to improvise. No matter how much equipment you bring, you could easily find you don't have enough, or the right kind. So you have to think like MacGyver. He's the super-resourceful action hero who finds himself in impossibly tight spots and always manages to extricate himself by rigging an ingenious solution from the materials at hand.

PRO TIP

MacGyver creator Lee David Zlotoff says he doesn't get his most creative ideas sitting at a desk. When he's stumped, he poses a question to himself, switches on the stereo, and dances, which he claims engages the other side of his brain. (He has a spacious office above a restaurant where he can dance undisturbed.)

For example, you've planned to shoot indoors in the reception area of a school or office building. You're prepared to shoot with movie lights (or any kind of tungsten lamps), but you see that the morning sun brightens the whole room, helped by the light-colored walls. So you might consider turning off all the interior lights and using a bounce board to redirect the daylight as the key, or primary, light (see Figure 5.2). This wouldn't require any lamps at all. You'd get lovely, soft light, and you'd also avoid the color-balance problems of intermixing tungsten lamps and daylight.

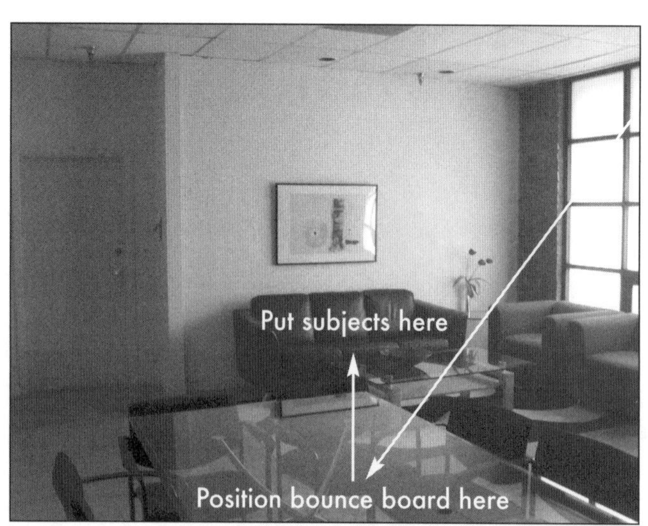

Figure 5.2
This office lobby is a perfect place to shoot using only the daylight coming through the frosted windows. Turn off the overhead lights and position a bounce board to redirect light back into the faces of your subjects.

If you prefer the mood that lamps would give or if you need the audience to think it's night, you should cover the windows (see Figure 5.3) and use lamps exclusively. (Here's where MacGyver would no doubt use a blanket or cut up cardboard boxes as a mask if he didn't have the professional tool, which is a roll of black felt.)

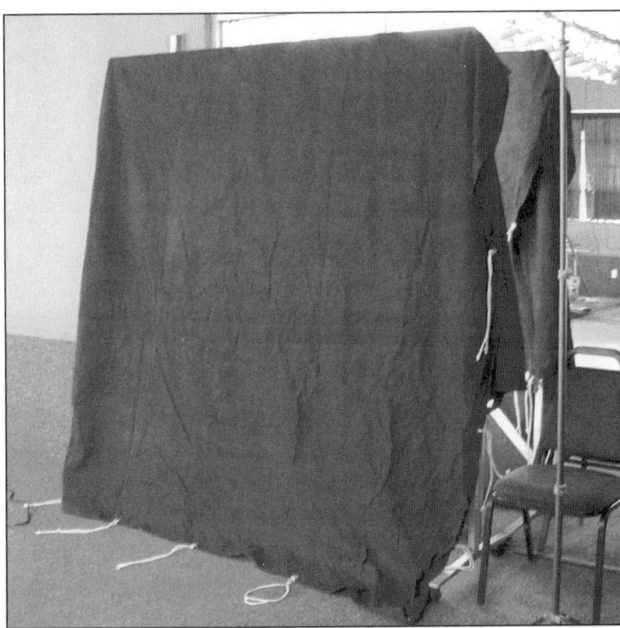

Figure 5.3

If you're lighting a scene with any kind of lamp (tungsten light) indoors, mask the windows to block the daylight. Otherwise, the color balance in the scene will be wrong, and it will be difficult if not impossible to correct when editing. Here black felt is draped over a metal stand, but you could also tape a blanket to the window sill. (Gaffer's tape can remove paint, so watch it!) Another professional solution is to put CTO (color temperature orange) gel over the window, which tints the daylight to match the color of the lamps.

Remember that one of your important objectives in lighting a scene is to keep the contrast low. Do this by masking the source of highlights or throwing more light in the shadow areas, or both. When you're shooting outdoors in bright sunlight, the contrast will almost always be too extreme for video. The best approach, using a minimum of equipment, is to move into the shadow of a building and use reflectors (see Figure 5.4) to redirect the sunlight and provide the key light (see Figure 5.5).

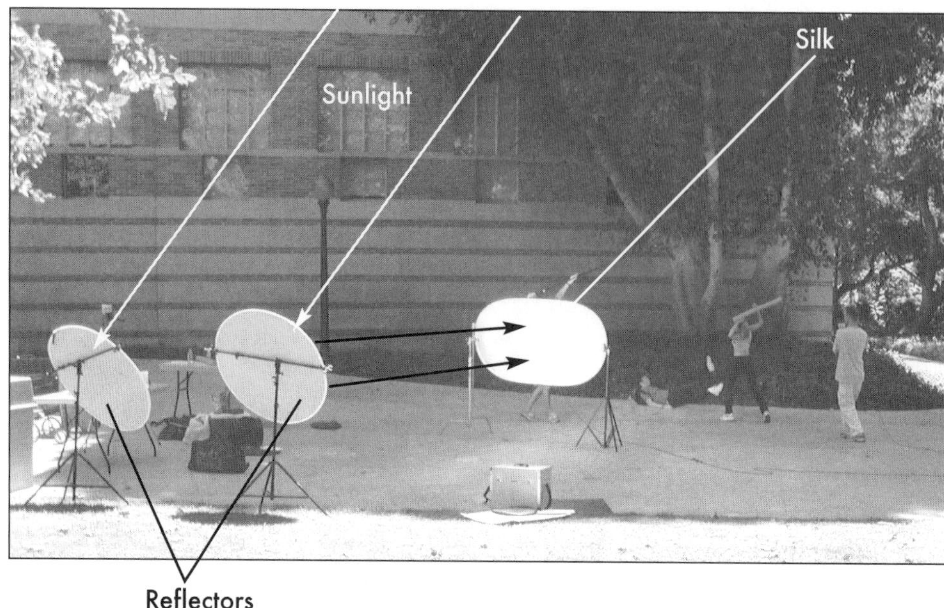

Figure 5.4
On a bright day, you can move into the shadow of a building where the light will be softer, reducing harsh contrasts. The sun can be redirected with shiny boards to provide key light. This was the set of our short "Selling the Punch."

Figure 5.5
To bounce sunlight, you can mount a photographic reflector on a stand, or a crewmember can hold a shiny board throughout the shot. You'll have to reposition reflectors and shiny boards during the day as the sun moves across the sky and the angle of the light changes. (To make a shiny board, tape aluminum foil to poster board.)

ARTISTIC LIGHTING TOUCHES

Recall that good lighting technique aims to illuminate the subject from three sources: key light, fill, and backlight. DPs may also add other light sources for artistic effect.

Eyelight aims a bright light directly into an actor's eyes (see Figure 5.6). It creates a sparkle in the eye that audiences find appealing and warm. Traditionally, movie-star heroes always get eyelight, and their villainous opponents don't, giving the "bad guy" a soulless look.

Kicker is an extra highlight located above or to the side of a subject to emphasize its contours. A kicker can make an actor's hair appear lustrous or can emphasize her jawline to make her seem more forceful or resolute.

Spotlight is a high-intensity beam on a small area, often in marked contrast to a darker area. For example, a bright light spilling from a doorway into a dark hallway could be created by a spotlight located behind the door.

Rim light is focused on the subject directly from behind to highlight its edges. It can make an actor literally appear to glow. In effect, it's a more intense type of backlight.

Background light throws extra illumination on the wall or scenery in back of the subject. Its purpose is usually to bring out details that would otherwise be lost in the shadows.

Figure 5.6

Besides classic three-point lighting, this closeup shows two artistic touches: 1) eyelight adds sparkle to her eyes and 2) a kicker focused on the top of her head adds luster to her hair.

Things to Keep in Mind on the Set: Lighting

Lighting involves the single most important set of decisions that will affect the quality of the video image. It determines what the audience sees, where they focus their attention, and the mood of the scene.

Here's a quick recap of the essential things about lighting to keep in mind as you're shooting.

To control lighting on the set:

1. Motivate the key light—make the audience think key light comes from a window or a lamp they can see.
2. Keep contrast low—tone down highlights and add fill lighting to shadow areas.
3. White balance manually each time you change the lighting source (or see the Tip below).
4. Make adjustments as light changes during the day.
5. Consider how highlights could add artistic touches and interest to your video imagery.

TIP

Adjusting white balance continually can be a hassle. If you're shooting either indoors or outdoors exclusively, your camcorder may have an overall white balance setting for Tungsten or Daylight. On the Canon ZR40, the menu command is CAM. SET UP > WHITE BAL. and either INDOOR or OUTDOOR.

Controlling Sound

As we discussed in Chapter 3, your main goal of sound recording on the set is to capture clean dialogue. For best results, use an external microphone and position it as closely as possible to the actor. (For suggestions on ways to do this, see "Audio Perspective" in Chapter 3.)

To use an external mic with the Canon ZR40 camcorder:

1. Insert the mini plug from the external mic into the camcorder's Mic jack (located under a plastic cover, near the lens).
2. As long as the external mic is plugged into the jack, the camcorder's built-in mic will be shut off automatically.
3. Especially when recording with an external mic, use headphones to monitor the audio during takes.

PRO TIP

Don't shoot silent with the mic turned off, even if you intend to build an all-music track. The pros call it shooting *MOS*, or *Mit Out Sound*. It's a joking term coined from the barked command of some old-time Hollywood directors whose native language was German (*mit* means *with*). As a matter of good practice, always capture the sound made by whatever the camcorder sees. You can use the audio as a *guide track* to time events, such as music cues, when you're editing, even if you don't use the actual sound.

Wear Headphones

At least one member of the crew should wear headphones to monitor the audio recording during takes. Ideally, two people should be listening: 1) the sound technician (who may also serve as the boom operator), and 2) the director (see Figure 5.7). And they should be paying attention to different things. The sound technician should make sure that the audio level is high enough for voices to be heard. She should pay particular attention to whether an actor ever goes *off mic* during a take—for example, walking or turning his head away from the mic, thereby dropping the audio level. The technician should also listen for noise during a take—for example, sounds of traffic, aircraft, or just crewmembers coughing. However, the sound technician shouldn't interrupt a take just because she hears a noise. It's usually best to keep the camcorder rolling and finish the take because it might still be usable in the edit.

Figure 5.7

The director's main purpose in wearing headphones is to pay close attention to dialogue. The actors' speeches should follow the script and be clear and understandable. The director is also the judge of whether their emotion and delivery serve the purpose of the scene. (Photo courtesy SOCAPA)

Even though we recommend it, using an external mic compounds the number of things that can go wrong with the audio. For example, an audio connector might come loose or a mic battery might go bad. So it's doubly important to wear headphones to make sure you're getting good audio from an external mic.

When the sound technician hears a noise during a take, she should signal the director silently by raising her hand. The director should then decide whether to cut or keep rolling. (The director may see something in the take worth keeping.)

Although the director should be aware of the technical quality of the audio, his main purpose in monitoring the recording is to concentrate on the actors' performances. He wants to be sure that they don't mumble their lines or speak so softly they can't be heard.

TIP

For both the sound technician and the director to use headphones, use a splitter cable (see Figure 5.8) connected to the camcorder's audio output to provide separate headphone jacks. To give them freedom to move around, you'll probably also need several mini cable extension cords.

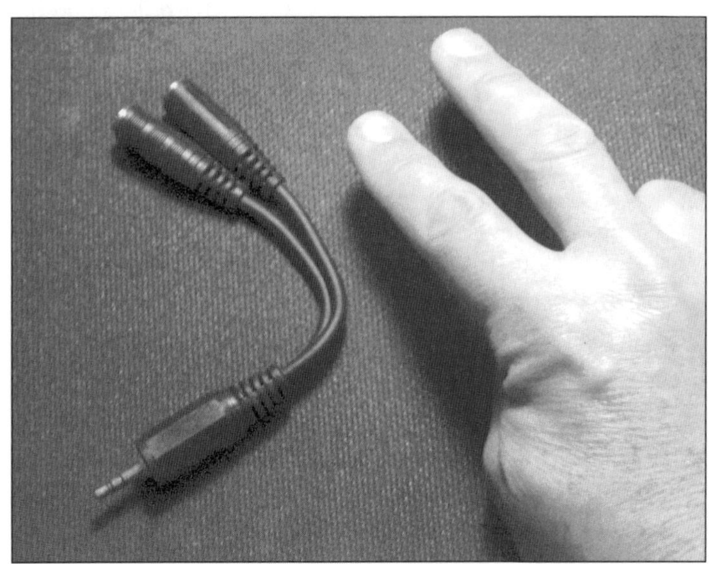

Figure 5.8

Use a splitter cable to divide the headphone output from the camcorder into two lines, one for the director and one for the sound technician or boom operator.

To set up the Canon ZR40 to use headphones:

1. Turn the camera power switch to the Camera position.
2. Press the Menu button.
3. From the menu, select VCR SET UP.
4. From the submenu, select A/V PHONES.
5. From the submenu, select PHONES.
6. Press the Menu button.

Watch the Mic

Unless you're shooting an interview, the mic shouldn't actually appear in the shot. If you're using a boom mic (or any kind of mic taped to a broomstick, as we've suggested), the camera operator should compose the shot so that the mic is outside the frame. And then he should pay careful attention during each take to make sure that the mic doesn't dip into the shot as the boom operator's arms grow tired (see Figure 5.9). To let the boom dip into a shot momentarily is a very common mistake—even on professional crews!

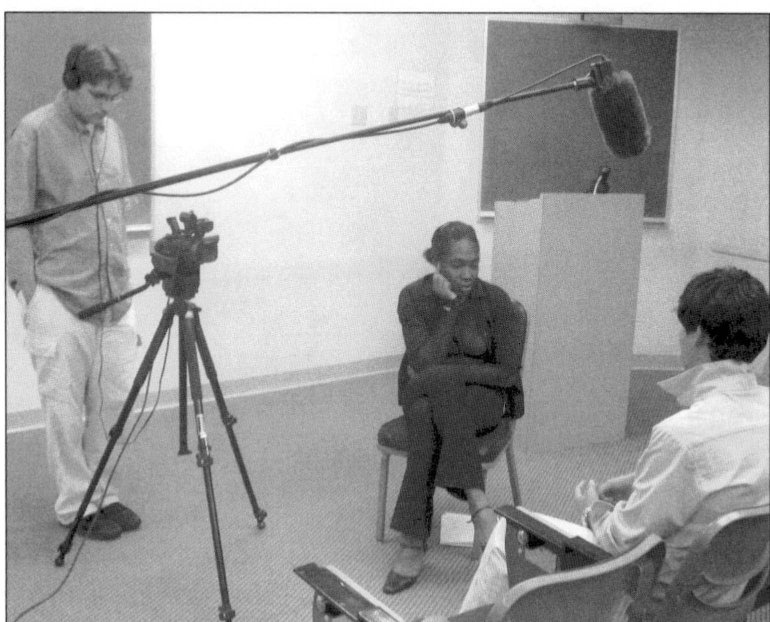

Figure 5.9

This crew appears to be monitoring audio closely. Notice that the director is also watching the action on the camcorder LCD screen. Besides judging the performance, it's very important to make sure that the boom mic doesn't dip into the shot! (Photo courtesy SOCAPA)

If you're shooting an interview with a handheld mic, the interviewer should always point it directly at the person who is speaking (see Figure 5.10). Watch how newscasters doing field reports on TV handle their mics. If you're the interviewer, it can seem as if you're wagging the mic back and forth a lot—and the first time you do it, you might think it's silly. But it's the best way to capture dialogue with a handheld mic.

Figure 5.10
The interviewer should point the mic directly at the person speaking, switching back and forth between herself and the subject. This mic is called a *shortie*, and it's the right type for singers and newscasters who work closely with a mic that is visible on camera. (Photo courtesy UnleashtheBeach.org)

USING A PRO MIC WITH CONSUMER CAMCORDERS

It can be a challenge to use a professional mic such as a shotgun boom with a consumer camcorder, for several reasons. The camcorder's audio jack is designed for a mini plug, but the pro mic uses an XLR plug (refer back to Figures 3.20 and 3.21). Furthermore, the operating voltage of the pro mic is lower than the consumer camcorder needs. Both of these problems can be solved by using an adapter like the BeachTek DXA-2 or the Studio 1 XLR-BP (see Figure 5.11). These adapters not only connect XLR to mini plugs, but they also overcome the voltage problem and provide a knob for adjusting the audio level.

Be aware that some kinds of pro mics require external power. (Sound technicians call it *phantom power*). Many pro camcorders have a mic connection for phantom power, but consumer camcorders generally don't. A common solution is a battery socket wired into the boom pole.

Another way to provide phantom power to a boom mic is to use a portable microphone mixer. It overcomes all the problems cited above, and also gives you much greater control over audio levels. Another useful function of a mixer on the set is to combine inputs from several mics, such as lavs, letting you control their levels separately. An example of a portable mixer used by many DV crews is the Shure FP33 (see Figure 5.12).

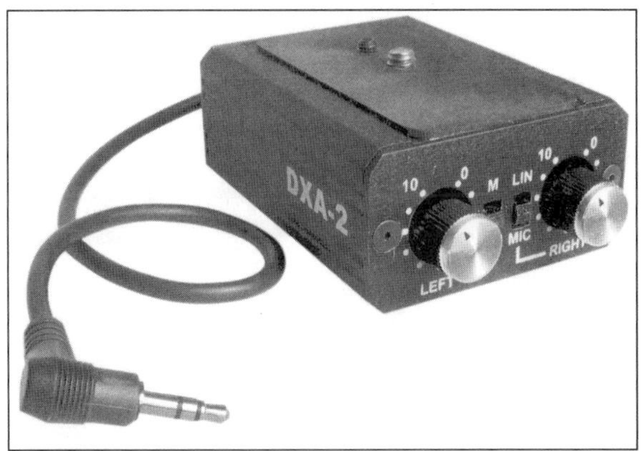

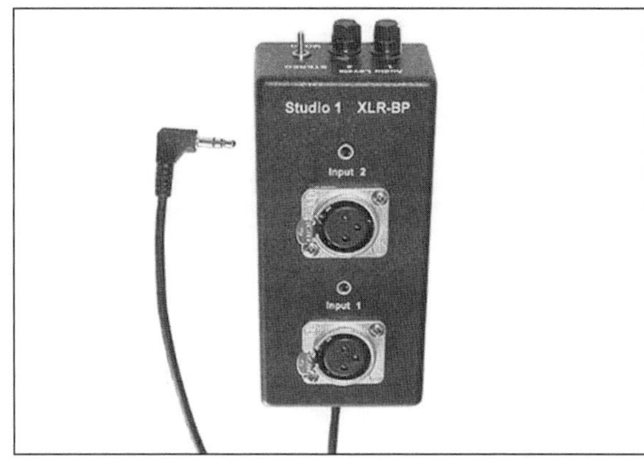

Figure 5.11

The BeachTek DXA-2 (left) XLR mic adapter screws onto the tripod mount at the bottom of the camcorder and plugs into the mini Mic jack. (Photo courtesy BeachTek) The Studio 1 XLR-BP serves the same purpose but is worn on the camera operator's belt. (Photo courtesy Studio 1)

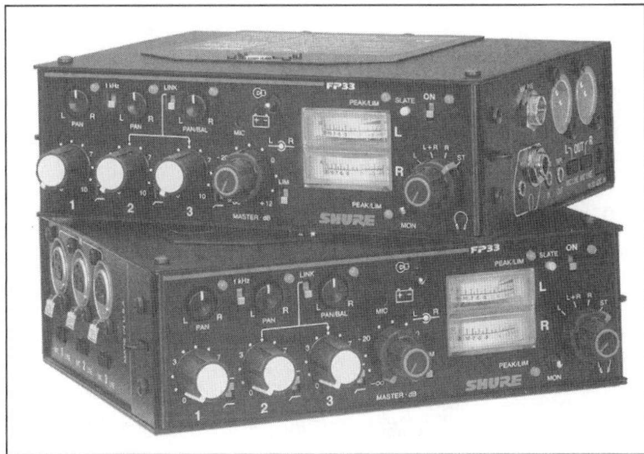

Figure 5.12

The Shure FP33 is a battery-powered mic mixer often used by DV crews that are shooting with a boom mic. It provides phantom power for the mic, as well as knobs for carefully controlling audio levels during a take. Although somewhat larger than the XLR adapters shown in Figure 5.11, it's compact enough to be worn on the boom operator's belt. Even though this unit costs almost as much as a consumer camcorder, you may be able to rent one inexpensively from a professional camera store. Two units are shown stacked so you can see the jacks and controls on either side. (Photo ©2005 Shure Incorporated)

Things to Keep in Mind on the Set: Sound

The most common shortcoming of low-budget independent movies—even by filmmakers who have some experience—is a poor-quality soundtrack. Somehow, it's all too easy to get caught up in the imagery, but remember that the audience gets much of the "story" from dialogue. If they have to strain to hear what the actors are saying, the audience become frustrated and uncomfortable. And, possibly, they won't be able to follow the story at all.

PRO TIP

When the pros screw up the audio (and they do), they send the actors back into the recording studio later to *dub* their voice tracks. The process is called *automated dialogue replacement*, or *ADR*. In practice, it's not all that automated. It's also done to replace strong language, correct errors, and create foreign language versions. ADR is tricky and expensive to do, and often, the result still isn't a perfect match with the original track. The best and least expensive solution is to avoid ADR totally by using an external mic on the set and monitoring audio carefully during takes.

Here's a quick recap of the essential things about audio recording to keep in mind as you're shooting.

To control sound on the set:

1. During a take when actors are speaking, concentrate on capturing clean dialogue and nothing else.
2. Wear headphones and listen to levels and noise.
3. Signal the director silently when you hear noise during a take, but keep rolling.
4. Record one minute of room tone (presence) after each take.
5. Remember to capture any wild sound effects you need in separate takes.

Working with Actors

A director's work with actors begins with casting, when you choose people for the roles. In your first projects, your choices may be limited to the students in your class or on your assigned production team. Or you may have to draw from the friends in your neighborhood who are free all day on Saturday for the shoot. But whether you hold auditions or select from a small group of friends, you should know what to look for in actors' performances.

PRO TIP

If you intend to distribute your movie to the public, including submitting it to film festivals, or use it for any commercial purpose, you must get permission in writing from your actors. This can be done by having them sign a *release form,* which is a legal agreement to use their recorded performances. If the actor is a minor (under 18 years of age, in most states), a parent or guardian must also sign. Remember that you need a release form for each actor or interview subject, even if he or she receives no pay for participating. We've included a sample player's release form on the DVD.

Actors should be able to say their lines sincerely and convincingly. They should speak the words in the script's dialogue as though they just thought of them. That's not particularly easy to do. If it were, acting wouldn't be the challenging profession that it is.

If you are the actor, the key to delivering a convincing performance is to concentrate on what your character is feeling at that moment in the story. The emotions that play on your face are just as important as the words you say, which is especially true in movies. What you cannot and must not do is be at all concerned about how you look on-camera.

Inexperienced actors and directors can fail to understand that acting is mostly *re*acting. Actors are naturally concerned with how they say their lines. But that's only one aspect of an acting performance. To an audience, actors are at their most interesting when they are reacting to things another actor is saying or doing. In particular, audiences pay close attention to the emotions they see on actors' faces when they are listening to some new information.

TIP

Here's a common mistake you can easily avoid: When shooting closeups, it's a common mistake of novice directors to think that all they have to get is the subject when she's speaking. A more experienced director will keep the camera rolling from the beginning of the scene to the end, especially on closeups, to capture her reactions as she listens to the other actor's lines.

For directors, a telltale sign of an inexperienced actor is any action, gesture, or emphasis of speech that is played for the benefit of the camera. The actor in that moment is more concerned with how he looks than what he's feeling. And the audience will know it.

In general, when coaching actors, avoid describing what you want in terms of the result you want to see on the screen. That would just get the actors thinking about how they look to the camera. Instead, talk in terms of their characters' objectives, preferably physical goals. For example, you shouldn't say to an actor, "I need you to go back into the house because you're not supposed to see what happens out front." A better suggestion would be, "You just remembered you forgot your keys. Go back inside for them." The actor's actions will seem more realistic, because his motivations, or his reasons for taking the action, will be more like a real person's in that situation.

Another way to encourage performances that look natural is not to rehearse too much. Good actors want to prepare in order to understand their characters and the space they'll work in, but there can be a tendency to try for perfection before the camera rolls. Resist that temptation. Answer actors' questions and do rehearsals, if time permits. Encourage them to try on their wardrobe, move around in the space (even if you can't go to the actual location), read their lines to each other, and practice their actions (especially stunts). But stop before they become too set in their ways. You want to allow for some discovery and experimentation on the set (see Figure 5.13).

Figure 5.13
If actors rehearse too much, their performances can become locked in before they get in front of the camera. Instead, the director should create a comfortable atmosphere of creative collaboration on the set. Allow for suggestions and some experimentation, but don't lose sight of your vision for the movie. (Photo courtesy SOCAPA)

PRO TIP

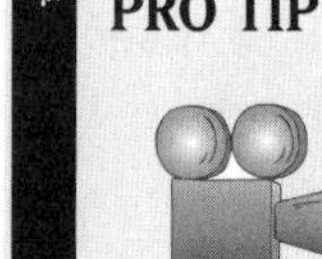

Traditionally, extensive rehearsals have been necessary both for live theater and for big-budget movies. In the theater, the goal is to nail the performances before opening night—when the play will run from beginning to end, with no second chances. In movies, film is expensive. So, when the camera rolls, the director and the actors must be ready. By contrast, DV tape is incredibly cheap. It costs next to nothing to do one more take if you don't get it right the first time, or even the tenth time. As a result, rehearsals for DV production can be less formal, resulting in performances on the set that seem fresher and more spontaneous.

One way to experiment in front of the camera is to try things different ways. While the director may have a clear idea about what she wants to see, actors will often have suggestions, particularly about what actions seem to make sense. So, if an actor makes a suggestion, do a take trying it his way. But remember—it's the director who is ultimately responsible for the movie's decisions. So also make sure to get at least one good take that fits your understanding of the scene and your creative vision.

Although actors shouldn't over-rehearse, ask—and expect—them to memorize their lines. However, despite diligent preparation, they may still have trouble recalling them on the set. In such situations, if the story permits the character to be reading from a book, tape the script page there as a *cue card*. Or pin the page to the other actor's shirt and shoot over his shoulder. You can also write out the lines in big letters with marker on poster board. If you're in a classroom, use the white board. Just make sure to display the lines as close as possible to the actor's *eye line* in the scene—in the direction the character should be looking. If the actor is speaking into the camera, or if you're shooting an interview, hold it directly under the lens. In a closeup involving dialogue, hold the card over the other actor's shoulder. The audience will know if the actor's eyes move, however slightly, to read a line. For best results, have the actor read and memorize the line just before you roll camera, then do the take without glancing back at the cue card.

TIP

A precaution we've often used is to print out only the dialogue in 30-point type the night before the shoot. If the actors need prompting, you can tape the pages to a bounce board. (An old trick in TV soap operas—which often had little, if any, rehearsal—was to cut script pages into strips and tape the lines to props the actors handled on the set.)

When you're shooting a scene, how many takes is enough? The pros talk about a director's shooting ratio, or the number of takes he shoots to get one he considers good. A director who knows what she wants probably shoots about 4:1, on average. In general, you should shoot as many takes as you need to get one that's both correct technically and satisfying creatively.

But it's easy to overdo it. Remember that a quest for perfection might be admirable, but you have a whole day's shooting to do, and your cast and crew could tire quickly from doing lots of retakes. If you find you're shooting more than six to eight takes for more than one shot, consider that maybe you're being too picky and you could move faster.

TIP

Remember also, the more you shoot, the more footage you'll have to deal with in the edit. Loading clips into your computer takes lots of time and gigabytes of precious disk storage!

That said, if a difficult scene requires a lot of takes, finish up by asking for one more "for energy." Your actors are probably tired from doing it again and again, and suggesting a fresh performance (and an end to the repetition) can get a good particularly result.

Things to Keep in Mind on the Set: Working with Actors

To summarize, here are the key things a director should keep in mind when working with actors on the set:

To keep performances under control on the set:

1. Don't rehearse too much.
2. Coach actors by giving them things to do, not by describing what you want to see.

3. Keep the camcorder rolling—capture actors' reactions as well as speeches. (You'll also need some extra footage as a cushion when you're editing.)
4. Ask interview subjects to repeat the question before responding. You'll be glad you did when you edit.
5. Keep everyone safe and comfortable. Provide meals, snacks, and breaks.
6. Remember to get signed releases, if you need them.

Getting Results from Your Crew

On a movie set, everyone in the cast and crew must know and acknowledge that the director is in charge. The most effective way for the director to work with the crew is to learn how to lead a team. Assign specific roles to each member of the crew. Make sure each has a job and knows which items of equipment and which supplies are his personal responsibility.

FEED 'EM!

One of the most basic ways to treat your crew right is to provide meals and snacks on the set. Especially when you're working with volunteers, food can help keep them in a cooperative frame of mind. But even on a professional movie set where people are well paid, the quality of meals and snacks is important to everyone. On a pro shoot, hot, sit-down meals are served by caterers, and a special unit called *craft services* is responsible for keeping snacks and beverages at hand throughout the day.

So you'll get off to a good start by providing donuts when the crew reports early in the morning on shoot day. Have snacks and beverages, including plenty of drinking water, for break times. And provide a full meal—whether it's pizza or sub sandwiches or a homemade casserole—rather than just encouraging everybody to fill up on snacks at lunchtime. And if you're putting in a long day and shooting into the evening, either provide dinner or give them enough break time to eat at a nearby restaurant.

A director's biggest challenge isn't to make creative decisions—instead, it's to communicate clearly and well. It's easy enough to think up cool stuff to do. The knack of great directing is to get those notions into the heads of the people who will make it happen. The better you learn to communicate, the better your results, and the more clearly your movie will express your vision.

Now, even though people have specific jobs, on a small crew everyone has to pitch in. It's one for all and all for one. On a professional crew, workers called *grips* have the job of moving things, like movie lights, from one setup to the next. But on a small crew, everyone, including the crew, the cast, and even the director, may have grip duties. Know your job, yes, but when the director tells you the next setup is over the hill and the sun is setting fast, all hands must cheerfully set to work to haul the gear over there.

At the beginning of this chapter, we talked about the role of the assistant director, who is always thinking ahead to the next setup. Particularly on a small crew, that's the mindset everyone needs.

The director should have a clear idea—preferably, as a written shot plan—what shots she needs and the setups necessary to get them. The crew doesn't have to know about all the setups in advance. But the director should keep them thinking at least one setup ahead.

PRO TIP

A pro tool for organizing crews and equipment is the *call sheet* (see Figure 5.14). Issued by the assistant director before the first shooting day and again at the end of each day, it gives specific reporting times the next day for cast and crew. It also lists transportation plans, special equipment, and contact information (such as cell phone numbers) for everyone.

Call Sheet

Production:	Neo's Ring	Shooting Day:	Saturday
Producer/PM:	Gerald Jones	Date:	Oct. 9, 20XX
Director:	Pete Shaner	Crew Call:	8:00 AM
AD:	Caleb Cindano	Shooting Call:	8:30 AM

SET	SCENES	PAGES	CAST NOS.	LOCATION
Stairway	1, 3, 6	5	1, 2	N.W. Anderson Bldg.
Pedestrian Bridge	2, 4	4	1, 2	same

NO.	CAST MEMBER	PART OF	MAKE-UP	SET CALL	REMARKS
1	Traci	Traci		8:30 AM	Running shoes!
2	John	Agent		8:30 AM	Black suit and tie

ATMOSPHERE / EXTRAS	PROPS	SPECIAL INSTRUCTIONS
	Backpack	

OTHER CALL TIMES:				VEHICLES & OTHER:
Director	7:30 AM	Camera		
First A.D.	7:30 AM	Sound		
Second A.D.		Grips		
PA		Electric		
Craft Services		Art Dept.		
Script Super		Make-up		
DP		Wardrobe		

NOTES AND CHANGES:

Lunch on the set at 12:30 PM (order in)

Figure 5.14

A professional call sheet is issued in advance of each shooting day by the assistant director. Its purpose is to organize cast, crew, and equipment to be in specific places at specific times. It also sets the director's expectations and promotes communication.

Plan to have spares of every item that you could use up or that might burn out. These include DV cassettes, lamps for movie lights, camcorder batteries, batteries for powered microphones, and items of wardrobe that might become ripped or soiled during a take. Also bring extra electrical extension cords (start calling them *stingers*), plug-in power strips, and audio connectors and cords, as well as all the improvised lighting supplies we've discussed—ropes, blankets, bounce boards, shiny boards, and stands.

> **TIP**
>
> Arriving at the location with a broken camcorder is a truly sad experience you can avoid. If you don't have a carrying case, pack the camera in Styrofoam (use the inserts from its shipping box, if you still have them) and slip it into a backpack.

One member of the crew should be responsible for keeping a written inventory of all your gear. Make sure you leave the location with everything you brought. You'll be particularly glad you did this if you borrowed someone's microphone or if you rented movie lights.

If you transport any gear in a vehicle, secure the gear by tying or wrapping it so the load doesn't shift while you're moving. Delicate gear can break from being jostled in transit. And using a pickup may be handy, but gear can actually bounce out on the highway if it's not securely tied down to the truck bed.

If you're shooting away from home or school, allow plenty of time on shoot day to travel to the location, to set up, and to take down (called *strike*) the set. Accidents are much more likely to happen when you hurry, and when you're striking for the day, you also risk leaving something behind.

Tell your crew that you expect quiet on the set. Some joking around is fine and inevitable as a tension-reliever after long takes. But everyone should know when that's okay and when it's not. Certainly, everyone must be quiet during a take. But they should also understand that you want to keep the camcorder rolling for a few moments after the last line of dialogue. That's good practice, not only for getting reaction shots from actors, but also for capturing some extra footage that will come in handy during the edit.

Things to Keep in Mind on the Set: Working with Your Crew

To summarize, here are the key things a director should keep in mind when working with a crew on the set:

To keep crew activities under control on the set:

1. Learn to communicate and work as a team. Everyone must agree that the director is in charge.
2. Keep thinking ahead to the next setup, safety first.
3. Be careful around any type of artificial lighting—lamps can get hot enough to burn you or cause a fire, and it's all too easy to trip over electrical cords, especially when you're in a hurry.
4. Take spares, including DV cassettes and several sets of batteries for the camcorder and other gear.
5. Leave the location as clean—or cleaner—than you found it.
6. Remember to feed 'em—well!

Get Your Shots: It's All About Coverage

When you're planning your setups for shoot day, your objective is the same as when you're developing a shot plan: You need to provide coverage, or all the shots the editor will need to assemble the screen story. And good coverage should also include several choices for each edit.

Whether you're shooting a carefully rehearsed scene in a script, doing an interview, or covering a live event—your goal should be to think about and get all sizes and angles of shots that the editor might need. To follow classic master-scene shooting, you must get:

1. Master scene—for example, a medium shot of actors in conversation, from the beginning to the end of the scene. (Get the entire scene on tape, even if you don't intend to use all of it in the edit. The master scene is the editor's all-purpose alternative for any take that's unusable.)
2. Closeups of the first actor and then extreme closeups on her.
3. Closeups of the second actor and then extreme closeups on him.
4. Inserts—extreme closeups of hands, objects, and gestures.
5. Establishing shot—a long shot of the building or location.
6. Wild sound effects, if you need them.
7. Room tone.

If you're covering a live event, you don't necessarily need to capture it all as a master scene. Consider, for example, that, while a birthday party might last a couple of hours, you'll do well to give your audience five compelling minutes of edited show. But you do need a variety of shots, particularly closeups, emphasizing not only what was said, but also people's reactions.

It's okay to move with the camera—for example, to pan or even to walk around with it—but use camera movement sparingly between stable shots. For this purpose, think of a stable shot as holding the camera in the same position and framing as it runs and you count to five. A series of stable shots will make good editing choices, but most of the footage from a constantly moving camera will be unusable.

PRO TIP

If you can, keep a written record of your takes. Use the camcorder time code (00:00:00 in the display) as a reference. Note which takes are good (OK) and which are no good (NG: out of focus, noise, poor line reading). This record will save you time when you're going through the footage to decide which takes to load into your computer for editing. A professional form for this purpose is the *camera and sound log* (see Figure 5.15).

Figure 5.15

A professional camera and sound log records the start and end points of takes as camcorder time codes. It's delivered to the editor as a guide for selecting takes from the camcorder tapes.

Date: Oct. 9, 20XX
Work Day: Saturday
Title: Neo's Ring
Director: Pete Shaner
A.D.: Caleb Cindano

Cam Roll	Snd Roll	Set	Scene	Take No.	Start	Finish	Description
01	01	N.W. Anderson Bldg.	13	1	01000000	01000213	NG
				2	01000216	01000301	OK
				3	01000306	01000518	Noise?
				4	01000520	01000735	OK
01	01	Long Stairway	15	1	01000749	01001702	OK
				2	01001710	01002820	NG
				3	01002859	01003934	OK
				4	01004001	01005314	NG

Wild Tracks		Remarks
Birds	01005316	
Fountain	01005421	13-1 Traci off mic
		13-3 Car alarm
		15-2 Focus
		15-4 Bus rumble

Script Supervisor

Shooting Action

In movies, you'll see actors drive cars the wrong way in traffic, fall down stairs and get hit by speeding cars, and impale their opponents on lances. The first thing you need to know about shooting action (chases and stunts) is that safety is the most important element. Everything in movies is make-believe, which means no one ever actually gets hit or hurt in any way. Every moment of a chase or a fight is carefully planned and rehearsed, and you should never do anything that puts your cast and crew in danger. It's not make-believe if somebody gets hurt.

AVOID ACCIDENTS, BUT BE PREPARED

The bottom line is to never attempt a stunt in which you cannot safely control all the elements—it's simply not worth the risk. Never do anything that makes an actor feel unsafe or even uncomfortable. Despite what we've said about taking suggestions from actors, never do anything, or permit them to do anything, that puts them in the slightest danger. Know what the risks are in advance, and plan to avoid them.

Professional movie crews always know the location of the nearest hospital emergency room. You shouldn't be attempting anything that would land you there, but it's good information to have. For example, a crewmember could suffer a serious arterial cut just from using a pocketknife on a piece of rope. As a precaution, at least one person on the set should have a cell phone to call 9-1-1 in case of an emergency.

Tips on Getting Coverage for Documentaries and Music Videos

We won't go into detail about all the types of projects you could shoot. Most of the movie-style shooting we describe involves dramatic acting—meaning scripted dialogue, as well as action, such as chases and fights. But we know that there are many other types of interesting projects you could pick, and here are just two examples.

You might, for example, shoot a live event and assemble the footage as a documentary. Examples would include a birthday party, a sporting event, or a family outing. As your camcorder rolls, keep in mind the advice we've just given about getting good coverage, especially holding on your subject and counting to five so you have usable footage for editing. But also set aside some time to do on-camera interviews with the people who participated. Perhaps after you've shot the action, take each person aside and get a few minutes of their personal reactions to what happened. Ask questions about how they felt, what they liked, what they hoped, and how they did it. When you go to put it all together in the edit, you won't necessarily use the "talking-head" video takes. But you can cut the audio "sound bites" of their reactions together to form much of the narration for your documentary.

Thinking ahead to how you'll edit your movie will suggest other ideas. For example, you can turn any documentary into a music video by later adding a song as your audio track. But if that's your plan, why not get some footage of your friends singing along with the song so you can cut it into the event stuff?

Spike Your Actors

One very effective way to ensure safety is to control carefully where actors come to a stop when they pause in a chase, or where they stand in a fight. You may have heard professional actors in TV interviews talk about "hitting marks." That's the practice of laying down small tape markers (see Figure 5.16) on the floor, called *spiking* their positions. It's often done on movie sets when lighting is so carefully done that it will only look right in a particular spot. But also when you're staging action shots, marking actors' positions can help keep them safe. For example, as we'll explain shortly, staging a convincing fight safely involves keeping the actors far enough apart so they never actually touch each other. If they're each standing on their marks, there will be much less chance of landing an accidental blow.

Figure 5.16

An actor's mark is two strips of tape laid down on the floor in a T to show her where to stand or stop. (The correct stance is usually one toe on either side of the T.) Traditionally used to position the actor just right within a lighting setup, this technique can also be used to mark safe positions in action scenes.

Shooting Chases

If you're tempted to shoot speeding automobiles spinning out of control, you won't find the instructions in this book! Although it might look easy, a foot race is challenging enough to shoot. And your approach to getting the shots is actually much the same, whether your moving subjects are on foot or aboard Roman chariots.

For safety's sake, as well as to keep things under control while you're learning the basics, we recommend you shoot your first chase scene as a foot race, as we did in our DVD short "Neo's Ring." Once you've mastered the principles involved, you can focus on speedier subjects who are tearing around on skateboards or bicycles.

An overall rule for chases is to keep lighting flat. That is, ideally the light should be much the same from all directions, as it is on an overcast day or in the shade of a building. What you especially don't want is to move the camcorder from a bright to a darkly lit area during the same shot or vice versa. If you're using autoexposure, the camcorder's circuitry will go nuts, and the result will be pretty ugly. If you're adjusting exposure manually, you probably can't adjust quickly enough either. If you're moving into the light, the lighter areas of the image will blow out suddenly, as if an explosion took place. Or, if you're moving into the darkness, the image will be enveloped in a sudden gloom. You might think these are nice artistic effects, but in video, they're not. The result just looks like you don't know what you're doing.

One adjustment you might try to make during a chase—or any fast action—is shutter speed. Reducing the shutter speed can enhance the "crispness" of the action and add excitement. But experiment and shoot some test rolls first because you don't want to blow it when you have your armies massed on the set!

To set Shutter Speed on the Canon ZR40:

1. Turn the Power switch to the Camera position.
2. Move the Program switch to P—where you should leave it all the time!
3. Press the Menu button.
4. Select CAM. SET UP by pressing in on the Selector Dial.
5. Select SHUTTER by pressing in on the Selector Dial.
6. Turn the Selector Dial to highlight the desired Shutter Speed and press it in to select.
7. Press the Menu button.

For fast action, start with a shutter speed of about $^1/_{250}$ and increase (make faster) or decrease (make slower) from there until you get the effect you want. Remember that a faster shutter speed reduces the amount of light reaching the camcorder's sensors for each frame. So, it stands to reason that very fast shutter speeds—such as $^1/_{1000}$—won't give you a good exposure and a clear picture unless you're shooting outdoors in full sunlight.

Some camcorders offer shutter speeds slower than $^1/_{30}$ (the ZR40 doesn't). This is slower than one exposure for every frame. The result is extreme blurring, which is an interesting special effect. We used it in the chase scene of "Neo's Ring" to suggest that the Agent was capable of moving faster than Traci could react to him. If your camcorder has these settings, you might want to experiment with them to see what kind of *time bending* effects you can achieve.

PRO TIP

To see the effect of varying shutter speed to capture action, as well as for professional advice on staging fights, rent the DVD *Gangs of New York* and run it with Martin Scorsese's Director's Commentary. The fight scene happens very early in the picture. It took weeks to shoot—longer than some crews take for an entire movie.

The Canon ZR40 also has a setting called *Sports Mode* that controls the shutter speed automatically during action shots. It might give better results than setting the speed manually.

To shoot in Sports Mode on the Canon ZR40:

1. Turn the Power switch to the Camera position.
2. Move the Program switch to P.
3. Press the Selector Dial. A menu of program modes will appear in the display.
4. Turn the Selector Dial to highlight SPORTS and select it by pressing the Selector Dial.

In "Neo's Ring," a mysterious Agent dressed in an ominous black suit runs after Traci in desperate pursuit. We see him follow her upstairs, downstairs, and across an elevated pedestrian bridge.

As you watch the short, notice that none of the shots is very long in duration. The chase is actually a series of very short actions, edited together. In the longest take, he chases her up two flights of stairs, which takes less than three seconds.

Shooting chases as a series of short actions adds to their excitement because editing must be a succession of quick cuts. But it also promotes safety—short takes are easier to do, easier to control, and the actors are less likely to tire and start making mistakes.

TIP

For chase scenes, pay attention to actors' wardrobes with safety in mind. For example, don't make an actor run in a long skirt that might cause her to trip.

If you study the chase scene in "Neo's Ring," you can easily see how the chase was shot as a series of short sprints. Here are some of the setups:

1. Traci runs up the stairs. She pauses and runs back down.
2. The Agent runs up the stairs. He pauses and runs back down.
3. Traci runs up the stairs, followed closely by the Agent. They pause, then run back down.

4. We get close shots on Traci's upper body as she runs, then on her feet.
5. We get close shots on the Agent's upper body as he runs, then on his feet.
6. Traci gives us reaction shots, looking backward.
7. The Agent gives us reaction shots, looking menacing.

And so on. The actors just do these same things in a few different locations, which we intercut to make the final chase.

Screen Direction and Continuity

Planning your shots for a chase involves a basic principle of filmmaking we haven't yet discussed, which is the relationship of screen direction to continuity. It actually applies to all shots and becomes extremely important during editing.

The chase scene is a good illustration.

Screen direction simply refers to where a moving subject appears to be going in the frame: left to right, right to left, bottom to top, top to bottom, straight at the audience or directly away, and so on.

There are many aspects of continuity, or logical visual flow, but screen direction is among the most important.

Continuity of screen direction is the logical flow of movement from one shot to the next in an edited sequence. For example, if one actor chases the other from left to right in one shot, they should appear to keep running in the same direction in the next shot. So its screen direction must also be from left to right. This makes the audience expect that the runner's goal is somewhere off-screen, to the right.

If then you show someone at his destination awaiting the runner's arrival, that person should appear to be looking to the left, the direction the audience expects him to be coming from.

You can change screen direction and preserve continuity in a sequence by inserting a shot with the actors running in a neutral direction—such as straight ahead, toward the camera. Another variation is to shoot them from a high angle, running up the street, from the bottom of the screen to the top.

PRO TIP

You don't always have to follow continuity of screen direction, particularly if you want to jar the audience. For example, changing direction without a neutral shot as a transition can convey confusion or disorientation. (Notice we did it a couple of times in "Neo's Ring.")

Following Action with the Camera

You can use the camera movements we've already described (pan, tilt, and zoom) to follow the action. For example, you can stand in front of the actors and pan handheld to follow them as they run past you, or you can swivel the camcorder on a tripod.

Other types of camera movement attempt to keep pace with a moving subject. *Trucking* moves alongside, staying even with the actor as both travel (see Figure 5.17). Whether the actor is moving or not, a *dolly* shot moves in toward, or out away from, the actor's position. And a *crane* shot raises or lowers the camera above or below the actor.

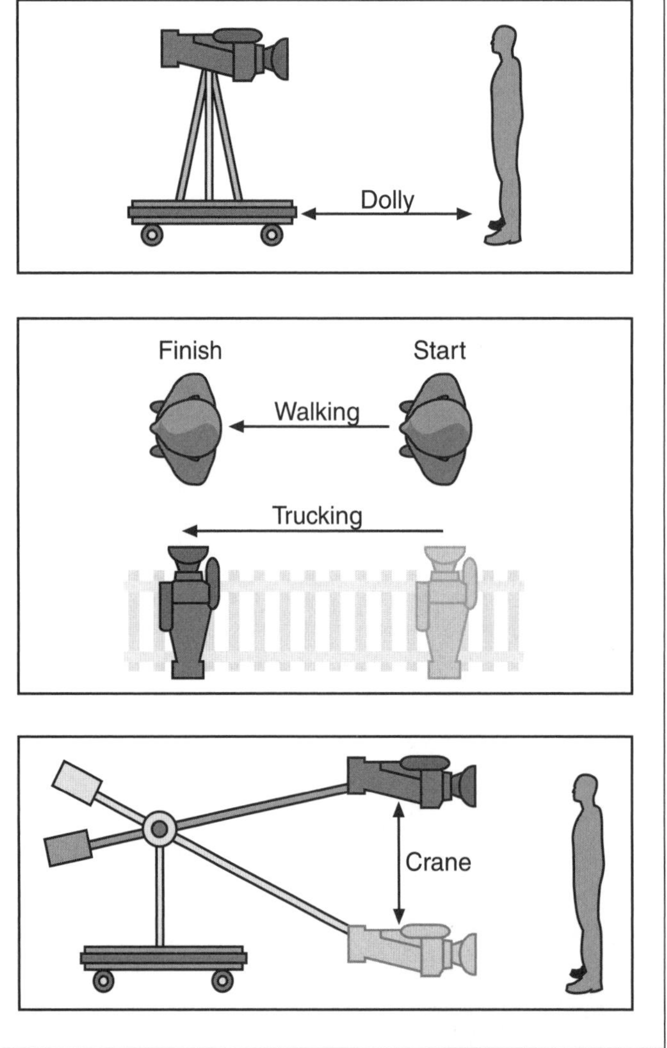

Figure 5.17
In a dolly shot (top), the camera moves toward or away from the subject. In a trucking shot (middle), the camera keeps pace alongside a moving subject. In a crane shot (bottom), a camera on a levered arm is raised above or lowered below the subject.

Hollywood crews have special equipment (appropriately called dollies and cranes) for doing these types of shots, but it's expensive and cumbersome gear.

You can achieve much the same types of movement by setting the camcorder and its operator on some kind of wheeled vehicle, such as a wheelchair, a shopping cart, a child's wagon, or a skateboard. We shot the closeups of Traci's feet in the chase scene in "Neo's Ring" by pushing the camera operator and his camcorder along as he sat curled up on a skateboard.

If you try one of these methods, the surface you roll over should be as smooth as possible. Every pebble the wheels hit in the road will cause the camcorder to jiggle. And the dolly grip who is pushing the operator should try to follow a straight path, keeping the speed uniform.

If you're shooting indoors on a smooth floor, such as a school hallway, a very effective improvised dolly shot can be done by seating the camera operator yoga-style on a blanket. Then have a crewmember pull the blanket by a rolled-up edge, sliding the operator across the floor.

Crane shots are trickier. You can try fastening a camcorder to the end of a broomstick with gaffer's tape, which will work as long as you're only raising or lowering it a few feet. But, particularly for high angle shots, you can get dramatic results by not moving the camera at all. Instead, find a high vantage point on a rooftop and use the zoom control to follow the subjects moving below you (see Figure 5.18).

Figure 5.18

A practical alternative to doing a crane shot for a high angle is to find a vantage point on top of a building looking down on the scene and then use the camcorder's zoom control to follow the action.

Are You Ready?

There's a lot of practical information in this chapter about what to do on shoot day. But if your scene involves stunt fighting or special effects, we'd encourage you to read a bit more before you set out. We'll describe how to carefully stage stunts in Chapter 7, as well as how to plan for special effects such as making a character mysteriously appear or disappear from a shot.

However, none of that will be useful without a basic understanding of how you follow through in the edit to make the movie magic work. So, we'll give you an overview of the editing process in Chapter 6 and then move on to disclose some secrets behind Hollywood movie magic in Chapter 7. (Come to think of it, everything about shooting makes more sense if you at least know what's involved in editing.)

It's a real challenge when you're on the set, the camcorder is rolling, and everything is happening all at once. And perhaps more than any chapter in this book, this one has a lot of rules to remember.

But having dished out all this advice, we'll go one more: Have fun. It's all about telling stories, and you should allow yours to be anything from stunningly horrific to downright silly.

Yes, there are rules that encompass the accumulated experience of more than a century of Hollywood filmmakers. These rules mostly have to do with creative techniques for assembling little snippets of reality called *shots* so that it all makes sense on the screen.

But the rules also include work procedures for keeping million-dollar movies on schedule and on budget. Fortunately, that's not your worry—yet.

So if you want to try breaking the rules—go ahead—you might discover something new and startling.

The future of digital filmmaking belongs to *you,* after all!

FROM THE DIRECTOR'S CHAIR

Here's a tip for coaching inexperienced actors.

If actors aren't responding to each other, the director can encourage better performances by simply reminding them to hold eye contact.

Director Garry Marshall (*Pretty Woman* and *The Princess Diaries,* among many others) sometimes appears in small parts in his movies, and he's also played roles on TV sitcoms. But he doesn't think of himself as an actor. In fact, he says he's fairly insecure about his acting abilities. However, he says he's found that, if he concentrates on making eye contact during a scene, the other actor will give him everything he needs for his performance.

Or, as Hollywood legend Jimmy Cagney reportedly put it: "Stand your ground, look them in the eye, and tell the truth."

One of the actors in "Neo's Ring" has professional acting experience. Can you tell which one? Hint: For most of the movie, you won't be able to tell whether he or she is following Marshall's advice.

6 Editing Your Show and Adding Music

Editing digital video on a computer with an application like Apple iMovie isn't particularly difficult. It's not much more complicated than editing text with Microsoft Word or AppleWorks.

And writing is a good analogy. Hollywood veterans say that a movie is written three times—first by the screenwriter, then by the interpretation of the director and the actors on the set, and finally by the editor. In this sense, editing is much more than the technical process of assembling clips to follow a script. That part of the job is the most like word processing.

But most of all, a great movie editor is a master storyteller. Editing is not just a matter of learning how to use iMovie. That won't make you an editor any more than knowing Word will make you a novelist.

But it's a necessary starting place. Even if you don't aspire to be an accomplished editor, just knowing how the process works will make you a better moviemaker. Because whether you're a writer or a director, an actor or a gaffer—you have only one ultimate goal—to get the editor the shots she needs to make a great movie.

We're going to describe the basic steps you can take in iMovie to assemble your shots to make a scene. From there, the main thing you need to become a skilled editor is lots and lots of practice. (If you have a Windows computer, see the sidebar "Windows Editing Software" in the Appendix.)

In fact, we'll show you how to create a movie even if you haven't shot any video. You can use iMovie in conjunction with iPhoto and iTunes to create a video documentary with music from any collection of still photos. (And if you've never done any video editing, this is a great first project for getting familiar with iMovie.)

Oh, and we'll also acquaint you with some audio tools that can make it easier for you to add an impressive music score to your soundtracks.

PRO TIP

Traditionally, Hollywood film editors have been called *cutters,* presumably because they actually cut film clips and cemented them together. But the origin of the term is actually older than that. The founders of the movie business came from the New York garment industry, where cutters followed dress patterns with scissors to cut pieces from bolts of cloth. Also from this industry, the early movie studios adopted the term *material* to refer to their own raw material—the screen story. For more information on how garment tycoons built the movie business, read Neal Gabler's history, *An Empire of Their Own: How the Jews Invented Hollywood.*

Basic Editing in iMovie 4

Almost all computer-based video editing systems, including iMovie, follow a three-step process:

1. Accumulate clips in a holding area called a *bin.* In film editing, a bin is a physical container used to hold strips of film. In digital video editing, a bin is a folder on your computer's hard drive.
2. Watch clips play in a *preview window,* which looks like a television screen. As you preview, trim the clip to the desired length.
3. Insert clips in story sequence on a graphic *timeline,* which always flows from left (start of movie) to right (the end).

Editing applications differ, however, in the terms they use for these three steps (and for other controls, as well). In iMovie, the bin is called the *Clips pane.* The preview window is the *Monitor,* and the timeline can be displayed in either of two modes—the Clips Viewer (see Figure 6.1) or the Timeline Viewer (see Figure 6.2).

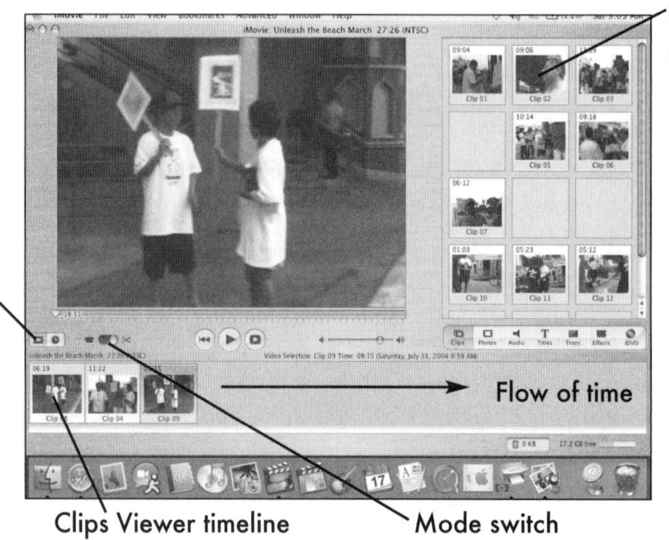

Figure 6.1
The clips shown in the Clips pane aren't in your movie yet. The pane is a holding area for clips you're preparing to trim, prior to inserting them in the timeline of your movie. Remember that, in any video editing application, time always flows from left to right.

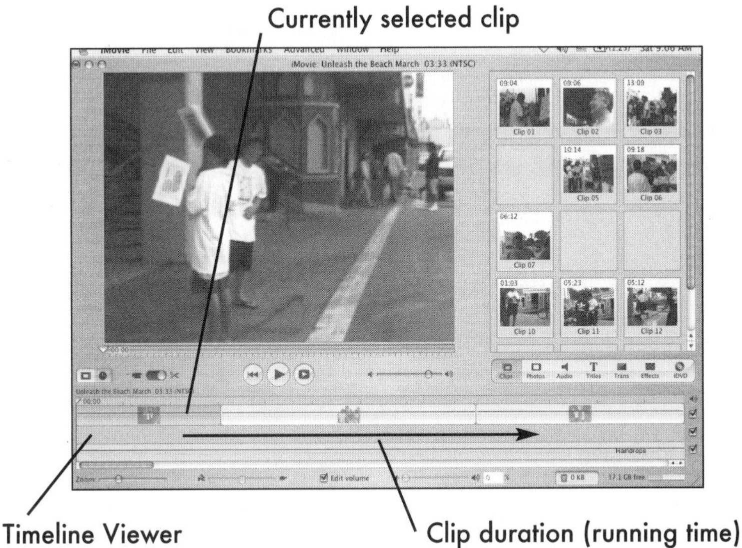

Figure 6.2

As you begin to tweak your edits, switch to the Timeline Viewer to see video clips and corresponding audio tracks. Note that the video track actually represents both the video and its locked audio track unless you extract the audio portion of the clip to work on it separately. Music and sound effects can be added to either of the lower tracks.

The basic editing process touches on the three steps, sort of like running the bases in baseball:

1. Upload (transfer) DV clips from your camcorder to the Clips pane, where you will see them represented as *thumbnail* views of the first video frame (see Figure 6.3).
2. In the Monitor, view the first clip in the sequence you're building and trim it by marking its *In point* (starting frame) and its *Out point* (ending frame; see Figure 6.4). Then *crop* it to the new length.
3. Drag the trimmed clip from the Clips pane to the Clips Viewer (see Figure 6.5). The clip's audio track will go along for the ride and will be inserted automatically in *sync* with the video.
4. Repeat Steps 2 and 3 for each clip you want to insert, each time adding the next clip in the sequence to the right end of the previous clip on the timeline.

Figure 6.3

In the Clips pane, each clip and its thumbnail represent a separate DV clip file on the computer's hard drive.

Figure 6.4

Beneath the Monitor, drag the pointer in the Scrubber Bar to locate and preview any frame within the clip as you watch for and mark appropriate in and out points.

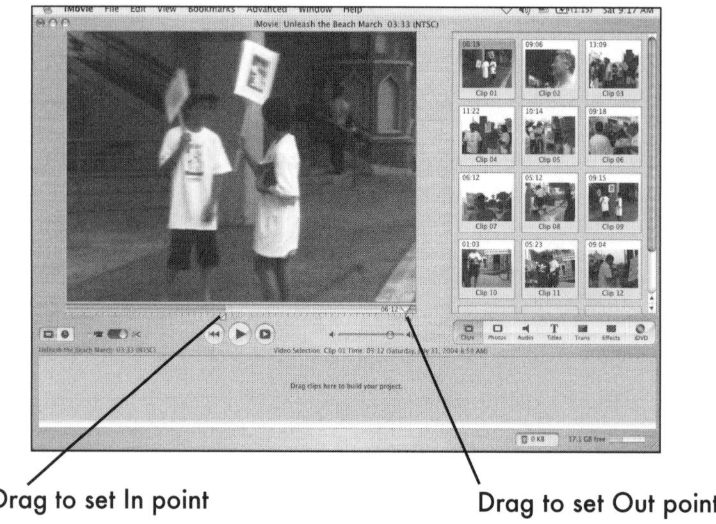

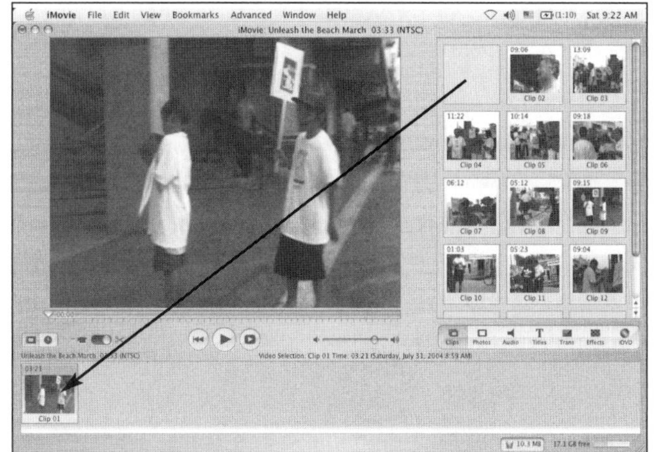

Drag clips to insert in sequence

Figure 6.5

The Clips Viewer is handy for seeing the sequence of clips, but it tells you nothing about their durations. (That's what the Timeline Viewer is for.)

NOTE

In the iMovie window, the Mode switch must be in Camera mode for Step 1 (refer again to Figure 6.1). Then switch to Edit mode, and leave it there for all the other editing steps. For details on uploading clips, see "Uploading DV Footage and Organizing Clips" in this chapter.

The trimming step (Step 2) isn't strictly necessary. You can simply drag any clip from the Clips pane into the Clips Viewer and then make adjustments later in the Timeline Viewer. But get in the habit of always trimming a clip before inserting it on the timeline. This will not only save you time, but also, as you gain practice, it will help you become a more skillful editor.

That's really all there is to *assembly,* building a scene or movie from a series of shots.

So, if you're in a great giant enthusiastic hurry to edit the scene you just shot—go right ahead.

TIP

Got footage? If not, on the DVD we've included the original camcorder takes from the opening scene and from the chase scene of "Neo's Ring." You can try cutting the opening scene on the park bench to practice with master-scene dialogue. Or, cut to the chase and try your hand at creating compelling action. If you get stuck, refer to the script we've included on the disc, or you can play back our finished short again to see at least one way the clips can fit together.

If you do go ahead and edit, you will discover for yourself the difference between simple, technical assembly and skillful, creative editing.

When you play back your first attempt at assembling a scene or movie, the viewing experience probably won't be satisfying. It will seem uncoordinated, like a band that can't find the beat. In movie language, its *pacing* will be all wrong.

One clue that the pacing is off will be that shots seem long and uninteresting, even if they include no more and no less than the dialogue in the script. Or, occasionally you'll see the opposite problem—an important moment will flit by, without a pause for its emotional impact to sink in.

In moviemaking, the result of the editor's assembly (with some tweaking) is called a *rough cut.* You can guess why. Even a pro's rough cut is, well, rough.

Most of what the editor does after the rough cut amounts to tweaking and fine-tuning—always with an eye toward adding interest and improving the pacing.

PRO TIP

Technically, an editor's first assembly with no tweaks is called a *string-out.* It's even rougher than a rough cut. A rough cut may also include a music track, or *scratch track,* although many, if not all, selections will eventually be replaced with a composer's original *score.* Any late version of the edit is called a *fine cut.* The finest of the fine cuts is the *final cut.* But the final cut is rarely final. Some studio executive will no doubt want to make changes based on audience previews. At some point close to the theatrical release date, the edit will have to be *locked,* barring further edits.

The first remedy for poor pacing is careful trimming. The master editor's rule for marking a clip's in and out points is also good advice for attending a Hollywood party: *Arrive late and leave early.* Enter the scene at the latest possible moment. Maybe it's just a breath before the criminal blurts out her surprise confession. Or just after the verdict the audience already knows. Or at the exact moment the cell door slams shut.

Then, leave the party as soon as you can—before it gets boring. After a phone conversation, you never see a movie character hang up, unless the reaction on her face as she does so gives the audience new information. (Screen acting means never having to say, "Good bye." This joke won't mean much to you if you never saw a rerun of *Love Story* on TV.)

TIP

It's a common mistake of novice editors to go for a fine cut on the first try. In and out points should be tight, but not too tight. When you trim, leave about an extra second on either end of a clip. Pros call the extra footage *handles,* and the term itself suggests why they'll come in "handy" in later steps as you refine your edit.

Another way to improve pacing and add interest is *intercutting,* which simply means inserting one shot inside of another. Here's where all that coverage you got by doing classic master-scene shooting will pay off. In master-scene editing, the first shot in the edited sequence is usually the medium-shot master. For example, two characters, Hector and Winona, are shown in heated conversation, framed from the knees up. But as soon as possible, the editor cuts to a closeup of Hector speaking. Then—sooner rather than later, while Hector continues to talk, the editor cuts away to Winona's reactions as she listens.

Now perhaps you realize why we harped so much on getting reaction shots during shooting. The audience will often prefer to watch the emotional reactions on the listener's face rather than the speaker's delivery, however expressive it might be. (Admittedly, in *Hamlet* when Laurence Olivier or Mel Gibson or Kenneth Branagh starts in, "To be or not to be . . . " the camera should stay on that guy for a good while.)

In fact, a skilled editor will look for opportunities to insert reactions at key moments, even if the director's coverage doesn't include them. For example, consider the situation where Hector and Winona are arguing. Having no clips with usable reactions for Winona, the editor might go searching for footage that catches the actor off guard between shots. The editor finds a moment where Winona, clearly impatient for the next take to begin, smirks and folds her arms. The editor then trims the reaction and intercuts it with the argument scene. Inside the argument, the gesture plays as disgust—a telling moment. The reaction not only breaks up the longer scene into which it's inserted, but it also heightens interest by adding an emotional dimension that didn't exist in the original performance.

Such an insertion could heighten the mood that the writer or the director intended for the scene. But it could just as easily change the way the audience understands the scene. And that's a good example of how an editor can rewrite a movie—in this case, by intercutting reaction shots that give the audience strong clues about the characters' inner lives.

The concept of intercutting goes beyond the editing of master-scene coverage. Moviemakers also use it to show parallel action—two or more scenes unfolding in separate locations at the same time. For example, intercutting back and forth between a speeding fire truck and a burning building is much more powerful than using either shot by itself. In fact, intercutting parallel scenes is the editor's staple for creating *time-fuse* sequences in action movies. In a time fuse, the hero has a limited amount of time—never enough, for an average human—to avert disaster. The moviegoers, always eager to be tricked again in new ways, are on the edge of their seats worrying that Hector won't get there in time. So as we watch him rush to Winona's rescue, we cut away repeatedly to her worsening plight. Each time we cut back to her, the fire is hotter, the menace greater, the disaster closer.

Uploading DV Footage and Organizing Clips

Okay, we've talked about editing theory, and we've advised you how to make sure you have the tools to do the job. Now it's time to get specific about how to achieve the tweaking and fine-tuning that editors fret so much about.

TIP

A pitfall when you're uploading clips is the annoying possibility of *dropped frames.* This happens when, for a variety of reasons, your computer can't keep up with the data flow and some video frames don't get captured to the movie file. If during uploading you see a message about dropped frames, simply recapture the clip. If it happens often, consult the Appendix for advice on configuring your computer for video editing.

To upload clips from your camcorder into your computer:

1. Power your camcorder and your computer from a wall outlet, not from batteries. Turn the camcorder power switch to Play (VCR). Turn the computer power on.
2. Connect the camcorder to the computer via a DV (FireWire) cable (see Figure 6.6).
3. Load the first DV cassette you shot into the camcorder.
4. Start iMovie. From the menu bar, select File > New Project.
5. Type a name for your show.
6. Click Save.

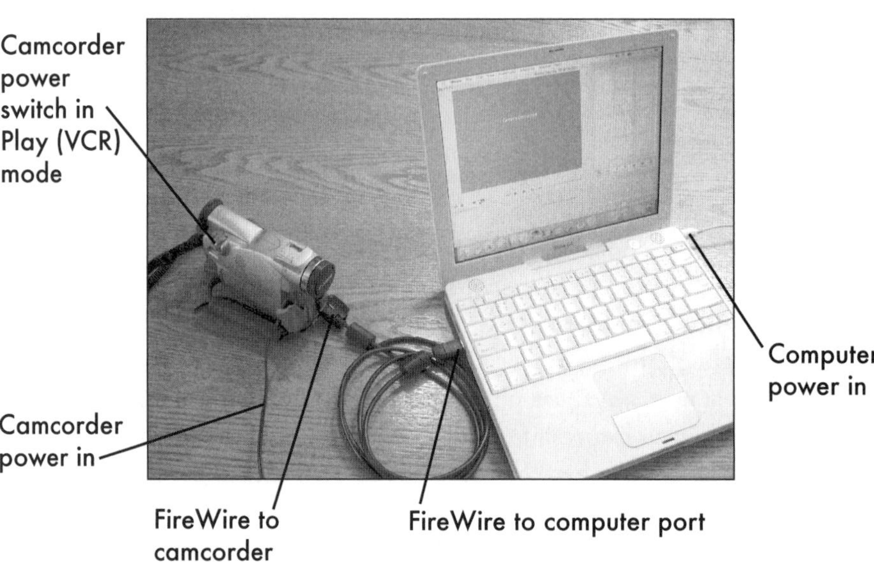

Figure 6.6

In preparation for uploading clips from a DV cassette, power on the camcorder (VCR mode) and the computer before you connect the FireWire cable.

NOTE

The optional disk location you select in the Where box determines the folder on your hard drive that will hold video data files, including your uploaded clips. By default, this is the Movies folder on your main hard drive. If your main hard drive has enough space to hold your uploaded clips, leave the setting alone. You can always copy your project folder to another partition or to an external drive before you switch to Edit mode to start trimming and assembly. Remember that you'll need 13GB of disk space for every hour of footage you want to upload. For more information on configuring your computer for editing, see the Appendix.

7. In the iMovie window, drag the mode switch to the left, to the Camera position. A blue screen with the message Camera Connected should appear (see Figure 6.7).
8. Click the Home button in the iMovie window to rewind the cassette back to the starting point of the first shot.

Click the Import button (or press the spacebar). All of the clips on the cassette will be uploaded automatically. (This will take up to an hour, depending on how much you've recorded.) Each time the camera operator presses the Record button to start a new shot, a separate clip file will be created and added to the Clips pane.

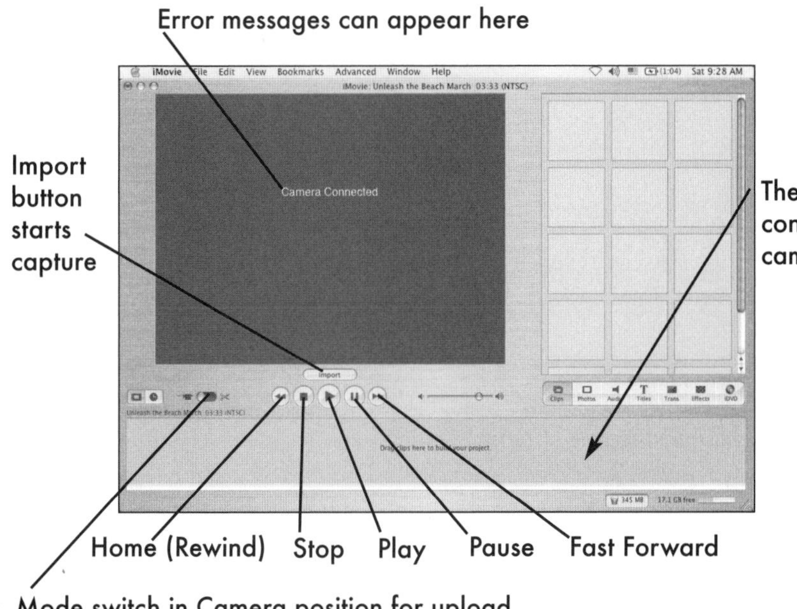

Figure 6.7

Drag (or click) the Mode switch into the Camera position only when you're exchanging video data with the camcorder. Put it in Edit mode at all other times. If there's a problem with the physical connection to the camcorder, you'll see a message in the Monitor window.

NOTE

For the *automatic scene detection* in Step 9 to work, your iMovie Preferences have to be set correctly. From the menu bar, select iMovie > Preferences and make sure there's a check mark in the box Automatically start new clip at scene break (see Figure 6.8).

Figure 6.8

Select iMovie > Preferences and make sure this box is checked to enable automatic scene detection, which permits you to upload the entire contents of a DV cassette while you're doing something more important—like having a sandwich!

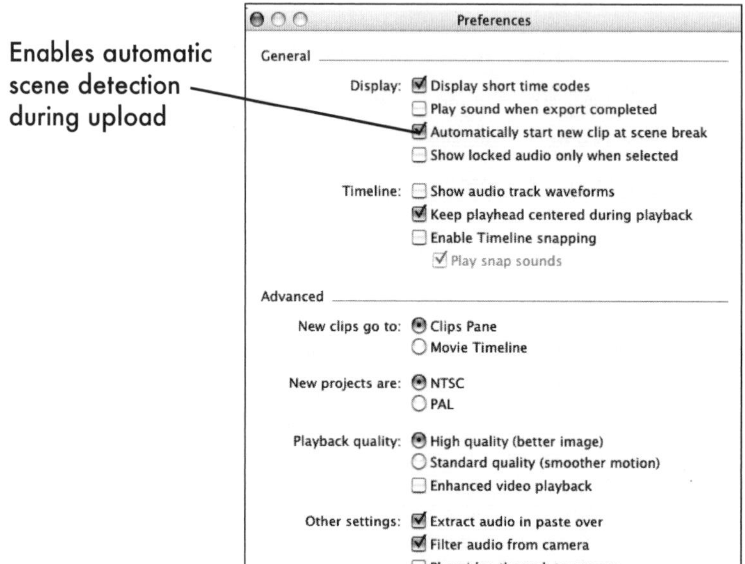

Trimming a Clip

Using the above procedure for uploading has the advantage of being quick and easy. But it has these drawbacks:

- It uploads both good takes and bad, eating up a maximum amount of disk space.
- It grabs the entire clip, starting the moment the camera operator pressed the Record button during shooting until he pressed it again to end the shot.

Trim as You Upload

A better alternative is to select and roughly trim clips as you're uploading them. This is more work for you initially, but overall it will probably save you a lot of time later.

To trim a clip as you're uploading it:

1. In Camera mode, press the Play button to start the preview.
2. At the In point, click the Import button (or press the spacebar).
3. At the Out point, click the Import button (or press the spacebar).

You'll probably have to play and rewind the clip a few times before you upload it to decide just where the In point should be. Ideally, you want to allow a second at each end for handles, jumping in a one-two count before the actual start of the usable shot, then waiting as you count one-two after the end to select the Out point.

Trim Before You Insert

No matter how you import clips into the Clips pane, you can trim them more carefully as you preview them in the Monitor.

To trim a clip in the Monitor:

1. In the iMovie window, switch to Edit mode.
2. In the Clips pane, click the thumbnail of the clip. Its first frame will appear in the Monitor.
3. The entire length of the Scrubber Bar beneath the Monitor represents the running time of the clip. Drag the right Crop Marker to the desired out point (see Figure 6.9).
4. Drag the left crop marker to the desired in point.
5. From the menu bar, select Edit > Crop (or press Command-K).

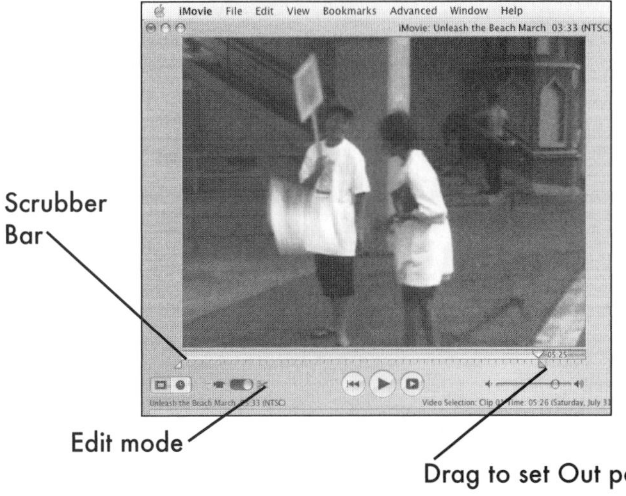

Figure 6.9

To trim a clip in the Monitor when using the Clips Viewer, drag the right-hand pointer in the Scrubber Bar first, to mark the Out point. Then drag the left pointer to mark the In point. Study your choices by playing back the clip and redo them if necessary.

> **TIP**
>
> Many pro editors say they can edit faster by using key commands. As an alternative in Steps 3 and 4, you can use the Left Arrow and Right Arrow keys to move the crop markers. Click the marker you want to move and then press the arrow key once to move one frame, or hold it down to keep moving. Pressing Shift-Right Arrow moves ahead 10 frames, Shift-Left Arrow, back 10 frames.

Trimming clips doesn't end here. You can—and surely will want to—adjust the in and out points of clips further in the Timeline Viewer, especially as you work on the timing of cuts between shots. (See "Cropping a Clip in the Timeline Viewer" in this chapter.)

Organizing Your Clips

No matter how you import clips, iMovie gives them file names: Clip 01, Clip 02, and so on. Those names aren't very descriptive, and as the number of clips grows, it will be more difficult to tell one from the other.

A good habit to make is to rename clips after you've imported them. If you're trimming them one at a time as you import, you can rename a clip before you capture the next one.

To work like a pro, rename clips according to scene, character, shot size, and take number. For example for Reel 1 (first cassette), Scene 1, Amy's closeup, Take 1, you might rename the clip file R1S1_Amy_CU_1.

To rename a clip:

1. In either the Clips pane or the Clips Viewer, click on the clip name, which appears just beneath its thumbnail.
2. Drag over the clip name to highlight it (see Figure 6.10).
3. Type a new name in the text box.
4. Click outside the text box.

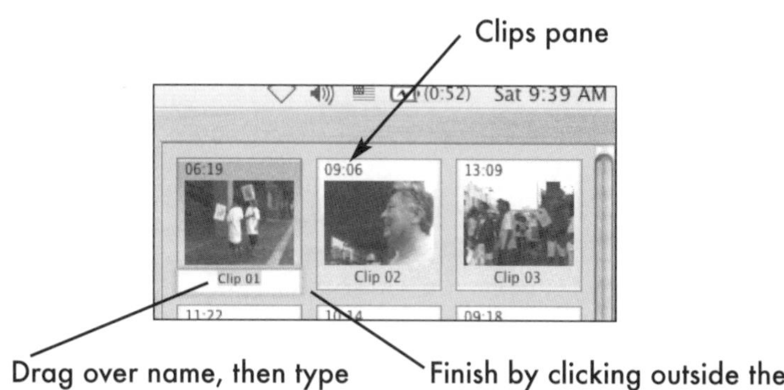

Figure 6.10

To rename a clip in iMovie, it's the same procedure you'd use in Mac OS—click on the name, type over it, and click outside the text box. (It's much the same procedure in Windows, by the way.)

Assembling Your Movie by Inserting Clips into the Clip Viewer

Once you've trimmed your clips, assembling your scene or movie couldn't be easier. It doesn't really matter whether the timeline portion of the iMovie window is set to Clips Viewer or Timeline Viewer when you do this. The result is the same either way. It's easier to see the overall sequence of clips in the Clips Viewer, and it's also easier to move them around if you want to change the sequence.

To assemble your clips:

1. Drag the first clip in your story sequence from the Clips pane into the Clips Viewer.
2. Repeat Step 1 for each clip in the scene or movie (see Figure 6.11). When inserting in sequence, add the next clip to the right edge of the previous clip in the Clips Viewer. To insert a clip between two others (out of sequence), drag it to the point of insertion.
3. If you want to change the order of a clip in the assembled scene, drag it from its original position in the Clips Viewer and drop it at the insert position.

Figure 6.11

You can shuffle the thumbnails of your clips by dragging them in the Clips Viewer to reorder the sequence of clips in your movie.

Playing Back Your Movie

After you've assembled your clips, play back the entire movie to see how it flows.

To play back the entire movie:

1. In Edit mode, in either the Clips Viewer or the Timeline Viewer, deselect any clips you're working on by pressing Command-D or clicking a blank area of the timeline.
2. Click the Home button (or press Function-Left Arrow; hold down the fn key while pressing the Left Arrow key). (See Figure 6.12.)
3. Click the Play button (or press spacebar).

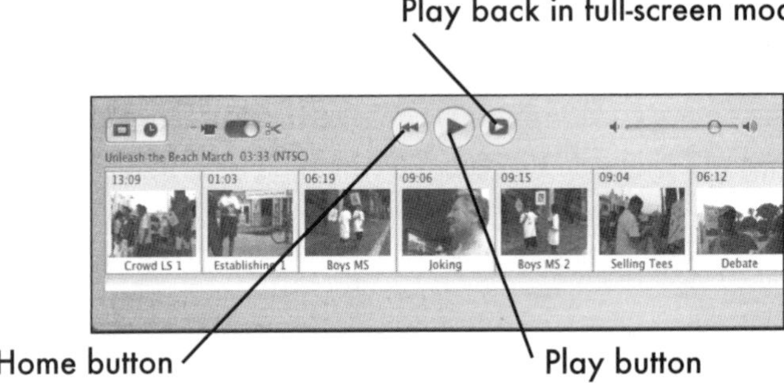

Figure 6.12
The secret to playing back the whole movie rather than just one clip at a time is to deselect all clips in the timeline first, rewind to the start, and then click Play. (The designers of iMovie didn't make this particular feature as obvious as it should be.)

> **TIP**
> If you don't move the playhead Home first (Step 2), playback might stop after the end of the first clip, even if it looks as though you've moved the playhead all the way to the left.

Switching to the Timeline Viewer

When you click the Timeline Viewer button (clock-face symbol), the clips in the timeline change to horizontal bars with lengths corresponding to their running times. And instead of one timeline, you see three separate tracks (see Figure 6.13). The top track is video, and the bottom two tracks are reserved for working with audio. (Actually, the top track holds both video and audio until you extract the audio when you want to work with it separately.)

Figure 6.13

There are actually three audio tracks in the Timeline Viewer. One is locked inside the video track on the top line. That's the locked dialogue track, which stays in there unless you extract it to work on it separately or mix it with music or effects.

Timeline Viewer Controls

The Timeline Viewer has its own playhead, a small inverted triangle, to indicate the frame that appears in the Monitor. As with the playhead in the Scrubber Bar, it moves from left to right as you preview clips or play back the entire movie.

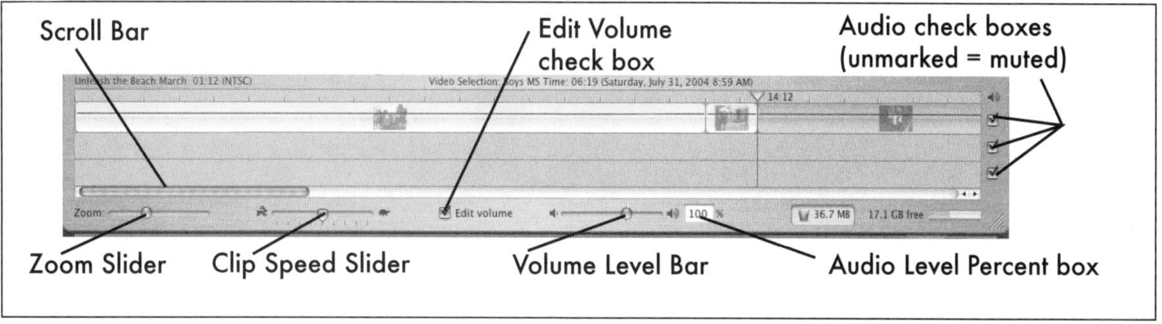

Figure 6.14

The controls in the Timeline Viewer allow you to fine-tune video and audio tracks separately, frame-by-frame, if necessary.

The Timeline Viewer also has some other controls you won't find in the Clips Viewer (see Figure 6.14):

- **Zoom slider.** Drag this control to the left to reduce or to the right to enlarge your view of the timeline. At the extreme left position, all the clips in your assembly should be visible (an overview). Enlarge the view (sliding to the right) to make adjustments to individual clips.
- **Scroll bar.** At larger zoom settings, drag the indicator in the scroll bar to the left or right to select the portion of the timeline you want to view.

- **Clip speed slider.** To make a clip play in fast or slow motion, select the clip in the video track and then adjust this slider. (Use this control sparingly!)
- **Edit volume.** Check this box to enable fine adjustments to the levels of audio clips. (Overall volume of a track can be changed whether or not this box is checked.)
- **Volume level bar.** Drag this slider to the left to decrease or to the right to increase the audio level in the selected clip in the timeline (or type a number in the Percent box).
- **Audio check boxes.** A mark in this box indicates the track's audio is turned on. Click a box to remove the mark, which turns the entire track off (mutes the track).

Making Edits in the Timeline Viewer

The Timeline Viewer is where you'll be working on the movie's pacing and inserting parallel action and cutaways.

Parallel action and cutaways are both types of intercutting, but you should think about them as different editing techniques. A parallel action usually interrupts a scene, replacing both its video and its audio. By contrast, a cutaway often occurs within a scene, replacing only its video clip as the audio from the original scene continues to play. Here's how to do each.

To create parallel action:

1. Upload the shot into the Clips pane that will be inserted into a longer clip that you already have in the timeline and trim it.
2. Select the longer clip in the Timeline Viewer. Drag the playhead to the point at which the parallel action will be inserted (see Figure 6.15).
3. From the menu bar, select Edit > Split Clip at Playhead (or press Command-T). The clip will be divided into two separate shots.
4. Drag the new clip from the Clips pane to the cut in the clip you created in Step 3. The new shot will be inserted in the cut (see Figure 6.16).

Figure 6.15

To insert a clip inside another, first mark the start of the insertion by moving the playhead to that location in the timeline. Then cut into the clip by selecting Edit > Split Clip at Playhead from the menu.

Figure 6.16

Dragging a clip into any cut in the timeline will cause the clip to be inserted in the sequence at that point.

To create a cutaway within a scene:

1. Upload the cutaway shot into the Clips pane and trim it.
2. Select the cutaway's thumbnail in the Clips pane.

3. From the menu bar, select Edit > Copy (or press Command-C).
4. In the Timeline Viewer, click the insertion point in the longer clip where the cutaway will begin.
5. From the menu bar, select Advanced > Paste Over at Playhead (or press Shift-Command-V). The cutaway video will replace the video of the longer clip. Its audio will be extracted automatically and inserted on the timeline in Audio Track 1. The audio level of the inserted clip will be muted automatically, permitting the extracted audio to play over it (see Figure 6.17).

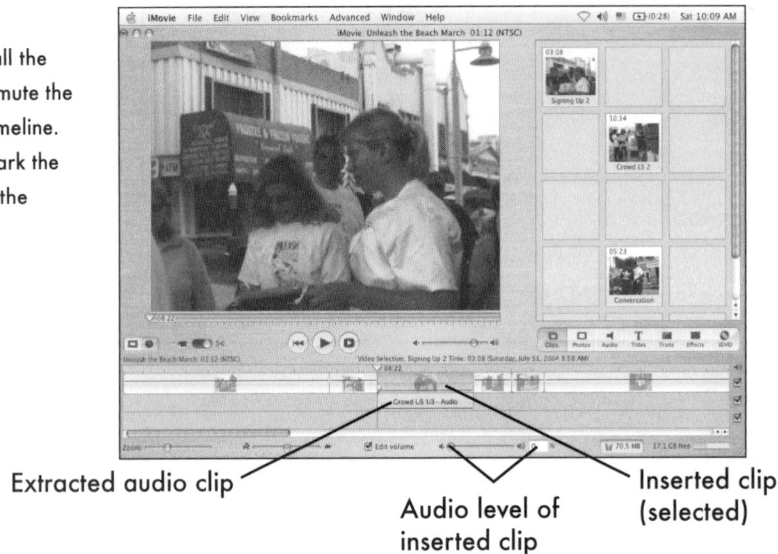

Figure 6.17

Drag the Volume Level slider all the way to the left (zero level) to mute the clip currently selected in the timeline. (To mute the entire track, unmark the check box on the right end of the track's timeline.)

Cropping a Clip in the Timeline Viewer

With the Timeline Viewer open, study your edits as you repeatedly rewind and play back sequences of clips. As you begin to concentrate on pacing, you'll find the exact moment when the cut will seem just right.

To trim a clip in the Timeline Viewer:

1. Select the clip in the Timeline Viewer.
2. In the Scrubber Bar beneath the Monitor window, drag the in point or the out point of the clip (see Figure 6.18), or both.
3. From the menu bar, select Edit > Crop (or press Command-K).

Remember that your trims will go into the iMovie Trash, and you can retrieve them if needed, as long as you don't explicitly empty the trash.

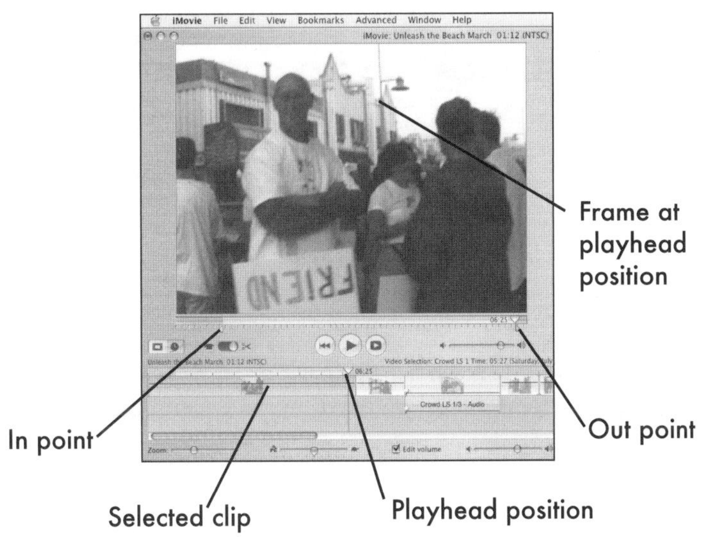

Figure 6.18

When you click the timeline scale just above a clip, its starting and ending points appear as small triangles. Drag them in the timeline to crop, or change the in and out points, of the clip. (There's an Edit > Crop command, but it's unnecessary if you select the points by dragging.)

GOOD HOUSEKEEPING IN iMOVIE

Most professional editing applications operate by a scheme of nondestructive editing. In those programs, your edits don't destroy any portion of the imported clips, which remain intact on your hard drive. And it's therefore possible to undo any edits you make at any point without re-importing the footage from your camcorder tapes.

However, the iMovie editing process normally does destroy portions of your footage. It does this mainly to conserve precious disk space. However, you can force iMovie to work in a nondestructive way by copying (rather than dragging) a clip from the Clips pane (Edit > Copy or Command-C) and pasting it (Edit > Paste or Command-V) into the Timeline Viewer. This preserves your original clip, but it eats up a lot more disk space.

Notice also that iMovie has its own Trash can, located in the lower right of the program window (see Figure 6.19). This is not the same as the Trash can on the Mac desktop. This one is dedicated exclusively to video. When you trim a portion of a clip, or when you delete a clip, the unwanted footage goes here automatically. You can restore a trim immediately after making it by selecting Edit > Undo (Move, Clear, or Crop).

Just to the right of the iMovie Trash can is a bar graph, which shows how much hard drive space you have free. You can watch it fill up rapidly as you upload clips from your camcorder. When the amount of free space is 2GB or less, it's time to make more room on the drive by deleting or backing up unneeded data files.

Another way to free up space is to empty the iMovie Trash (File > Empty Trash). However, if you do this, you will not be able to recover the lost footage.

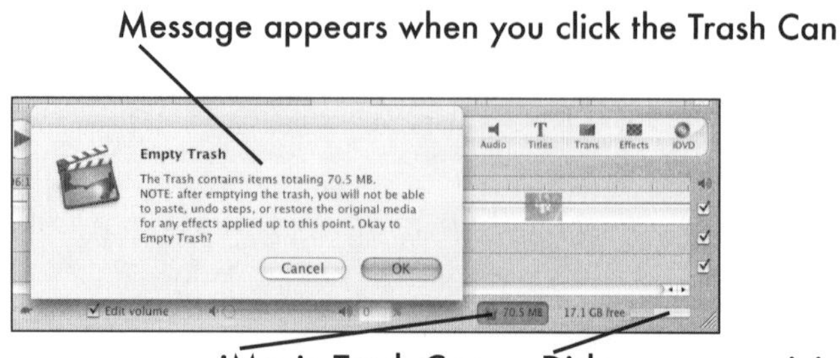

Figure 6.19
The iMovie Trash can is a separate holding area from the one on the Mac desktop. Trimmed video clips can be recovered until you select File > Empty Trash. Empty the trash or delete other unneeded data files on your hard drive if the capacity bar graph shows less than 2GB.

Adding Transitions

The most common type of transition between shots is a cut. Historically, the term meant joining two pieces of film together. When you drag a clip into the timeline in iMovie, the transition created automatically is a cut. You don't have to do anything else to achieve a cut.

A cut works because it spans a logical flow of action on the screen—proceeding from a medium shot to a closeup for the next line of dialogue in a scene, for example. So, the key editorial skill in making a cut is to select clips for *matching action.* Then trim them carefully so that the out point of the first—followed immediately by the in point of the second—makes a transition that seems logical to the audience.

A transition from one shot to another that breaks the continuity, or logical of visual flow, is called a *jump cut.* Jump cuts transport the audience instantly to an unexpected location or time. As with any other cut, an effective jump cut results from your selection shots and the timing of their respective out and in points.

The second most common transition is a dissolve, which in iMovie is called a *cross dissolve.* The first shot fades out while the next shot is fading in over it. A dissolve usually signals to the audience that a time is passing.

As with all other types of transitions except cuts, the editor can vary the duration of a dissolve. A long dissolve (also called a *lap dissolve*), indicates a leisurely transition, a marked changing of pace. And a quick dissolve (lasting perhaps only a few frames) is sometimes an editor's trick for covering a bad cut.

The two other types of transitions you should consider are *fade in* and *fade out.* Fade in gradually at the beginning of your movie; fade out at the end.

> **TIP**
>
> Transitions and effects can add running time to clips. This is another reason to allow some extra footage, or handles, when trimming clips before inserting them in the timeline.

The iMovie application offers many other types of transitions, which go by names like *radial* and *twirl.* Generally, avoid them in your narrative projects. It's not that fancy transitions require advanced skills—they don't. But overusing complex or unusual transitions is the mark of a rookie who is more in love with effects than storytelling. (Exception: If you're making a fast-paced, eye-popping music video, knock yourself out.)

Within your movie, try to stick with cuts. Use dissolves sparingly, usually only to indicate that the next scene occurs at a much later time.

To add a transition between clips:

1. In either the Timeline Viewer or the Clips Viewer, click the boundary between clips where the transition should occur.
2. Click the Trans button to switch to the Transitions pane.
3. Click the type of transition you want to apply, such as Cross Dissolve.
4. Drag the Speed slider to vary the duration of the transition. Click the Preview button to view the transition in the Monitor.
5. When you're satisfied with the duration, drag the name of the transition from the Trans pane into the cut in the timeline (see Figure 6.20). A transition symbol will appear between the clips in the timeline.

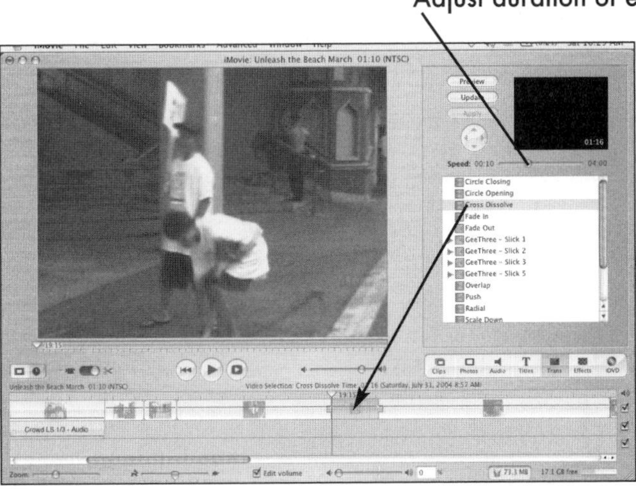

Figure 6.20

As an alternative to the numbered steps listed here, you can drag any transition effect into the timeline and then adjust its duration there—just as you drag the endpoints of a clip.

Extracting an Audio Clip

By default, iMovie keeps audio locked and hidden, in effect, in the video track so you don't have to fool with it and risk getting it out of sync (a real headache to fix).

And for scenes that contain dialogue, you should keep the audio locked most of the time. In general, especially as you're learning to edit, you want to use the sound the camcorder recorded during the take when the actor was speaking.

However, when you're intercutting master-scene coverage, you might prefer to use the dialogue from one clip under the video of another. This is especially true for documentaries, where you may want to use the audio from an on-camera interview as narration under cutaway scenes.

Insert the audio in the timeline first, before inserting the video cutaways.

To work with a clip's audio clip separately:

1. In the Timeline Viewer, insert the video clip that contains the audio at the point in the timeline where you want the audio to begin.
2. With the video clip selected in the timeline, from the menu bar, select Advanced > Extract Audio (or press Command-J). The clip's audio will be inserted directly underneath it (still in sync) in Audio Track 1 (see Figure 6.21).
3. To use only the extracted audio under other clips, select the video clip in the timeline and select Edit > Clear (or press the Delete key).
4. You can now insert cutaway shots from the Clips pane into the video clip directly above the extracted audio (see Figure 6.22).

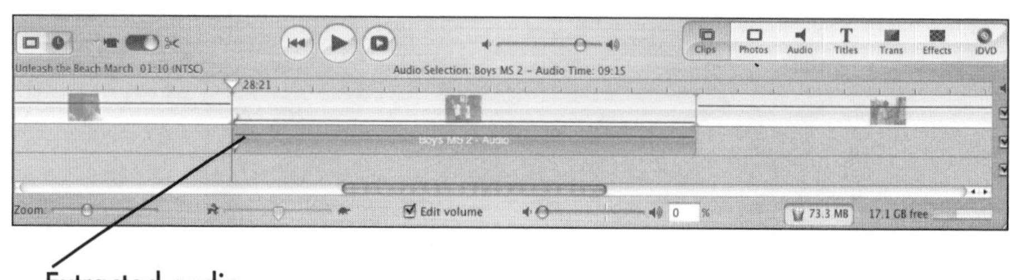

Figure 6.21
When you extract an audio clip, it appears in the empty track area beneath its video clip. However , it remains locked to (in sync with) the video unless you deliberately unlock it. (As a rule, don't unlock a dialogue track without a very good reason.)

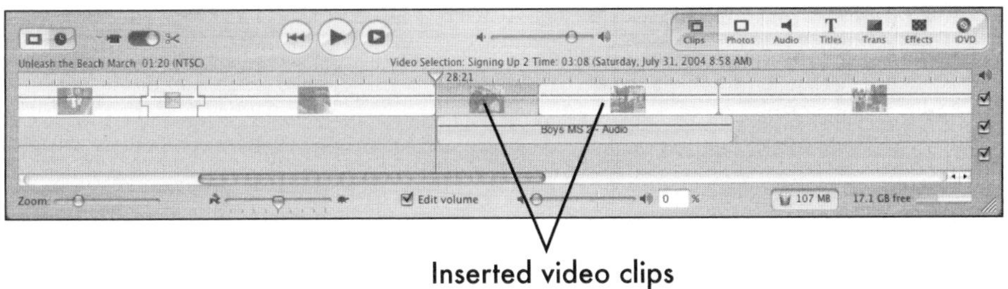

Figure 6.22

One reason to insert a video clip above a separately recorded audio clip is to play a scene with voiceover narration. (Remember to mute the video clip's audio by zeroing its Volume Level slider.)

Controlling the Audio Level of a Clip

There are several ways to control the audio level, or volume, of a clip.

To adjust the overall volume of a clip:

1. In the Timeline Viewer, make sure the corresponding audio check box for the track is marked.
2. Select the clip you want to adjust. If the audio hasn't been extracted, select the video clip. If extracted, select the audio clip directly beneath the video.
3. Drag the Volume Level slider up or down (or type a number in the percent box; see Figure 6.23).
4. Play back the clip, listen, and repeat Step 3 to make further adjustments.

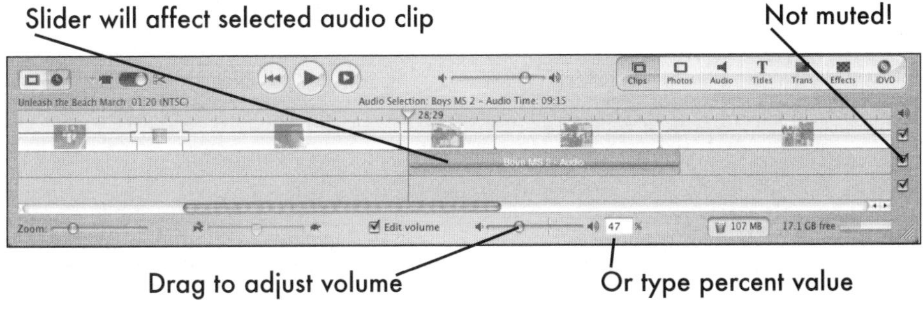

Figure 6.23

The Volume Level slider controls the overall audio level of the clip, whether the audio is embedded in the video track or shown on a separate track. The horizontal bar shown within the clip rises or falls as you adjust.

You might want to adjust the audio level of just a portion of a clip—for example, to dip the volume temporarily to soften a car horn or dog bark. Or you might boost the volume a bit if an actor goes off mic.

To adjust volume up or down during a clip:

1. In the Timeline Viewer, mark the Edit Volume check box. A flat horizontal line (volume level bar) indicating the audio level will appear within each clip in the timeline.

2. Drag the volume level bar in a clip up at a point where you want the level to fade up, down to fade it down. A small circular marker will appear at the point where the level changes (see Figure 6.24).
3. Each volume marker has a tiny companion marker, a dot that appears to its left. Optionally, drag the dot down to create an audio fade-in (see Figure 6.25). Drag it to the left or right to control the duration of the fade.

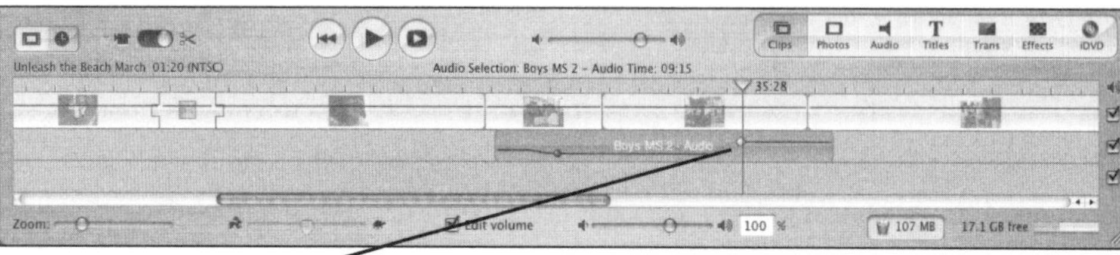

Figure 6.24
Varying the volume within a clip involves clicking and dragging any point on the horizontal volume level bar.

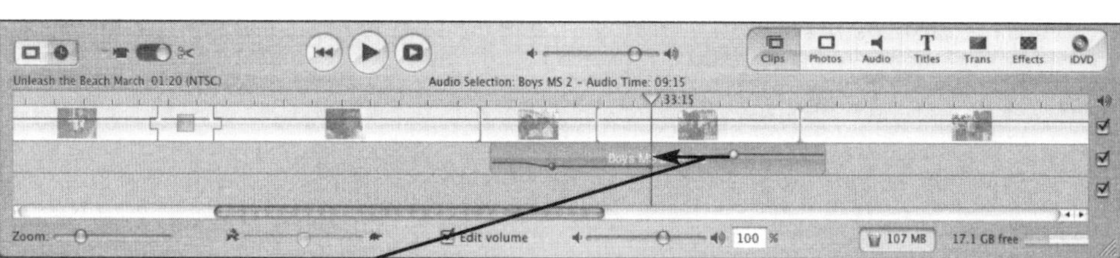

Figure 6.25
Dragging the companion dot of a volume marker changes the in point of the fade and possibly also its duration.

PRO TIP

When you drag the markers in Step 3, you're actually working with key frames. That is, you're specifying the starting point and ending point of an effect, and the program is calculating all the intermediate frames in a process called *interpolation*. You'll find extensive key-frame capabilities in Final Cut Pro for doing custom tweaks to transitions and other effects. And key-frame manipulation is a core capability of Adobe After Effects and other applications that combine and transform video imagery. The term *key framing* derives from traditional movie animation. Lead artists would draw characters at the positions where major movement occurred. Then, in a process called *in-betweening*, apprentice artists would draw the frames in the interval to create smooth motion.

Overlapping Audio Clips

The iMovie Timeline Viewer can display as many as two separate audio tracks. And, if you don't extract the audio and leave it locked in the video track, that gives you a maximum of three tracks to work with. For example, if you leave the dialogue in the video track, you might use the Audio 1 track for music and the Audio 2 track for sound effects.

NOTE

Technically, the camcorder audio track isn't "in" the video track. DV audio is recorded on the tape separately from the video as two tracks—Stereo Left and Stereo Right. However, since iMovie normally keeps video and audio locked together, the program shows the clip to you in the timeline as a single track.

You might think that three audio tracks are all anyone would need, but you'd be far wrong. Professional movies typically have many, many layers of audio for each scene. For one thing, editors often extract and separate dialogue for each actor into a separate track in a process called *cleaning* the dialogue. For another, sound effects in particular can be extraordinarily complex. Remember that the goal of sound techs on the set is simply to capture dialogue. Later, in the final phases of editing, specialist *sound editors* create a rich audio environment instead of the dull echo of a studio sound stage. And original music scores usually contain separate tracks for each instrument in a group or for each section of the orchestra.

Pro editing software can show a great many audio tracks on the timeline, and this is a major difference with iMovie. Final Cut Pro, for example, allows you to work with many separate audio tracks (see Figure 6.26).

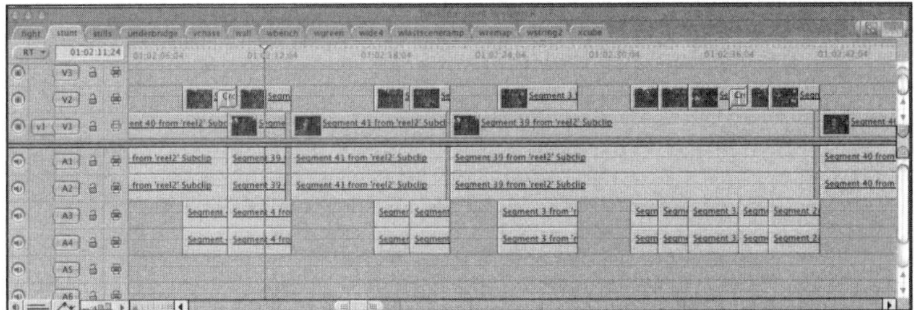

Figure 6.26

The Final Cut Pro window bears a strong resemblance to iMovie, but it supports manipulating many separate audio tracks for greater richness and control.

But if you're finishing your project in iMovie, don't despair. Even though the application limits you to three audio tracks, it gives you the ability to overlap, or merge, an audio clip with either of the separate audio tracks (Audio 1 or Audio 2) on the timeline. And it doesn't limit how many overlaps you create. For example, you could add one sound effect after another to the same track.

There is a disadvantage to this process of overlapping audio. In an editing application like Final Cut Pro or in a music composition program like GarageBand, keeping audio tracks separate preserves your ability to tweak them separately. In particular, it's handy to be able to adjust their levels. But in iMovie, once you overlap one audio clip with another, you can only adjust the overall level of the merged track.

TIP

To find downloadable sound effects on the Web, surf to Sound Hunter (www.soundhunter.com).

The iMovie program has a variety of sound effects to choose from. And you can also import audio files (including both music and effects) from CDs or from Internet downloads.

To add a sound effect to an audio clip by overlapping:

1. Click the Audio button to open the Audio pane.
2. Select iMovie Sound Effects from the pop-up menu at the top of the panel. The sound effect files contained within the Movies folder will appear in a list (see Figure 6.27).
3. Drag the effect you want onto the audio track in the timeline.

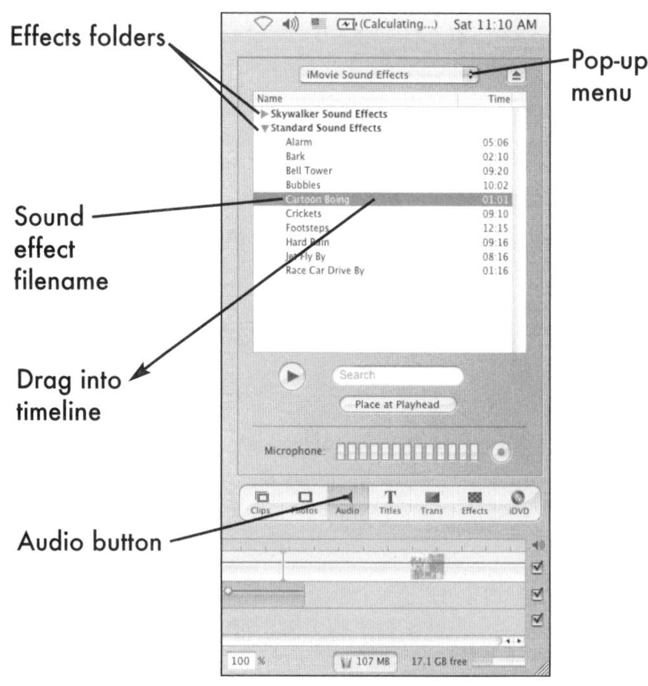

Figure 6.27

The pop-up menu at the top of the Audio pane shows different folders that contain audio files you can import. Within the iTunes folder can be separate folders for each playlist you've built.

Creating a Split Edit

Here's an editing technique you can use to add a truly professional touch—the *split edit.*

In a split edit, at a cut, the transitions between video and audio clips occur out of phase, at slightly different times. Either the video of the incoming shot precedes its audio (called an *L-cut*) or the audio precedes the video (a *J-cut*).

If you watch for it, you'll see this technique used in the movies a lot. It's often done to create a smoother transition when intercutting close-ups during master-scene dialogue. In particular, it's useful for cutting away to reaction shots as quickly as possible before the person who's reacting begins to speak.

TIP

Making a split edit can be tricky, and you probably won't be satisfied with the result the first time. Give yourself some "wiggle room" by starting with clips that have handles on each end.

To create a split edit:

1. Start with two adjoining clips in the Timeline Viewer. Click a transition point just to the left of the cut—about a second long.
2. From the menu bar, select Edit > Split Video Clip at Playhead (or press Command-T).
3. Drag the playhead to the other side of the cut—by exactly the same distance (running time) to the right—as far as the first cut was to the left.
4. Select Edit > Split Video Clip at Playhead (or press Command-T).
5. Select just the two small clips on either side of the cut (Shift-click; see Figure 6.28).
6. From the menu bar, select Advanced > Extract Audio (or press Command-J).
7. From the menu bar, select Advanced > Unlock Audio Clip (or Command-L).
8. To create an L-cut, click the top-right video clip and select Edit > Clear (or press Delete). Then do the same to delete the bottom-left audio clip. To create a J-cut, delete the top-right video and the bottom-left audio (see Figure 6.29).
9. When you're satisfied with the split edit, select the remaining small video and audio clips (Shift-click) and select Advanced > Lock Audio Clip at Playhead (or press Command-L).

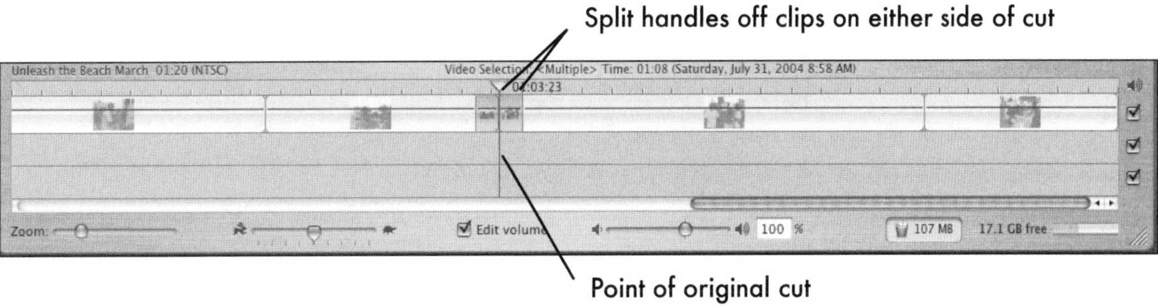

Figure 6.28

To prepare a clip for a split edit, first split the clip to the left of the cut by a duration that's about the same length as the handle you added when you trimmed the clip.

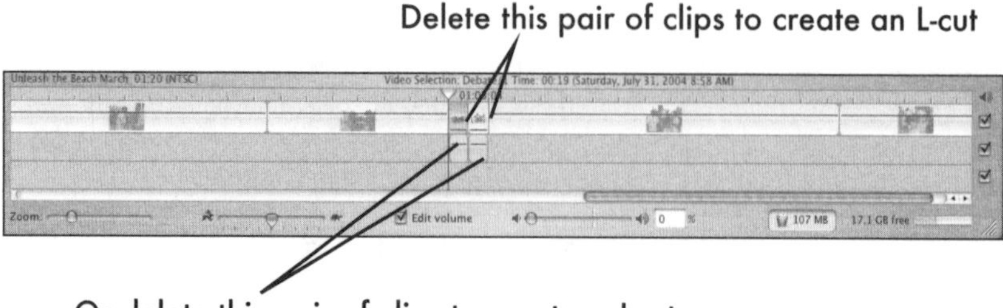

Figure 6.29

To create an L-cut or a J-cut, select a diagonal set of handles you left on either side of the clip when you trimmed it. Then delete the handles. When the program rejoins the cuts after the deletion, the video and audio tracks will be out of phase by the duration of the cuts you deleted. Split edits can be tricky to do, and it will probably take several tries to get one right.

Importing Music from the iTunes Library

As you undoubtedly know, the iTunes application can manage and play digital music files you upload from CDs or that you download from the Internet. It's also designed to work seamlessly with iMovie so that you can transfer music clips directly into the timeline of your movie projects.

To import music from iTunes:

1. In the Timeline Viewer, click the point where you want the music selection to begin.
2. Click the Audio button to open the Audio pane.
3. Select iTunes or a specific playlist name from the pop-up menu at the top of the pane. A list of song titles will appear (see Figure 6.30).
4. Click the title of the song you want to insert.
5. Select the Place at Playhead button.

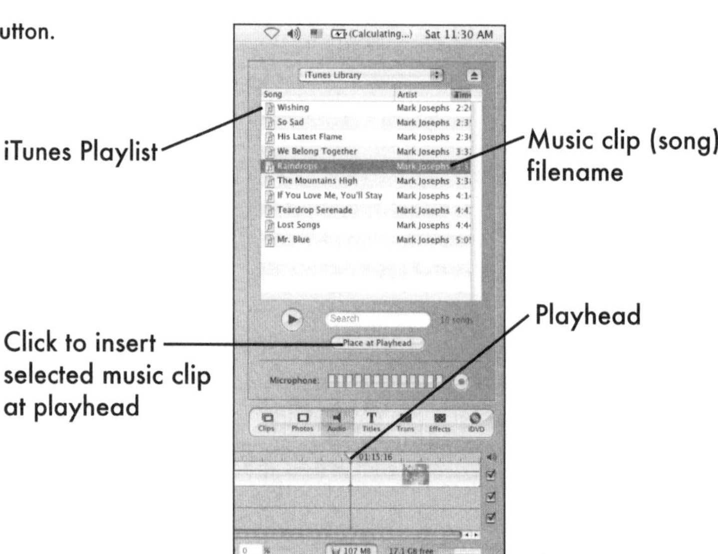

Figure 6.30

You can use iTunes to manage any collection of audio files on your hard drive, in a variety of file formats (such as MP3 and AIFF), including both music and sound effects.

PRO TIP

Remember that all recorded music is copyrighted—and believe it or not, so are sound effects. Don't use someone else's copyrighted music or effects for your project if you intend to exhibit it for the public, show it on the Internet, sell it on tape or DVD, or submit it to film festivals. Library music and loops you use from applications like Sonicfire Pro are okay to use, as long as you have a paid license for the software. And, compositions you create in GarageBand, even if they contain Apple Loops, are your own property.

Importing Music from Sonicfire Pro

We've included the demo version of SmartSound Sonicfire Pro on the DVD. It's one of the best tools we've found for building music soundtracks without a lot of technical fuss or musical skill. Sonicfire Pro provides prerecorded music that has already been cleared for copyright purposes—as long as you paid for the software. There are lots of commercial distributors of so-called library music for movies. However, editing prerecorded audio clips can be tedious, and it's usually hard to match the duration of the music clip to the duration of your video scene.

SmartSound has solved this problem by developing software that automatically recomposes its music clips to exactly fit the running times of your scenes. (In fact, that's exactly how the composer of an original music score works—by fitting her passages for each scene to the running times in the editor's fine cut.)

This technology has a further level of sophistication, which is the ability to automatically "compose" new music selections from prerecorded short passages called *blocks* (see Figure 6.31). Once you've selected a music style, you simply drag the blocks onto the timeline (just as you would an entire song), and the software recomposes the transitions so that it all fits together musically.

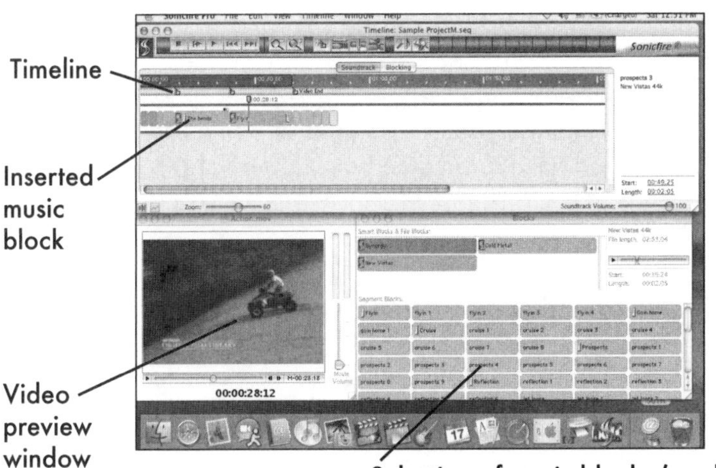

Figure 6.31

In Sonicfire Pro, you load your entire movie by opening it as a project. You can then view its clips in a preview window and add music blocks at any point along a timeline. The application recomposes musical transitions between blocks so the selections sound as if they were scored especially for your movie. It will also alert you as to whether a block is a better intro or finale, for example.

Importing Music from GarageBand

With the release of iLife 4, Apple began to include the GarageBand music composition application. If you have some music training—and particularly if you're producing a music video—you should try building your own music.

The GarageBand window is set up much like the audio timeline of Final Cut Pro, permitting multiple tracks by which you can build many-layered soundtracks (see Figure 6.32).

Figure 6.32
The GarageBand application in the Apple iLife suite lets you compose your own music from a variety of sources, including MIDI recordings, keyboarded passages you create, and imported, prerecorded loops.

The building blocks you can use for your music compositions in GarageBand include your original instrumental performances (imported as MIDI files), imported music clips, and Apple Loops. In music composition software, a *loop* is a musical passage that you can play back repetitively. A drum bed (or any rhythmic percussion) is a good example of a basic loop. But any musical passage can form a loop, even a few notes you played yourself on a keyboard.

We can't begin to tell you how to compose music because there isn't space, and we're not particularly skilled at it.

From the standpoint of using GarageBand with iMovie, it's sufficient to know that you can import any audio file you create with GarageBand through the Audio pane, just as you can with iTunes.

Making a Documentary from Digital Stills with the Ken Burns Effect

Another application that iMovie plays happily with is iPhoto, which helps you manage collections of digital photos as special folders called *albums*. You can use iPhoto to upload stills from your digital photographic camera, or you can scan old snapshots from a paper family album and import them into your iPhoto digital album.

Either way, when you click the Photo button in iMovie, the application will automatically detect any album files you have stored in iPhoto. The Photo pane works much the same way the Clips pane does.

To create a movie from still photos:

1. Drag the photo's thumbnail from the Photo pane into the timeline (either the Clips Viewer or the Timeline Viewer).
2. For the photo you just added, adjust settings in the Ken Burns Effect section of the Photo pane: For the start of the effect, drag the slider bars for Duration or Zoom, or both (see Figure 6.33).
3. Adjust Duration or Zoom for the finish of the effect.
4. Repeat Steps 1–3 for each photo you want to add to the movie.
5. Click the Audio button and add a music track or narration (or both) to the audio tracks.

Figure 6.33

The Ken Burns Effect in iMovie automatically applies a pan or zoom effect to the current slide on the timeline. You can vary the duration of the effect for variety and to keep pace with your music track or narration.

In Step 2, the Duration is the length of time the image will appear on the screen. The Zoom setting controls the speed of the zoom effect.

The types of transitions you set in Steps 2 and 3 are named for documentary filmmaker Ken Burns. In 1990, Burns produced a miniseries for PBS called *The Civil War*. It was immensely popular, and it broadened the popularity of historical documentaries. He's also produced historical TV documentaries on baseball, jazz, and the Statue of Liberty. In developing the visual style that now bears his name, Burns relied almost entirely on vintage photographs and the occasional on-camera interview with noted historians. He let his camera dwell much longer on his still imagery than most producers thought modern audiences would tolerate. And he used the traditional animation techniques of *pan and scan* and *pan and zoom*, adding visual interest by moving the camera around on the still imagery.

PRO TIP

The minimum resolution for still photos is 640 × 480 pixels—larger if you'll be panning or zooming. The resolution of a still DV frame is actually less than required. You'll therefore get ugly, blocky images if you try to use the Ken Burns Effect on stills you grab from your camcorder footage.

The Ken Burns Effect is a very effective way of turning what would otherwise be a straightforward slide show into a dynamic visual experience.

And, as we've said, it's a great way to get some hands-on time with iMovie, even if you don't have any camcorder footage.

Think about it—you can turn the photos of your camping trip into a video that rocks—and use iTunes, Sonicfire Pro, or GarageBand to deliver a music track to match.

Watch the Pace

As quick and easy as iMovie is to use, we just covered the basics in this chapter. There's lots more to discover, and the best way is simply to experiment with assembling your footage, polishing the dialogue, and adding music and sound effects.

At some point, you need to step back from the detailed work, play back your movie, and take a critical look at its pacing. Most of the time, it'll be waaaaaaaay too slow. So, you'll have to do more tweaking to get the scenes to move along crisply. (The advice about Hollywood parties will always serve you well.) You may even find that you don't need some of the dialogue from the script. The actors' gestures, inflections, and body language may tell the story without the words. Send those extraneous words "to the cutting room floor."

Pacing is absolutely fundamental to visual storytelling. To achieve it, directors and editors need to collaborate closely. Remember that the audience only sees and hears what you show them. And, especially in dialogue scenes, you have just two tools to control pacing and to give the scene emotional impact.

The two tools are pauses and closeups, especially extreme closeups.

When a dialogue scene is paced correctly, every pause should be significant. That is, the editor shouldn't permit any pauses between characters' speeches unless it's a "sink in" moment. The audience will understand that a pause is significant only if the pace leading up to it is brisk.

The same holds true for extreme closeups—insert them sparingly. Overdone, they're meaningless.

But combine a rare pause with an extreme closeup of the actor's expression just as he realizes he's touched some emotional third rail—and you have what the pros call a "movie moment."

A movie moment is rare and precious. In an entire feature film, there might be only five or six of them.

Whenever there isn't a major pause, show no mercy. Writer-director Frank Pierson advises filmmakers to grab the audience by the throat in the first scene, and then keep slamming their heads against the wall until the final fadeout.

If you can do that—interspersed with some heavy movie moments—you'll have a real thriller on your hands.

They can breathe on the way home.

FROM THE DIRECTOR'S CHAIR

OR

MEET WALTER MURCH—AN EDITING GOD

The topic of film editing deserves a book of its own, and unfortunately, you won't find a user manual included with iMovie. We cover the basics here, but there are many good books that deal with iMovie exclusively.

If you have professional aspirations as an editor, our favorite book on the art and craft was written by our colleague, Charles Koppelman, *Behind the Seen: How Walter Murch Edited* Cold Mountain *Using Apple's Final Cut Pro and What This Means for Cinema.* Check it out—or better for Charles, buy it!

Walter Murch *(Apocalypse Now, The English Patient, Cold Mountain)* is not only one of the most respected editors working today, but he also worked closely with Apple Computer to make recent versions of Final Cut Pro more useful to professional editors.

7 Shooting and Editing Fights and Special Effects

What's the matter—those long, steamy dialogue scenes not your cup of java?

Just in case there's anyone out there who'd rather stage a fistfight than a breakup or a kiss-and-make-up, this is your chapter.

NOTE

SIR PERCY KNOCKABOUT (V.O., clearing his throat importantly): My view, I like to see both action *and* a love story—all in the same ripping movie—but a certain *impetuous zeal* for situations that betimes break the Marquess of Queensbury rules is quite understandable. (If you have no idea what he's talking about, Google it, and you'll find some pages on the formal rules of boxing.)

Be Safe Out There

We've said it before, and we'll say it again, especially as your actors suit up to clobber each other with Styrofoam maces: **Movie fights are totally fake.**

Action-hero actors and professional stunt performers don't like getting hurt any more than you do. (They need to go to work the next day.) In most stunt fights you see on-screen, the actors *appear* to do a lot of swinging and bashing, but they rarely ever touch each other. Unless it's accidental—and it can happen to the best of them—their strongest blows are little more than taps and pats.

In this chapter, we'll shamelessly spill out our guts about how fake these tough-guys are, and how they pull it off so you think they're getting seriously stomped.

So—with this advice—there should never be any need for any member of your cast or crew to ever be at the slightest risk.

TIP

On the set, never, ever do anything—or ask anyone else to do anything—that's even slightly dangerous. A good basic rule is, if it makes the person uncomfortable to even think about it, then don't try it.

Selling the Punch—Staging a Convincing Fight Scene

The most basic element of any fight is the punch. When Hollywood pros talk about *selling a punch,* they mean taking specific steps that can make a fake blow look real. In our short "Selling the Punch" on the DVD, two professional stunt actors show you exactly how to throw a punch, and how to make the audience think it was bone-shatteringly real. We'll summarize the steps here, but, of course, it's much more fun to watch the video!

In practice, short sequences of punches are put together in *combinations,* and from these the pros use a series of combinations to create lengthy and complicated fights—in much the same way we've told you how to construct a long chase scene from a series of short sprints. We'll also let you in on a few things besides punches you can use to add excitement to your fights, and we'll tell you how to apply stage blood and makeup to simulate the gory results.

Even if the audience is supposed to think the victim is taken by surprise, every punch in a movie fight is carefully rehearsed. A Hollywood punch is a precisely choreographed movement where both characters know exactly what will happen and when.

Throwing the Right Cross

The basic punch is the *right cross.* As with most other types of movie punches, the right cross never involves any actual physical contact.

Let's consider what happens in the fight from the standpoint of the actors: The two of you stand facing each other, with the person who will be receiving the punch staggered slightly to one side. Make sure there's enough distance between you so that the person throwing the punch can get a full extension on her swing without actually contacting her opponent (see Figure 7.1).

Use tape to spike your positions and hit your marks! If you're the aggressor, before you throw the punch, make sure you make eye contact with your partner. This safety measure will prevent you from catching him off guard (and possibly hitting him accidentally).

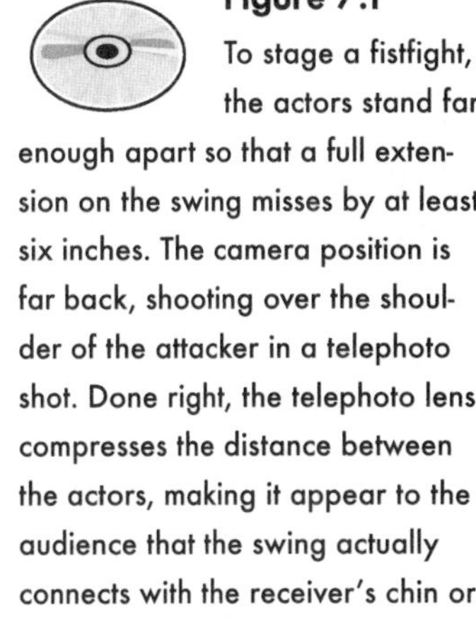

Figure 7.1

To stage a fistfight, the actors stand far enough apart so that a full extension on the swing misses by at least six inches. The camera position is far back, shooting over the shoulder of the attacker in a telephoto shot. Done right, the telephoto lens compresses the distance between the actors, making it appear to the audience that the swing actually connects with the receiver's chin or body.

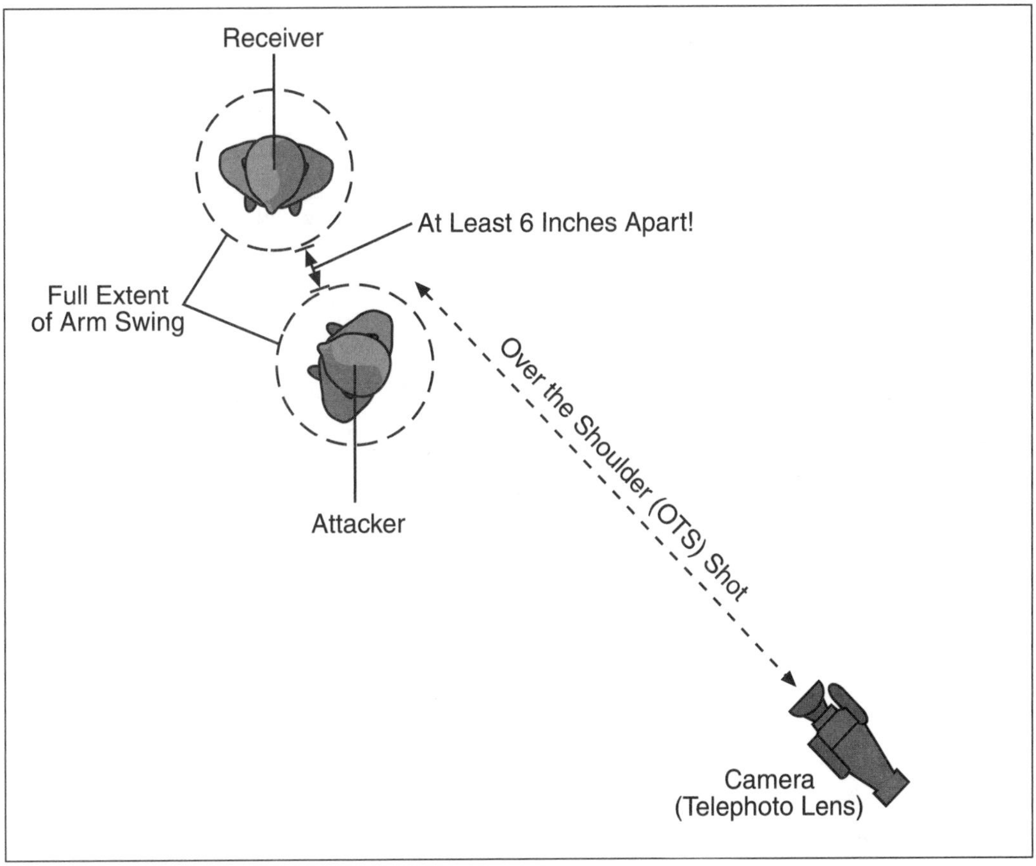

The punch itself is actually quite simple. Just swing past your partner's chin, making sure that you miss it by at least six inches. If you're the person being hit, your reaction and its timing are really important. Snap your head to the side the moment the fist crosses in front of your face.

And that's all there is to it.

In setting up to shoot the punch, camera position must be just so. Locate the camera far enough away from the fighters and zoom in to a telephoto shot to frame the scene. Normally, the camera should be behind the person who is throwing the punch, a little off to the side. In "Neo's Ring," Traci uses exactly the same technique when she appears to clobber the Agent with a swing of her backpack (see Figure 7.2). To the audience, the telephoto lens will seem to compress the distance between attacker and opponent, so it appears to them that the fist (or the backpack, in our example) actually connects with the chin, rather than scoring the wide miss that happens in reality.

Figure 7.2
When Traci clobbers the Agent with her backpack in "Neo's Ring," she actually misses him by about a foot. The illusion of being struck is helped by the Agent reacting to the blow with his body, and by a sound effect created by simply dropping a loaded bag on the sidewalk.

Four Secrets to Selling Punches on the Screen

No matter how well you rehearse your punches, the fight won't look real unless you do four things exactly right:

1. The person throwing the punch has to complete her swing with a follow-through. If you stop the swing in front of your opponent's face, the blow won't look convincing.
2. The person receiving the punch has to time his reaction so that it matches the swing. Snapping your head too early or too late will spoil the effect. It's also helpful if you react to the pain of being hit. Staggering backwards and rubbing your chin will show the audience how hard the blow was.

3. The camera must be in the right place. Usually, you'll want it looking over the shoulder of the person throwing the punch. For some variety when you're editing, the camera can also be directly behind the person being hit. If the camera isn't in one of these two places, the audience will see that the punch isn't real.
4. In editing, you must pick an appropriate sound effect to sell the punch. Although you can find pre-made sound effects of various punches, it can be more fun to create your own. Hitting a head of lettuce or snapping a stalk of celery is the standby in Hollywood. But experiment a little and create some sounds of your own. Then, when you edit, try a selection of different sounds with the scene. Each one will make the punch seem different. You can even record an actor's "oof," "ah!" and "ugh!" as wild sound effects—and mix the reaction with the sound of each blow during the edit.

Other Types of Punches: The Jab and the Uppercut

Once the cast and crew have mastered throwing and shooting the right cross, try these two other punches.

Jab. The jab can be thrown with either hand, but usually with the left. It's a short, quick punch aimed directly at the face, typically thrown two or three times in rapid succession. Note some differences between the jab and the right cross. There's no follow-through in the jab. After throwing the jab, pull the hand quickly back into position for the next punch. If you're the receiver, react to the punch by snapping your head straight back and grimacing or grabbing your face to show how much it hurt.

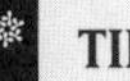

TIP

Make sure the person receiving the punch is standing far enough back so he will not actually be hit when the puncher's arm is fully extended. This will prevent any accidental contact. Help the actors remember where to stand by spiking the safe distance with tape.

Uppercut. It's similar to the right cross—except the motion of the punch goes straight up instead of across the face (see Figure 7.3). The target of an uppercut is your opponent's chin, and to simulate getting hit, the receiver snaps his head up and back.

Figure 7.3

When executing an uppercut, the attacker shoots her fist straight up, and the receiver snaps his head back smartly to indicate a hard blow to the chin. As with the right cross and the jab, the attacker never actually touches her opponent.

Once again, safety is paramount. When throwing an uppercut, make sure there are at least six inches between your swing and your opponent's chin.

Staging a Fight as a Series of Combinations

You can take the three basic punches—the cross, the jab, and the uppercut—and put them together in combinations of three or four punches at a time. An example of a combination would be two jabs followed by a right cross.

You can then build a longer fight scene as a series of short combinations. Shoot just one combination at a time, after which the director would call cut, change camera positions, and shoot the next combination. That way, the entire fight from beginning to end never actually happens all at once on the set. Instead, you shoot the pieces one at a time and then put them together during editing. Breaking a fight scene down like this makes it easier to shoot and safer for your actors, since they only have to concentrate on two or three punches at a time.

Staging a fight as a series of combinations is both easier and safer than shooting a continuous take of a long fight, which is the exception to always shooting one long take of the master scene. You won't necessarily have one take that captures the whole event from start to finish. But breaking the action into combinations can enhance the drama by escalating the apparent violence and the pace from one combination to the next. Achieving this is largely a matter of masterful editing, which we'll explain shortly.

Tips for Safe Choking and Hair Pulling

Besides punches, there are some other pieces of action you can add to give excitement to a fight. Two possibilities are choking and hair pulling. Each of these elements involves physical contact between the actors, and each of them looks very painful. But the secret to each one is that the person who looks like he's in pain is actually in total control of the stunt.

TIP

If the "victim" doesn't feel in control at all times, then stop because you're doing it wrong and someone will get hurt!

To simulate choking someone, the attacker puts her hands around the neck of the opponent, and the opponent grabs onto the wrists of the attacker, and—here's the trick—instead of actually trying to choke the opponent, the attacker tries to pull her hands *away* from the opponent's neck while the opponent tries just as hard to hold the attacker's hands in place (see Figure 7.4).

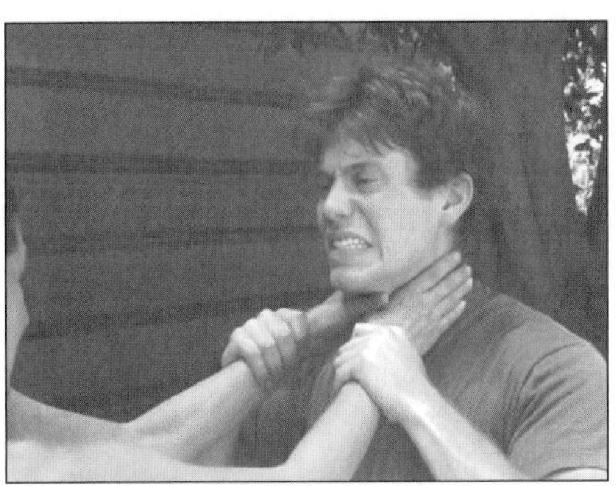

Figure 7.4

In a correctly staged choking, the physical strain of the struggle is caused by the attacker trying to pull her hands away from the victim's throat as the victim struggles just as hard to keep them there. Done properly, the victim is always in control of this stunt.

When done properly, both actors are truly struggling against one another, and the exertion on their faces is real. But no one is in any danger of being hurt.

The hair pull is done in similar fashion. To the audience, it looks as if one actor is dragging the other by his hair. Once again, this is just an illusion. The attacker places her hand on the opponent's head and grabs a handful of hair. The opponent grabs the attacker's wrist with both hands (see Figure 7.5). The trick here is that the opponent is actually being dragged by his arms, and there is no strain on his hair at all. The handful of hair is just for show. Of course, as with any stunt, it's the opponent's acting that makes it look like he's in pain.

Figure 7.5

The technique for the hair pull is much the same as for a staged strangling. The opponent holds tightly to the attacker's hand, and there is never any strain on the hair.

Striking with a Weapon

Sometimes in a fight, you'll want to have the attacker hit his opponent with, say, a club or a light saber. This is easy to do, but there are two very important things to keep in mind.

First, never use a real weapon. Use something made of light plastic or foam rubber that looks like the real thing, but won't cause any harm if contact is accidentally made. In theatrical supply houses and novelty shops, you can find every type of weapon from baseball bats to nun chucks, all made out of lightweight foam rubber. These are designed specifically for use in stage fighting, and it's the skill of the performers along with some excellent sound effects that make the blows seem real.

The second important point is that the weapon need never actually touch the opponent. Just like a stunt punch, there is always at least six inches between the weapon and the opponent. It's the opponent's reaction along with the editor's sound effect that make it seem as if the weapon has landed a blow.

Faking Injuries with Makeup

For most fights, makeup is fairly simple and will consist mostly of some blood and a little bit of bruising.

Creating and Using Stage Blood

The blood is easy. You can either buy stage blood, or make your own by mixing corn syrup with a little red food coloring. The corn syrup is thick and sticky just like real blood, and it has the added benefit of tasting pretty good. The most common places to use blood during a fight are underneath the nose or at either corner of the mouth. Apply it with a cotton swab or makeup eyeliner brush to paint gashes and scars.

Using Makeup to Create Bruises

Bruising is also pretty easy, and is accomplished by using makeup sticks of red, purple, and black. The key to making a "good-looking" bruise is not to use too much color and to blend the colors together carefully (see Figure 7.6).

Figure 7.6

Build up a fake bruise in layers with makeup crayon—a large red area, a smaller yellow area within it, and a touch of blue at the center. Blend the edges outward into the surrounding skin. Touch up the center with a gob of stage blood. In a fight sequence, build up the bruise in stages, adding a bit more to it after you finish shooting each combination. (You can buy these makeup sticks in the cosmetics section of any drug store.)

Now here's the second reason that fights are broken down into combinations and filmed separately: Stopping the fight after each combination allows you to add the makeup a little at a time, in stages. That way, the injuries build up gradually over the course of the fight, making it seem more realistic.

Editing a Fight Scene

We said there were four things you have to do to sell a punch, but we left out the finishing touch, which is editing a series of combinations so they play like a single, continuous fight.

Here are a few basic rules for cutting a winning fight:

1. **Edit for matching action.** Marry the swing and follow-through to the correct reaction shot. For example, if the attacker throws an uppercut, cutting to the receiver's reaction to a right cross won't match. Also, preserve continuity. Don't cross the *stage line* (an imaginary line drawn between the actors) from one shot to the next (see Figure 7.7). That is, if the attacker is on the left side of the screen when throwing the punch, she should still be on that side when you cut to the receiver's reaction shot.
2. **Edit for pacing.** Don't cut away too soon from the attack—remember to show the follow-through. However, don't leave any pauses within the combination. Remember that a pause is a "sink-in" movie moment. Save those for closeups of the receiver's reaction, giving the audience the first glimpse of the shock on his face at the force of the blow and the extent of his bloody wounds.
3. **Time the sound effect.** When you're editing in iMovie (or in any video editing application), you must align the audio peak of the blow to match exactly the visual moment of contact.

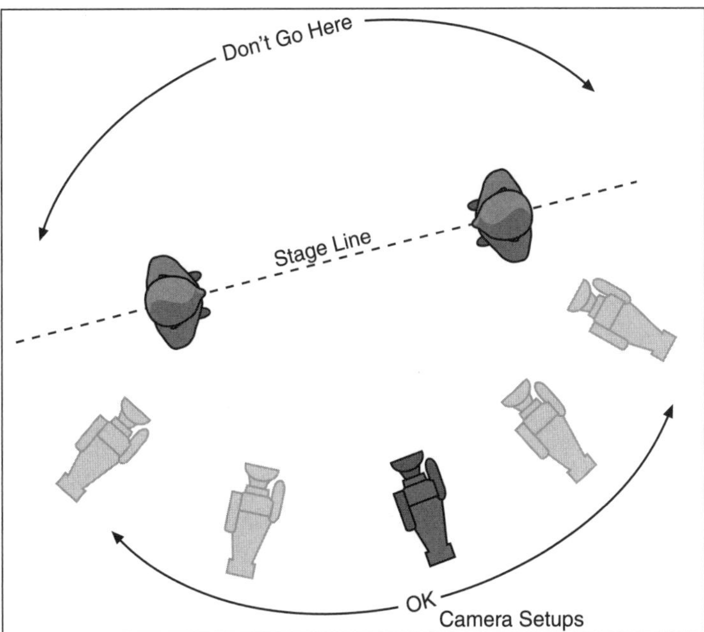

Figure 7.7

The traditional director's rule of not crossing the stage line with the camera when shooting a scene also applies during editing, especially when assembling a fight sequence. Selecting takes from either side of the line will cause actors to jump inexplicably from one side of the screen to the other.

To align picture and sound in iMovie:

1. From the menu bar, select iMovie > Preferences (or press Command-Comma).
2. In the Preferences window, mark the Show audio track waveforms check box (see Figure 7.8).
3. Close the Preferences window. Waveforms showing the peaks and valleys of the audio level will appear in the clips in the timeline.
4. Click the sound effect audio clip in the timeline to select it.
5. From the menu bar, select Advanced > Unlock Audio Clip (or press Command-L).
6. Drag the playhead in the timeline to show the visual point of impact in the Monitor.
7. Drag the sound-effect audio clip so that its first peak aligns vertically with the playhead (see Figure 7.9).

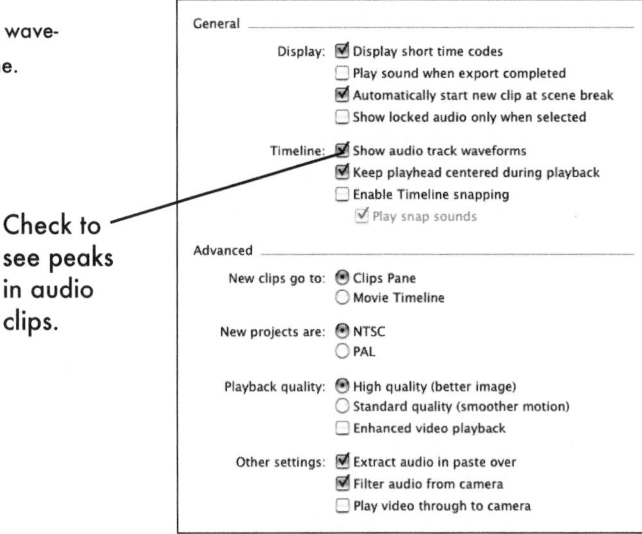

Figure 7.8

Mark this check box to display audio waveforms in the clips in the iMovie timeline.

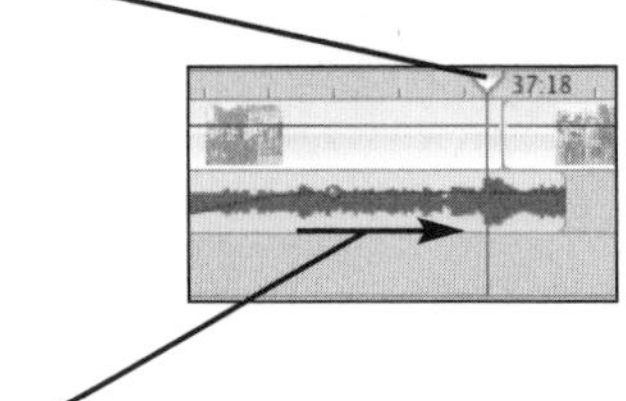

Figure 7.9

By dragging the unlocked audio clip to the right or left in the Timeline Viewer, align the leading edge of a sound-effect peak with the video frame that shows the landing of the blow.

Stunt Fighting Recap

Here's a summary of the basic things you need to do to create a convincing fight scene:

1. Position actors so a full swing will miss the receiver by at least six inches.
2. Although there can be variations, shoot from over the attacker's shoulder with a telephoto lens, from a distance. This will compress the apparent distance between the attacker and the receiver so that the audience will think the blow makes contact.
3. The attacker should follow through with her punch.
4. The receiver should react to the blow to convince the audience of its severity.
5. Pick an appropriate sound effect to sell the punch. Adjust its timing during editing so that it coincides exactly with the landing of the blow.
6. Shoot fight sequences as a series of short combinations.
7. Edit for matching action and continuity. Especially during a combination, don't pick takes that cross the stage line.
8. Edit for pacing, permitting no pauses between punches, perhaps pausing at the end of a combination on the receiver's reaction shot.
9. Add stage blood and bruise makeup to worsen the appearance of wounds at the end of each combination.

Movie Magic Debunked—Shooting and Editing Special Effects

All right, my pretties. Gather 'round, and we'll show you how to dissolve the evil witch. Or make the hero pop magically out of thin air.

You shoot both tricks the same way. And it's so simple, you'd think the deception put over on movie audiences for more than a century would be so stale that no one today would believe it.

To shoot someone magically appearing or disappearing, put the camcorder on a tripod. Actually, that's the most technical part of it. You need to keep the camcorder absolutely still for the duration of the shot. Shoot the actor in the scene, and then keep rolling as she steps out. Or do the opposite—roll on an empty set and let the actor step in. This is exactly what we did to make Traci magically disappear from the opening park bench scene in "Neo's Ring" (see Figure 7.10).

Figure 7.10

To make an actor appear or disappear, simply hold the camera in the same position and have her step out of the shot. The magic is done in editing by omitting the "stepping out" part (middle photo) and joining the two remaining shots with a cut or a dissolve. As with stage punches, a sound effect helps to "sell" the illusion. This example is from the opening scene of "Neo's Ring."

It really doesn't make any difference which order you shoot them in—or whether you intend for the actor to appear or disappear. In editing, you'll cut out the middle part—the stepping in or out—and cut from "now you see him" to "now you don't." (Or, the other way.) To make the illusion slicker, you can dissolve at the transition. Or you can splice a blown-out white frame between the before and after shots, which will make the actor appear (or disappear) in a blinding flash!

Add a suitable sound effect (POP! or BOING! or BUZZZZ!), and you'll effectively sell the audience on your trickery, just as surely as you peddle those fake punches.

Preparing for Compositing—Shooting a Green Screen

With the addition of some inexpensive software, you can use iMovie to combine video imagery in a process called *compositing.* You'll see several examples of it in "Neo's Ring," including the sequence where Traci keeps popping into scenes from distant lands after she vanishes from the park bench.

The trick to doing this is only a little more complicated than making her appear or disappear.

To make it possible to combine Traci with vacation travel footage, we shot her against a solid green screen (see Figure 7.11). In a later editing step—called *chroma keying,* which we'll describe in detail in the next chapter—you can combine a clip of the actor standing in front of the screen with another clip showing the scene you want in the background. In the compositing process, iMovie substitutes the background scene for every pixel in the original shot that's green.

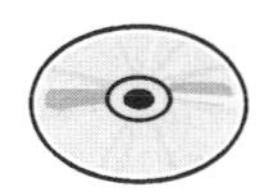

Figure 7.11
Shooting Traci against a videographer's green screen made it possible to create a composite special effect during editing that substitutes video scenery for the green areas in the shot.

You can buy a small portable green screen in a professional photo shop. They also make blue ones. In general, green works best outdoors, blue indoors.

PRO TIP

You can also use solid white or solid black for a background, in a composite process called *luminance keying*. However, using white instead of green or blue can be very difficult to do, especially outdoors, for two reasons. First, the white area you want to substitute must be totally overexposed (100 percent, or blown-out). So areas that are merely very light gray won't work. Secondly, any blown-out highlights in the subject will also be substituted, causing the background scene to show through the sheen in the actor's hair, for example. Similarly, using black as the key color means you can't permit shadows to fall in the wrong places. So, you have to light the scene very carefully using flat lighting to avoid highlights, and the subject can't move around too much, to avoid catching a reflection that will be recorded as white.

When you're shooting, whichever color you choose as a chroma key, there are two main things to remember:

1. Light the screen evenly. Any shadow or highlight falling on the screen, including the actor's shadow or a shaft of sunlight, will register in the camcorder as a different color and won't be included in the substitution process (see Figure 7.12).

2. Avoid using wardrobe or prop items that contain the key color. Also, don't shoot shiny objects like jewelry or sequins that might reflect it.

Figure 7.12

The main thing to remember when rigging a green (or blue) screen is to light it evenly. Here, for shooting in full sunlight, we rigged a silk over the actor's head to soften highlights and shadows.

Ho hum. It's really all too easy...

Unless, of course, you try something *really tricky* like a *dolly counter-zoom.*

Okay, Go Ahead and Try a Dolly Counter-Zoom—If You Must!

The incredibly complicated-sounding shot called the *dolly counter-zoom* is simple enough in principle: You dolly in while zooming out. Or you dolly out while zooming in. For the effect to work, the two actions must happen at exactly the same time, at exactly the same speed, so that the size and framing of the subject doesn't change.

It's a totally cool effect, and one it seems every film student feels obliged to try at least once. (If there's one telltale sign of an enthusiastic and talented newbie in filmmaking, this shot showing up in her work is it.)

The effect of dollying in while zooming out on an actor's closeup makes a transition from telephoto to wide. It can convey a sudden and frightening revelation: The criminal in the dock realizes he left a telling clue that will send him to the gallows.

PRO TIP

Alfred Hitchcock made breathtaking use of the dolly counter-zoom in *Vertigo* to emphasize the hero's fear of heights when he took a dizzying peek down a spiral staircase. Steven Spielberg, who makes no secret of his admiration for Hitchcock, used the effect in *Jaws* when Chief Brody sees the little boy eaten by the shark.

The effect of dollying out while zooming in on an actor goes from wide to telephoto. It can convey alienation or abandonment: The little child in the forest realizes there isn't a friendly creature for miles around.

Done well, a dolly counter-zoom is artful, even if it's overused. Done badly, it's awful.

So go ahead and try it. Get it out of your system.

But be warned from two guys who've been there. If you set out to shoot a scene and you try this, you'll spend all day trying to get the effect right, and you'll never have time to shoot the rest of the scene!

FROM THE DIRECTOR'S CHAIR

OR

YOU'RE WAY COOLER THAN QUENTIN, DUDE

Trying to recreate dazzling effects you see in the movies can help you develop your ability to brew your own movie magic. In trying to second-guess how the effects were achieved, you'll discover a bag of tricks that can serve your own imagination.

For example, consider the remarkable freeze-frame technique from *The Matrix* when the hero dodges a hail of bullets in ultra-slow motion. This effect has been so widely imitated that it's now called *bullet time* in the industry.

We tried this kind of effect in "Neo's Ring," when Josh fights the Agent. Here's how we did it:

1. When shooting, coach the fighters to move in slow motion—about half speed.
2. As the attacker lands his punch, tell the actors to freeze in position.
3. While the actors try to remain as motionless as possible, the camera operator circles around them, doing a steady handheld shot (see Figure 7.13).
4. When the camera has gone full circle, tell the actors to resume the fight.
5. When editing the scene in iMovie, vary the Clip Speed slider during the shot to distort the viewers' perception of time.

Keep up this kind of experimentation, and you won't be able to stop. You could well discover an effect no one has done before. Then film school students of the future will be imitating Truffaut, Hitchcock, Spielberg—and you!

Figure 7.13

In the Josh-Agent fight in "Neo's Ring," the actors appear to freeze and the camera circles around them. To enhance the perception of altered time, we varied the playback speed of the shot in the edit. The movement of the camera during the freeze helps disguise slight movements the actors make as they try to hold their poses.

8 Polishing Your Blockbuster

Once you've wrapped the shoot and done a rough-cut edit, you might think you're nearly done.

You're not.

The post-production phase of moviemaking is meticulous and time-consuming. Although it certainly has its creative side, most of the work is technical. It involves not only editing to achieve just the right pacing but also a variety of polishing steps. And, in many ways, careful polishing is what separates the wannabes from the pros.

Remember the last time you waited for the much-anticipated sequel of some mega-hit movie to be released? Perhaps it was *Star Wars, Lord of the Rings, Harry Potter,* or *The Matrix.* At some point, the media reported that shooting had wrapped and the movie would be released *some time next year.* And you wondered, "What is taking them for-*ever?*"

Sometimes, studio executives decide to hold off releasing a movie until, say, the holiday season. But the main reason it can take a year or longer to finish a movie is postproduction. This phase consumes as much as 90 percent of the effort of manufacturing your run-of-the-mill, 100-million-dollar, "eye-candy," action-adventure movie.

Choosing and assembling the takes can be done fairly quickly. A rough cut for a two-hour feature usually takes a few weeks, at most. Simply, it's the tweaking that takes the time. Sound editing, music scoring and mixing, special effects, and titles for a feature film typically consume six to eight months—with an entire team of editors and other technicians working long hours, day in, day out.

In this chapter, we hope to give you some appreciation of why postproduction can be so complex. And, although you probably won't be adding 3D virtual imagery and surround sound to your first productions, we'll suggest ways to polish your show to make a more professional presentation.

Now, you probably don't want to throw yourself into a year of sweating and fretting over a five-minute production. But it's not as unlikely as it sounds. Once you get involved in these details, it can be hard to stop. No matter how long you've been at the process of refining your movie, you will always have the nagging suspicion that there's something you can still improve. You'll want to find just the right sound effect, match the skin tones better from one scene to the next, or make a music passage even more stirring.

No editor, student or professional, ever feels completely finished and totally satisfied with a project. Before you think you're done tweaking, someone who has the authority to do it—usually, a producer or a sponsor—declares it done and takes the project away from you to meet a deadline. And many student filmmakers fall into this trap. Somehow they don't realize that perfection isn't possible—or even desirable. It's much better to ship your project off to an upcoming film festival on time and start writing your next script or planning your next shoot.

Polishing Your Soundtrack

By far the most common shortcoming of student films—and even of some indies you see in theaters—is a poor-quality soundtrack. At times, actors' speeches are either inaudible or distorted. The audience can't understand what the characters are saying, and has difficulty following the story. Or some background noise—such as city traffic or a strong wind—is so loud that it drowns out the lines.

If you find that your soundtrack is plagued with these problems, you'll resolve to do better next time. As it is with those nasty diseases they warn you about, the best and least expensive cure for a case of bad sound is prevention, which, in this case, would require a good external mic and someone who knows how to use it on the set.

But that was then, and this is now. What do you do if you find out at this late stage that the audio is so bad that the audience can't follow the story?

Confronted with a less-than-ideal dialogue track, the professional sound editor has three alternatives. In order of increasing hassle and difficulty, these are:

- Clean and separate the dialogue
- Minimize noise and distortion
- Rerecord the dialogue

Cleaning and Separating Dialogue

A technique that sound editors use to improve the quality of production sound is to separate characters' speeches into separate audio tracks. This process is called *checkerboarding* because the resulting audio clips appear in alternating positions along the timeline (see Figure 8.1).

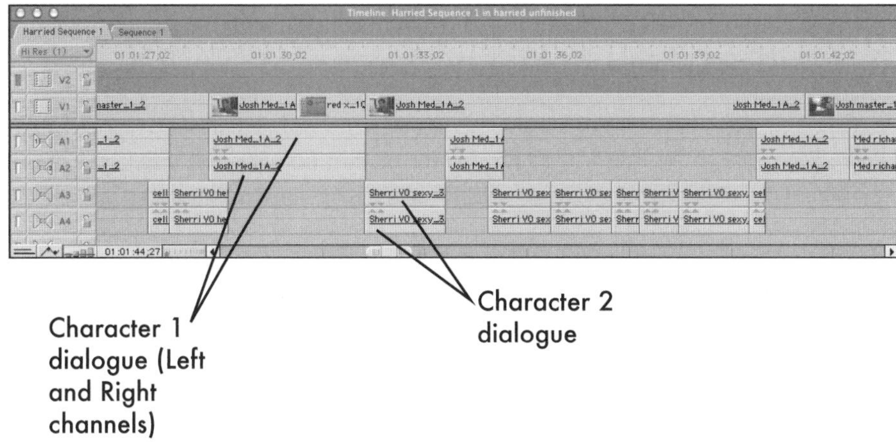

Figure 8.1

Checkerboarding is a routine practice for cleaning dialogue, but it's a bit cumbersome to do in iMovie because of the limited number of audio tracks and the fact that audio dissolves aren't supported. Here's an example showing the timeline of a project being edited in Final Cut Pro.

By separating lines of dialogue, checkerboarding is the first step in *cleaning* the audio tracks. The purpose of cleaning is to remove or reduce noises that commonly occur just before or just after an actor's speech. Examples are coughing, breathing, lip smacking, and throat clearing.

Checkerboarding works best when you've left handles, or a little extra footage, on either end of the selected takes. Having a pair of adjoining handles at the cut between the takes gives you the extra running time you need to insert a cross-dissolve transition in the audio track. The audio dissolve smoothes the transition, especially if there's a marked difference between audio levels or background noise from one shot to the next.

PRO TIP

In a program like Final Cut Pro that does nondestructive editing, you can actually create handles in the audio timeline simply by dragging the in and out points outward from the cut. Or you can set a default Handle Size to automatically add a second or so on either end of the take during video capture. However, in iMovie, the duration of a clip, once trimmed, can't be extended in the timeline. If you find you need to add handles to a clip in iMovie, restore the unedited version of the clip from the Trash (or upload it again from the camcorder tape), trim it in the Clips Viewer, and reinsert it in the timeline.

Unfortunately, in iMovie 4, you can't apply the Cross Dissolve (time-lapse) effect to an extracted audio track. But if you apply a cross-dissolve to adjoining video clips without extracting their audio, the effect will be applied to both video and audio.

If you need to extract and separate the audio tracks in iMovie, you can try a repair that works almost as well as the cross-dissolve.

To reduce noise at the cut in iMovie:

1. Extract the audio from adjoining clips that have handles.
2. In the handle portion of each clip, after the character has finished speaking, drag the Volume Level Bar down to near zero (see Figure 8.2).
3. Overlay the muted portion of the audio track at the cut with a short audio clip of room tone.

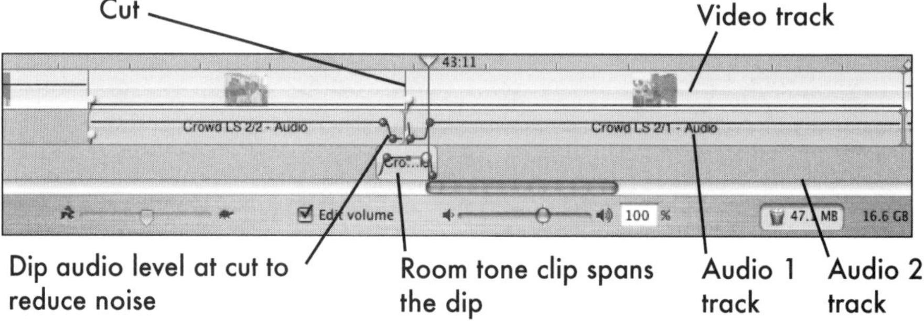

Figure 8.2
To minimize noise at the cut in iMovie, drag the Volume Level Bars down on each side of it. Add a brief clip of room tone over the dip, or there will be a noticeable dead spot in the audio.

Another benefit of checkerboarding is to isolate character speeches that are so bad they need replacement. If the character is off-screen, you may be able do this easily by borrowing the audio from another take. But if the character is on-camera, the audio from another take might not be in sync with his lip movements. In such cases, turn on waveform display, unlock the audio, and drag the audio clip to the left or right slightly to align the waveform peaks with the lip movements. (This will only work if the needed adjustment is slight, however.)

PRO TIP

A professional software tool that can help sync dialogue to lip movements is VocAlign Project (www.synchroarts.co.uk). The program aligns the peaks in two separate audio clips, compressing or expanding the audio slightly in the second clip to align its peaks with those of the first. You can use VocAlign Project to sync audio from a different take with the original audio from a video clip. After the second clip is aligned, insert it in the timeline beneath the corresponding video and then mute the original audio. (Don't delete the original—keep it in the edit as a guide track.)

Fixing Audio Problems

If checkerboarding and cleaning don't solve the problems, here are some other pro sound engineers' tricks you can try:

Dip to duck noise. If a car horn, for example, occurs during a brief pause in the actor's speech, mute the track briefly to hide it by dragging down the Volume Level Bar on each side of the sound peak. Insert a corresponding clip of room tone in the Audio 2 track to span the dip (see Figure 8.3).

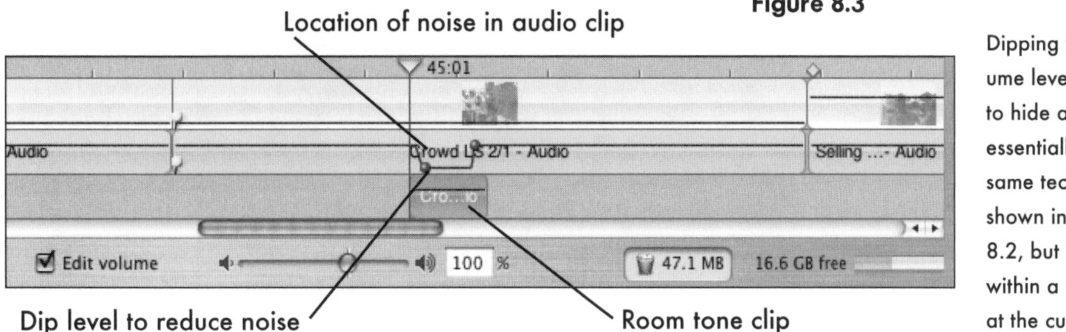

Figure 8.3

Dipping the volume level briefly to hide a noise is essentially the same technique shown in Figure 8.2, but it occurs within a clip, not at the cut.

Need more room tone? If you find you haven't recorded enough room tone, copy and paste a sequence of room-tone clips together on the timeline. Apply cross-dissolves to the cuts between them as video clips and then extract and unlock the audio. Delete the video portion, then restore the edited sequence to the Clips Viewer so you can reinsert it or trim clips from it whenever you need to insert pauses or cover audio edits. (If the room tone has faint noises, clean the clip before you duplicate it, or you'll hear them repeated over and over throughout the spliced segment.)

Can't cut noise? If a phone rings or a car horn blares or a dog barks when the actor is talking and you don't have a clean take, it may be better to incorporate the noise in the scene rather than try to eliminate it. Insert the noise as a sound effect a few times in the scene leading up to that point. The audience will become used to the noise as part of the audio background, and it won't draw so much attention when it occurs under the actor's line.

Increase audio level without distortion. If you have to increase the volume level of an audio clip over 100 percent for it to be loud enough, you could create a distortion problem that's just as bad. In such cases, extract the audio, increase the level to 100, make a second copy of the clip, and insert the copy in the Audio 2 track just below the first. Thus "stacking" duplicate audio clips can have the effect of making them louder without adding distortion.

What to do about distorted digital audio? Analog audio recording permits a certain amount of distortion, but digital audio doesn't. Adjusting the audio level over 100 percent is always a bad thing, whether you're recording or editing. If the original camcorder track is so loud that it's distorted, there's no repairing it. You'll have to replace it by either finding audio from another take or rerecording it.

Replacing Dialogue

Recall that the pros sometimes do automatic dialogue replacement (ADR), also called *looping,* to dub actors' voices after the fact (see Figure 8.4). They do this to create foreign language versions, to replace strong language for television or airline versions, to add voiceover narration, and to replace production sound that's beyond repair.

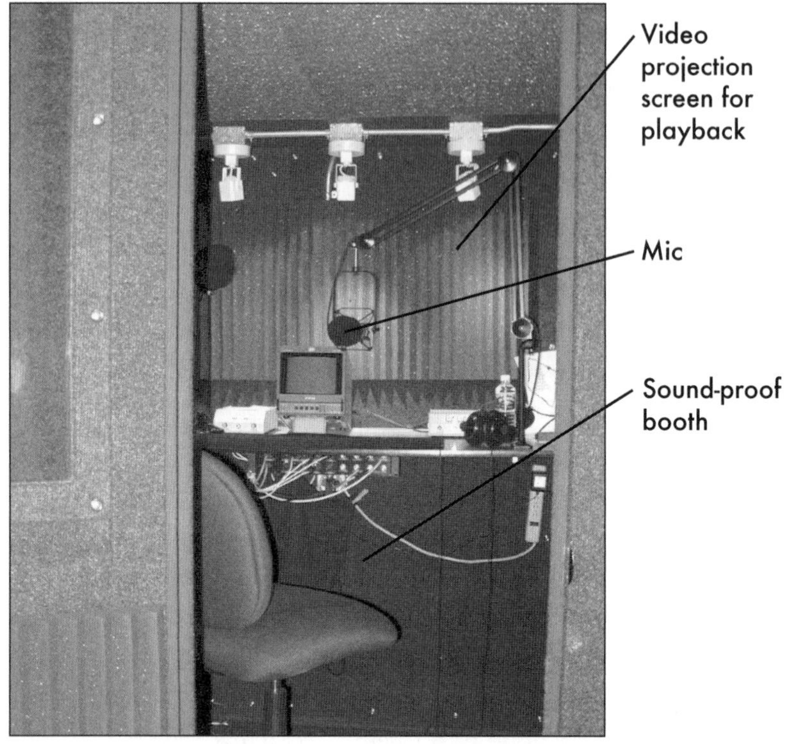

Figure 8.4
Professional sound studios for doing ADR range in size from this one—used for recording voiceover narration—to larger sound stages where the entire cast of a scene can be assembled while they watch the visual playback and record their dubbed lines.

PRO TIP

Particularly for music videos, another reason for ADR is *double tracking,* by which vocal or instrumental artists can record additional tracks to accompany themselves.

Recording replacement dialogue can be challenging, and even when it's done right, the results can be disappointing. In particular, the room tone of the ADR recording probably won't match—even if you return to the shooting location.

But you can do a down-and-dirty type of ADR with your consumer camcorder. To match presence, record indoors if the scene was an interior, outdoors if exterior. If the camcorder has an Audio Dub feature (as the ZR40 does), you can use that (but read the following note).

NOTE

The Canon ZR40 will permit you to record audio over a scene you recorded previously. You do this in VCR mode, by selecting Audio Dub > Audio In from the VCR Set Up menu. However, dubbing will only work at SP speed using 12-bit audio, and you must have made your original recording with those settings. Remember also that audio dubbing doesn't replace the audio on the original recording. Your ADR is simply added to one of the stereo tracks. Since iMovie doesn't let you edit Stereo Left and Right tracks separately, it'll generally be easier to use the procedure described in the text below to record a fresh tape.

Or print the scene to VHS tape (File > Share in iMovie) and watch on a separate player and monitor while the narrator or actors speak into the camcorder's built-in mic as you record on a fresh cassette.

To more nearly match room tone in your edit, add a room-tone audio clip to the Audio 2 track under the entire take (or overlay it on the rerecorded audio track).

Use the procedure described in Chapter 7's section, "To align picture and sound in iMovie," to line up the audio peaks in the ADR track with the lip movements in the video.

Fine-Tuning Music

In Chapter 6, we described briefly how you could use various applications, such as iTunes, GarageBand, and Sonicfire Pro, to add music to your movie soundtrack. We won't go into all the details of music scoring, but we'll acquaint you with some techniques for enhancing the effect of any music you choose.

Unless you're producing a music video—where the music itself is the center of attention—the effect of music in your movie should be subtle and reinforcing. It's an old Hollywood maxim that movie music shouldn't be memorable in itself. In fact, you'll notice that when a feature film is used as a vehicle to launch a hit song, the song often plays under the end titles. There it can play for its full three minutes or so and not compete with the story line for your attention. (*Men in Black II* has an entire music video spliced onto the end.)

Many people think that movie music exists to manipulate the emotions of the audience. But that isn't quite right. Editor Walter Murch points out that movie music can't instill an emotion that doesn't already exist in the scene. Used correctly, music should be introduced just *after* an emotional moment in the story, which the music serves to amplify.

There are some exceptions. Notice on the DVD that the student films from the School of Cinema and Performing Arts (SOCAPA) fall into two categories, which correspond to specific course assignments. In the first group, the movies were all shot as single takes. The films in the second group were shot and edited according to classic master-scene technique. "Sweet Reward" is a short in the first category that's an homage to the Charlie Chaplin comedies of the silent cinema. At the beginning of the 20th century, piano players accompanied silent movies with live performances in the theaters. The soundtrack of "Sweet Reward," which plays throughout the movie, recreates such a live performance.

But, in general, playing a music selection under your entire movie is a bad idea. It's overkill—and it can compete with the dialogue. Instead, use different music passages selectively, as Murch advises, to amplify significant moments. Chase scenes and fights are particularly good places to add stirring music. Dialogue scenes typically aren't. But you might want to cue the violins right after he says, "I love you."

Composers who write for the movies usually don't begin their work until after most of the visual editing is done. At that point, the running times of a scene are fixed, and the new music can be fitted to it with frame-accurate exactness.

You can work the same way. Hold off until after you get the pacing right before you start to add music clips to your short.

In fine-tuning your music selections, timing is everything. Here are some tips:

Cut to the beat. In the editing program, turn on waveform display. The peaks in a music track generally will correspond to musical beats. Listen carefully as you sync up the music to the video, and cut on the *downbeat* (first and strongest beat in each musical measure). When you're cutting rapidly—in a travel sequence, or in a chase or fight—pick music with a strong beat and cut on the downbeats.

Backtime for precise cueing. When inserting a music clip, you may want its crescendo or climax to coincide with a video event—whether it's the blowing of a kiss or the falling of a blow. When you're composing original music—or if you're building music with an application like Sonicfire Pro—you can fit the duration of the music clip exactly to the scene, as well as time the climax to match the visual event. But if you're using a prerecorded clip, you don't have this kind of flexibility. In such cases, professional sound editors use a procedure called *backtiming.* That is, they align the music crescendo and the visual action first on the timeline. Then they work backward along the timeline, fading down the level of the music to zero at the beginning of the scene and raising it to an audible level just before the climax (see Figure 8.5). A related technique called *sneaking in* the cue involves raising the audio level of the music selection very gradually from the opening of the scene (see Figure 8.6).

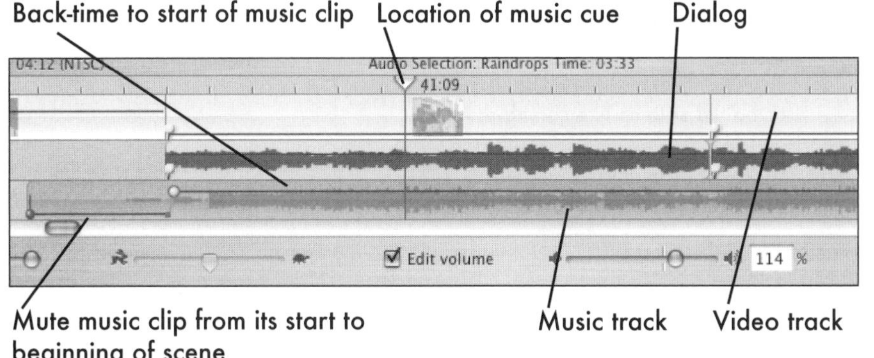

Figure 8.5

Backtiming a music cue involves choosing the point at which the crescendo will occur and then working backward to set the in point at the beginning of the scene. The exact timing of the fade-up will depend on what's going on in the music at that point.

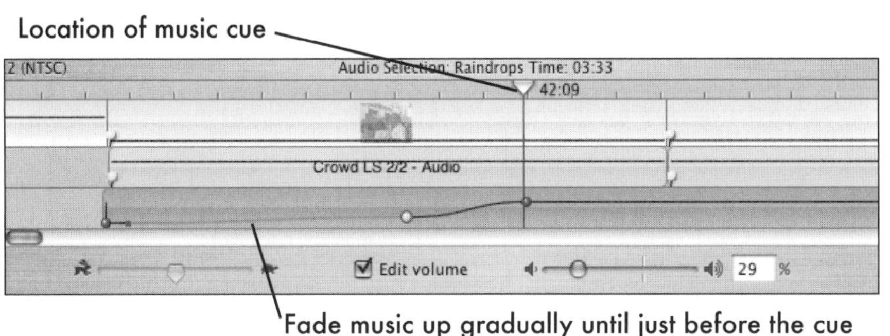

Figure 8.6

Sneaking in a music cue involves fading it up very gradually so the audience isn't aware of just when it was introduced.

Manufacturing Sound Effects

The iMovie application comes with a small selection of sound effects, accessible through the Audio pane. You can also find ready-made sound effects on the Internet at www.soundhunter.com. Some of these are royalty-free—you don't have to pay to use them, even for commercial purposes (refer to the Web site for terms of use).

But it's much more fun to create your own sound effects. Simply point your camcorder at something that makes a sound, capture it on tape, upload it as a clip, and extract the audio. If you try this, you'll discover something sound engineers have known for decades—that the ear is easily fooled. We gave you two examples in Chapter 7—the sound of the payoff punch in many movie fights is nothing more violent than the breaking of a stalk of celery or the tearing of a head of crisp lettuce.

With just a few household items, you can create a whole library of sound effects:

- Crumpling paper sounds like a crackling fire.
- Popping a bubble-pack dimple sounds like a gunshot.
- Rapping a water glass with a spoon sounds like a bell. (You can change its pitch by adjusting the water level.)

- Hitting the bottom of a frying pan with a spoon sounds like heavy swords clanging.
- Shaking a box of cereal sounds like a battalion on the march.
- Shaking a large sheet of poster board sounds like rolling thunder.
- Tearing a piece of gaffer's tape sounds like the violent tearing of clothes.
- Peeling a piece of tape off the roll sounds like a structure fracturing.
- A clothes dryer running empty sounds like a giant motored vehicle on the move.
- An electric hair dryer sounds like a jet engine.

In fact, the history of movies is full of audio trickery. For example, in reality, walking through grass doesn't make much sound at all. But in the movies, it has a characteristic noise that the audience expects to hear. Traditionally, it was done by a special effects technician called a *Foley walker* treading in a bin of discarded magnetic tape. (The technique and the artists who perform it are named for veteran Hollywood sound-effects wiz Jack Donovan Foley.)

Enhancing Imagery

The topic of digital video image manipulation and computer graphics is huge, so we'll give you a kind of bird's-eye view. Also, this is one area where iMovie has very limited capabilities. For a taste of what you can do with more sophisticated tools, see our discussion of professional postproduction software in Chapter 10.

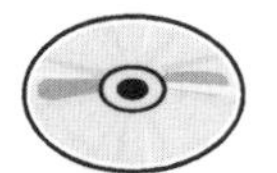

PLUG-INS FOR iMOVIE

Although iMovie doesn't have all that many whiz-bang features for manipulating imagery, its capabilities can be extended with plug-in software. The iMovie application comes with a small assortment of ready-made plug-in video effects, and there is also a huge selection of third-party plug-ins you can buy separately. Some of these effects can be found on the DVD in the Gee Three Slick Sampler. (There are lots of plug-ins for Final Cut Pro, too.)

Think of plug-ins as the microwavable dinners of video editing: They can lend visual sophistication without the bother of starting from scratch. Besides Gee Three, vendors include Stupendous Software, Virtix, CSB Digital, ImageIP, BKMS, eZedia, and Mouken. They sell sets of ready-made audio and video effects at modest prices, and some offer fully workable samples as downloads from their Web sites. (For a list of vendors with Web links, surf to apple.com/ilife/imovie/ and scroll down to the bottom right of the page.) Once installed in iMovie, you select these plug-ins from the various panes as you would any of the built-in transitions and effects.

Some types of image manipulation you may want to try in iMovie are:

- Adding titles
- Adding effects
- Correcting color
- Compositing with chroma key

Adding Titles

You need to give your movie a title, and presumably your cast and crew would like their names to appear in the screen credits. Traditionally, there are three places where titles appear in movies and documentaries:

Main title. The title of the movie usually appears right after the opening fade-in. In some feature films, an opening scene plays as a kind of prologue before the titles appear. This technique is called *delayed titles.*

Credits. In a Hollywood movie, big-name credits appear right after the title. Traditionally, these are called *above-the-line* credits, and they appear in the following order: stars (lead actor first), producer, screenwriter, and director. Other cast and crew credits usually come at the end for *below-the-line* personnel.

Lower thirds. This term refers to the lower-third horizontal area of the screen (see Figure 8.7). Particularly in news clips and documentaries, names and job titles or affiliations of interview subjects appear here. In narrative films, especially in historical dramas, lower-third titles at the opening of a scene are often used to identify its time or location. When you use lower-third titles to identify an interview subject, it's a good rule to show the person first, wait a second or two, and then add the title—much as your host would introduce you to a guest at a party, with a visual greeting followed by an introduction. And if the title might distract the audience from the subject's speech, wait until her first pause before showing her name. In general, show the person's name and identification (Bob Marley, Singer) the first time he appears in the movie. If he reappears much later in the show and you think the audience needs a reminder, show just his name, briefly.

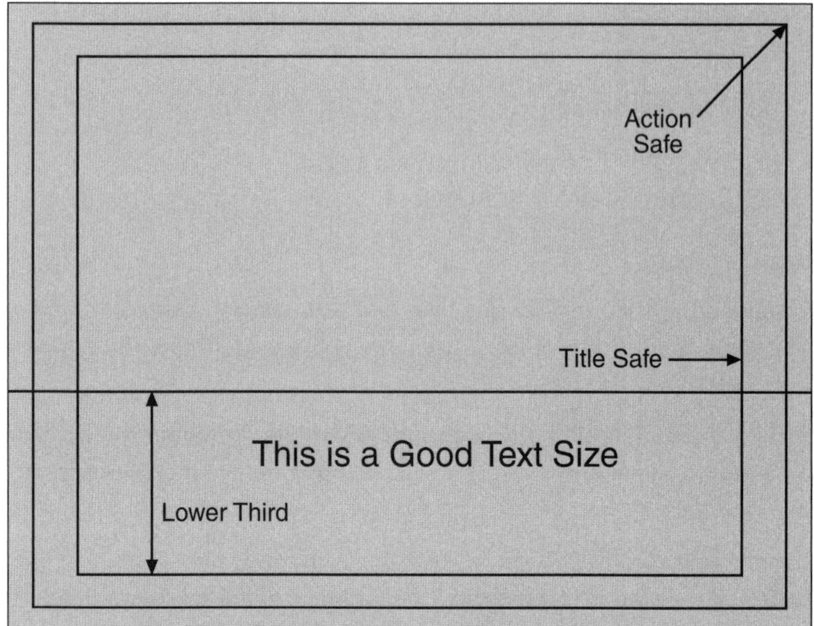

Figure 8.7
When supering titles that identify interview subjects, keep them in the lower third of the screen. Keep all text within the Title Safe Area. And keep any significant action, such as actors' gestures, within the Action Safe Area. Text size should be large enough so it's readable by a viewer sitting a distance of four times the screen height away, and that's a good guideline for any kind of visual detail—such as a newspaper headline you expect the audience to read.

For main title and credits, a basic choice is whether to show them on a plain background (usually, black) or to superimpose them over a scene (called a *supered* title, for short). A key difference is that choosing a plain background will increase the running time of your movie, but supering it won't unless you add extra footage as a background.

If titles appear on black, a good choice for text color is white. It has a clean, elegant look. However, white doesn't work well for supered text if there are bright highlights in the background. The best all-around choice for text color that will be readable supered over any scene is yellow-orange. (You'll see it often in the lower-thirds of TV news clips.)

PRO TIP

Regardless of the text color, you can make any supered title read better by adding a drop-shadow effect. A drop-shadow is a same-sized copy of the text, layered behind it and offset slightly. It's usually done in a color that contrasts with the text on the top layer. For example, the drop-shadow could be black if the text on the top layer is white or yellow. The edges of the drop-shadow can be hard, which makes the text look dimensional, or soft, which makes the text appear to float above the image. Many plug-in title effects have drop-shadows built-in, and you can create them yourself in applications such as Final Cut Pro and After Effects.

Many of the plug-in title effects animate the appearance of the text. As with fancy transitions, use these sparingly, if at all. You might try applying animation to a main title. But it's usually a needless distraction on credits and lower-thirds. If you do choose to animate titles and credits, the traditional method is called a *vertical crawl*. In iMovie, you'll find this effect listed in the Titles pane as Scrolling > Rolling Centered Credits.

To create a title in iMovie:

1. In the Timeline Viewer, move the playhead to the point at which the title will appear.
2. Click the Titles button to open the Titles pane.
3. Select the name of a title effect from the list box. The various options for that effect will appear in the pane. (If a control is dimmed, that option is not available for the effect you've selected.)
4. Type the title in the text box at the bottom of the pane.
5. Adjust the sliders to control Speed (duration in seconds from the in point), Pause (delay), and Size (text height). (Special effects may have other options.)
6. Optionally, click the Color box to select a text color. Then make a selection in the Colors box that pops up (see Figure 8.8) and close the box.

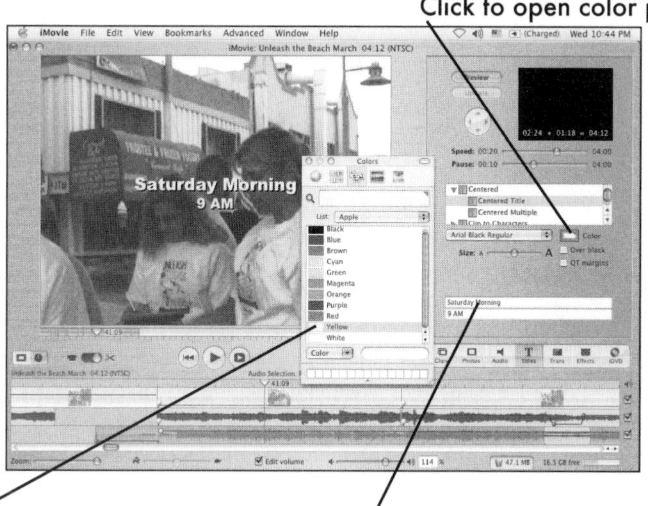

Figure 8.8

Clicking the Color button in the Titles pane opens a color wheel from which you can select the text color. Buttons across the top of the box provide different ways of viewing color choices, and the palette at the bottom of the window holds your most recently used choices.

> **TIP**
>
> To improve readability of supered titles, reduce the brightness of the background scene by adjusting Brightness & Contrast in the Effects pane.

Other options that apply to most selections in the Titles pane are:

Over Black. This option shows the title over a plain black background. The duration of your movie will increase by the number of seconds in the Speed setting.

QT Margins. By default, iMovie keeps titles within the *TV safe area,* a broadcast standard that prevents text from being cut off at the edges of a picture due to variations in television sets. If you mark this option, the permissible boundaries will increase slightly to the QuickTime standard used for streaming video on the Web.

> **TIP**
>
> A classic example of a vertical crawl occurs in the opening of all the *Star Wars* movies, showing text receding in extreme perspective into the star-sprinkled distance as the words disappear off the top of the screen. This effect is an homage to Saturday matinee serial thrillers of the 1930s and '40s, including several that starred a popular detective-adventurer named Boston Blackie and others that celebrated the exploits of spaceman Flash Gordon. This animated title effect comes ready-made with every copy of iMovie. Appropriately enough for *Star Wars* fans, it's called Far, Far Away.

Adding Effects

A video effect transforms the imagery in a selected clip. Another term for an effect is a *filter* because it changes the way the audience perceives the image. For example, a straightforward type of filter can transform a full-color image to black-and-white.

There are lots and lots of effects, especially when you include all the varieties of plug-ins you can buy. The only way to discover what they do is to experiment with them. For example, the names of some of the effects included with iMovie suggest what they do: Earthquake, Fairy Dust, Fog, Lens Flare, and Soft Focus.

As with unusual transitions and animated titles, you should apply effects sparingly. (Of course, if you're doing a music video that's intended to shock and awe, ignore this rule.)

An example of a filter applied to an entire movie is "Sweet Reward" on the DVD, which was converted to sepia, replacing the full-color camcorder footage with a brownish monochrome.

To apply an effect in iMovie:

1. In the Timeline Viewer, select the clip to which the effect will be applied.
2. Click the Effects button to open the Effects pane.
3. Select the name of an effect from the list, such as Sepia Tone.
4. Drag the Effect In and Effect Out sliders (see Figure 8.9) to set the in and out points of the effect in the scene (measured in seconds).
5. Other options available for that particular effect will appear in the pane. Adjust them as you like.
6. Select Preview at any point to watch the effect on the scene in the Monitor window.
7. When you're satisfied with your adjustments, click the Apply button to add the effect to the selected scene.

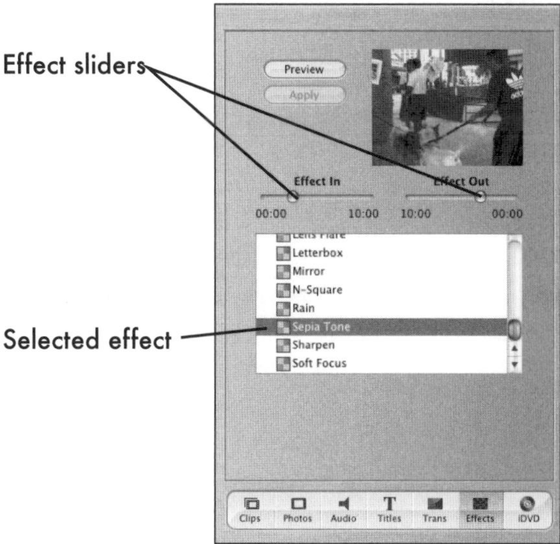

Figure 8.9

The Effect In slider controls the in point and the Effect Out controls the out point of the selected effect. Timings are in seconds from the position of the playhead in the timeline.

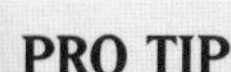

PRO TIP

Most editing software these days includes one or more plug-ins for making video look like film. In iMovie, the effect is called Aged Film. If you set its option sliders to the max, your show will look like a vintage movie, showing film grain, scratches, dust, and *jitter* (dancing image caused by movie projectors). However, if you decrease the option adjustments to minimize these effects, your video can have the look of newly-shot film. Experiment with this effect, perhaps in combination with the Letterbox effect, if you want to imagine how your production would look as a big-screen movie.

Correcting Color

If you want to achieve a professional look, this is one category of effect you probably shouldn't avoid. If you're shooting with available light, now indoors and now out, chances are your scenes aren't color balanced from one to the next. Your subjects might look green or blue in some shots, orange in others. Two correction filters are included in iMovie 4—Adjust Color (see Figure 8.10) and Brightness & Contrast.

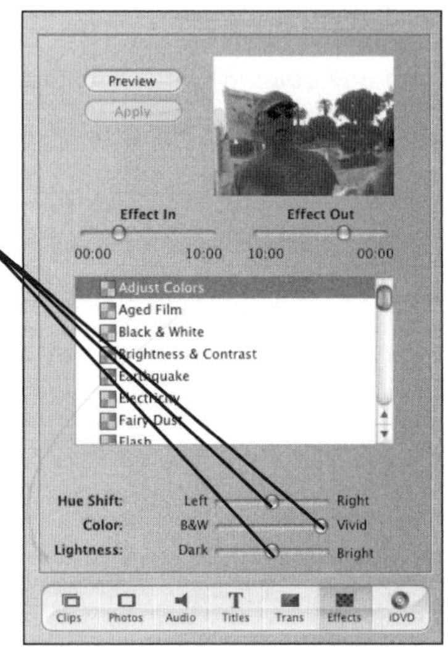

Figure 8.10
The Adjust Color options in the Effects pane are built into iMovie. The Brightness & Contrast effect can also change the viewers' perception of color.

You'll find a more robust set of color controls in Gee Three Slick Volume 6. The name of the filter is Color Correction (see Figure 8.11). It will even generate broadcast-safe colors automatically.

All of these effects change the *color cast* of the entire video frame. If you need to adjust color on specific objects—such as changing skin tones on faces without affecting the color of the sky—you need a more sophisticated postproduction tool, such as After Effects.

Click here with White Eyedropper to adjust white balance

Eyedropper button

Drag to adjust tint

Figure 8.11

The Gee Three Color Correction filter has a more extensive set of options and controls than you'll find in iMovie's Adjust Color effect. For quick results, to let the program adjust the colors automatically, click the White Point eyedropper and then click an area in the image that's blown-out (pure white). This technique does much the same thing as setting white balance in the camcorder.

PRO TIP

You needn't worry about selecting broadcast-safe color unless you intend for your movie to be shown on commercial television. However, this isn't all that far-fetched a possibility, since all local cable television stations are required by law to air some *public-access* programs. Call the station to find out how to get your show on the air, which may involve taking a course they offer in video production for a nominal fee. Remember, however, that broadcast-safe colors will look faded (*desaturated* is the technical word for it) compared to your original footage. From a practical standpoint, it might be better not to select the broadcast-legal option and let the engineering department at the television station deal with the color, if you're so fortunate as to get an air date.

Compositing with Chroma Key

In Chapter 7, we described how we shot the elements we needed for the composite scenes in "Neo's Ring" using a portable green screen. In postproduction, the green areas serve as a chroma key, or *digital matte.* When two images are combined in postproduction, the second image (called an *overlay*) is substituted wherever that special color is found in the original scene.

The iMovie application doesn't come with chroma-key capability, but plug-ins are available for it. One example is in Gee Three's Slick 4 package, and once installed it appears in the iMovie Effects pane listed as Slick Vid Mix.

To generate composite imagery using a chroma-key matte with Slick Vid Mix:

1. Shoot a scene with a green (or blue) screen background (refer back to Chapter 7 for tips).
2. Shoot a matching scene to use as an overlay.
3. Upload the green-screen scene into your iMovie project.
4. Upload the overlay scene into a separate iMovie project (File > New project) so that it resides on your Macintosh HD as a separate .MOV file.
5. In your main project, add the background clip to the Timeline Viewer. (It should be highlighted as the currently selected clip.)
6. Click the Effects button to open the Effects pane.
7. In the list of effects, select Gee Three – Slick 4 > Slick Vid Mix.
8. Click the Configure button. The Slick Vid Mix window will open (see Figure 8.12).
9. Click the Choose Overlay Movie button. The Choose a File window will open, permitting you to navigate the Macintosh HD directory to locate the overlay .MOV file. (Hint: It should be inside the Movies folder under the project name you gave it.) Click Choose to select the overlay file.
10. Make sure the Color to Replace is the same as the chroma-key color in the matte.
11. Click OK to generate the composite imagery.
12. Click Apply in the Effects pane to replace the selected scene in the timeline with the composite.

Figure 8.12
Using the Slick Vid Mix filter for compositing requires the overlay scene to be in a separate iMovie project file. Click the Choose Overlay Movie button to navigate to the file location on the hard drive and select it. The Brightness Replacer button does luminance keying (which is even trickier than a green or blue screen), and the Cookie Cutter button permits you to define the matte by choosing a still image file that holds a shape.

In Step 10, you can select the Brightness Replacer for luminance keying, but read our cautions about that in Chapter 7. You can even try this if you haven't shot chroma-key footage but have a scene in which the background is blown-out (100 percent white).

Getting Feedback

When you feel you've arrived at a fine cut in your editing, here's a word of advice you might not like very much:

Show your movie to some people who couldn't care less.

Your natural instinct will be to screen it first for your loyal fans. Of course you'll do that, and you should. Everyone is no doubt looking forward to the party where they finally see themselves on-screen, hoot and holler at inside jokes about good times on the set, and generally celebrate their contributions to cinema literature. Just be aware that your cast, your crew, and your devoted families can't help loving your movie, warts and all—even if, by objective standards, it might be regarded by the world at large as, well, ahem—a real stinker.

If you've read our cautions about the importance of pacing in editing, it will come as no surprise if your movie moves too slowly, or if its flow seems erratic. Even if your indifferent test audience doesn't say a thing—you can learn a lot from their body language as they watch your masterwork unreel.

Showing your work to a potentially uncaring audience is difficult advice to take, especially when you've put hours and hours into the production. But at some point, after your friends' cheering has stopped, you need to find out what the rest of the world will think.

Whatever you learn from that experience will probably help you decide what you want to learn by doing your next project.

FROM THE DIRECTOR'S CHAIR

The pros cut and recut. After the director of a feature approves a fine cut (called the *director's cut*), a high-powered producer usually steps in and wants more changes. Then, and only then, will the studio conduct test screenings with the public. And the movie probably will be recut again based on reactions the audience marked on "bingo cards." Big-name Hollywood directors complain they don't get approval of the *final cut,* but that's how the game is played (and many of them command million-dollar salaries, so it's hard to feel too sorry for them).

In fact, filmmakers have been second-guessed throughout the history of the movies. Legendary studio executive Harry Cohn, who ran Columbia Pictures like a tyrant for years, once commented that he could tell a picture was bad during a screening when his butt started to itch. This prompted industry insiders to joke that, if only science could find a way to attach electrodes to Cohn's backside, the studio would have a sure-fire method of predicting a hit.

(continued)

FROM THE DIRECTOR'S CHAIR (CONTINUED)

Simply put, when the audience starts to squirm, that's a sure sign you need to recut and pick up the pace.

When you watch "Neo's Ring," pay attention to its pacing. When Traci appears to pop from one location to another (through the magic of chroma key), if it were too fast, the audience would be as disoriented as her character appears to be. Too slow, and the audience could start paying too much attention to the effect itself.

The same is true when the Agent is chasing her. Too fast, and it plays as comedy. Too slow, there's no excitement or flow to the chase, and the audience can become aware that it's just a strung-together sequence of separate shots.

9 Releasing Your Extravaganza

Once upon a time and not so long ago, the only way for a student filmmaker to make a film was to shoot it *on film*. The student format of choice was 16mm, which was somewhat less expensive than the 35mm used for professional shooting and the 70mm used for widescreen theatrical projection. But even in that narrow-gauge format, the cost of the film itself and laboratory processing for a 10-minute short could set you back a few thousand dollars. And that didn't begin to take into account the cost of renting camera and movie lights, much less feeding and transporting a cast and crew.

So it's no wonder that film school was once considered a rich kid's playground.

Today, if you have a computer with a DVD burner, you can release your movie for under $5–the cost of a raw disc. And, in many ways, the technical quality of its imagery and stereo sound will be better than the best 16mm movie ever achieved.

Let's dispel one notion right away–there's no longer any need for you to convert your DV movie to film. That would run you about $10,000 for a short movie, and you'd gain nothing by it. These days, most film festivals gladly accept submissions on DVD. Commercial television stations–should one agree to air your news segment, documentary, or commercial–can convert a DV cassette copy of your show to any of their required tape formats. (They may charge you as much as $200 for the service, though.)

But your options for distribution media don't begin and end with tape and disc. You have a variety of release formats to choose from. Each has a different standard of quality, and each its own particular use. Your options are:

- Printing to tape
- Burning a CD

- Creating video files for the Internet
- Authoring and burning a DVD

Printing to Tape

In the days of analog video, most editing was done on tape, and making a copy was called *dubbing* (not to be confused with the same term used for ADR). Nowadays, outputting to tape from digital editing software is called *printing.* (Some people call it *exporting,* but they are mostly hopeless nerds.)

NOTE

We're not sure, but it's possible that the origin of the term *printing* for digital copying was meant to convey that the result is another original, not a copy. A digital copy is identical to its source material with no sacrifice in quality. And that's true no matter whether you copy from the original data file or from one of its copies. They will all be of the same high quality. However, *dubbing* implies a loss of quality. When you copy from one analog tape to another, signal strength diminishes slightly and noise increases. A copy is therefore of lower quality than the original, and a copy of a copy is lower still.

Printing to digital tape from iMovie is about as easy as it gets. Most of the hassle is involved in connecting the equipment.

To print a movie to tape in iMovie:

1. Save the movie project file to your hard drive (File > Save Project or Command-S).
2. Connect your DV camcorder to the computer's FireWire port via the DV cable.
3. Turn the camcorder power switch to the Play (VCR) setting, and insert a blank DV cassette. (Check the camcorder manual for the proper mode, which may be designated VTR instead.)
4. Make sure the camcorder's DV jack is set up for recording input. (On the Canon ZR40, press the Menu button, select the VCR SET UP menu, and make sure AV-DV is set to OFF.)
5. From the iMovie menu bar, select File > Share. A window with several output choices will appear (see Figure 9.1).
6. Click the Videocamera icon.
7. Optionally, change settings for Wait time (a few seconds for the camera to warm up and start rolling) and the number of seconds of blank tape at the *head* and *tail* of the movie. (The default settings of 5, 1, and 1 should work fine for most camcorders.)
8. Click the Share button. The recording process will start, and recording is complete when the output window disappears.

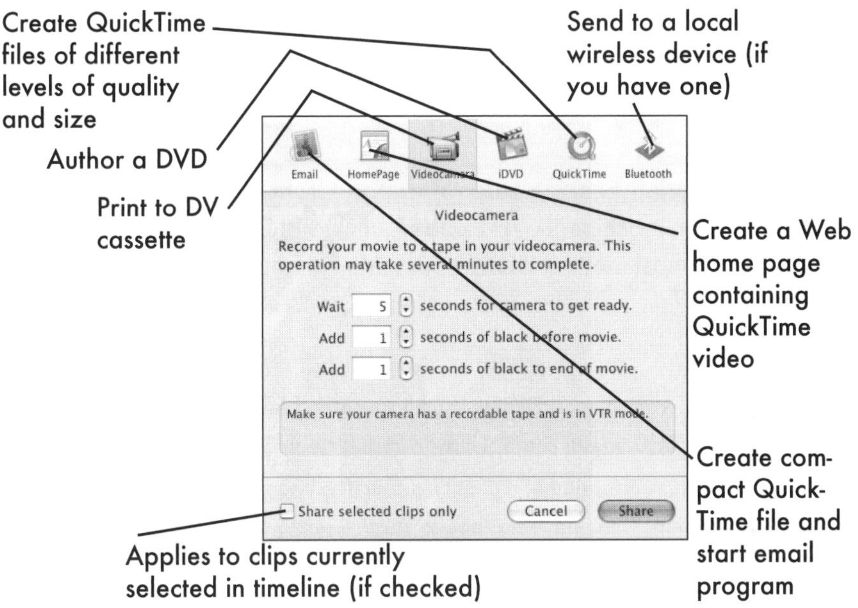

Figure 9.1

The output window has a row of buttons at the top representing various distribution media. Selecting the Videocamera button will activate the FireWire link between your computer and the camcorder.

The printing process will take at least as long as the actual running time of your movie, possibly longer. In general, the more special effects you've included in your movie, the longer it will take for the computer to *render* the imagery before tape recording actually starts.

PRO TIP

If your movie is longer than an hour, you'll have to create it as separate projects, each under the 60-minute running time of a cassette. (Don't use 90-minute cassettes or long-play [LP] camcorder mode. You could lose data.) End each segment at an *act break,* or intermission. Television movies (called *movies of the week,* or *MOWs,* in the industry, no matter when they're shown) are typically divided into seven act breaks, where commercials are inserted. The ideal act break is at a *cliffhanger* moment in the plot, which leaves the audience wanting to know what happens next—so they won't switch channels during the commercials.

Copying a DV Cassette to VHS Tape

If your computer has a video output card, you may be able to print your movie directly to analog videotape, but it's not the best way to go. Even if your goal is to create a VHS tape, always print a DV cassette version first. Unless something goes weirdly wrong with the computer or the camcorder, or unless the tape itself is defective, the digital videotape will be an exact and error-free copy of your movie project. You can then use it as a *duplicating master* for making analog dubs. No matter how good your recording equipment is, analog videotapes will always be poorer in quality than your digital masters.

TIP

Perhaps it's obvious, but let's state for the record that anything less than Full Quality DV format won't be suitable for broadcast, videotape duplication, or for creating high-quality DVDs.

Although VHS tapes seem to be disappearing from the video stores and from our daily lives, an analog VCR makes a dandy movie-duplication machine. A VHS dub is quick and inexpensive to make, and you can rest assured that even your most nontechnical relative will find a way to play the cassettes you make.

To make a VHS dub of your movie:

1. Using the special cable that came with your camcorder, connect its analog video and audio outputs to a VCR (see Figure 9.2). On the Canon ZR40, it's a single yellow jack labeled AV.
2. The other end of the cable has three RCA-type plugs, typically colored Yellow, White, and Red. Connect the Yellow plug to VCR Video In. Connect the White to Audio-L(eft) In. Connect the Red to Audio-R(ight) In.
3. Switch the VCR to Input mode, typically done via a button on the remote control. (On some VCRs, the correct mode may be Line1 or Line2—check the manual.)
4. Switch the camera to Play (VCR) mode. Set the camcorder's controls for DV playback. (On the Canon ZR40, this involves pressing the Menu button and then changing the VCR SET UP option AV/PHONES to AV.)
5. Insert a blank VHS cassette in the VCR and rewind it fully.
6. Insert the recorded DV cassette in the camcorder. Make sure that it is rewound to the beginning of your movie.
7. Press the Record button on the VCR.
8. Wait a second or two for the VCR to gain speed; then press the camcorder's Play button.
9. VHS recording will begin. It will take exactly as long as the running time of your movie.

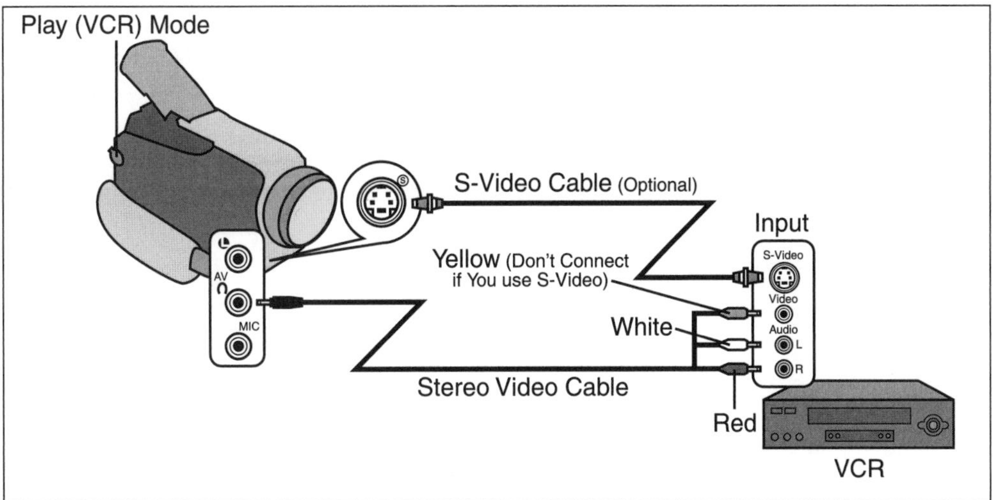

Figure 9.2

A camcorder AV cable, used for dubbing to a VCR, has a special three-contact mini plug on one end for insertion into the camcorder's AV output jack, and three RCA plugs on the other for insertion into the VCR input jacks. If both the camcorder and the VCR are equipped with S-Video jacks, use that video connection instead and leave the Yellow RCA plug disconnected at the VCR. (S-Video provides a higher-quality signal.) However, if you use S-Video, leave the Red and the White jacks connected for stereo sound. That's because S-Video carries only the video signal.

Burning a CD

An alternative to printing your movie to a DV cassette is to save it to a hard drive as a QuickTime full-quality DV movie file (File > Share > QuickTime > Full DV Quality). (Technically, full-quality DV is defined as 29.97 fps, 720 x 480 resolution, and high-quality 48*kHz* stereo sound.) You can then load a blank disc and simply drag and drop the file in the Finder to the CD icon on the desktop. This will create a full-resolution video that can be played back on any Mac with a QuickTime player, but the disc won't work in most DVD players and may be unreadable by some Windows PCs.

> **NOTE**
>
> For historical reasons that nobody understands or cares about, a magnetic computer storage device, such as a hard drive, is spelled d-i-s-k and the optical variety, such as a CD or a DVD, is a d-i-s-c. This distinction is so pointless, perhaps a decade from now there will be a single, standard spelling.

A typical CD can hold about 700MB—less than four minutes of full-quality DV. A DVD can hold about 4GB. So if your computer can burn CDs but not DVDs, either your movie must be fairly short, or you'll have to choose one of the QuickTime *compression* options, which reduces the quality of the movie and also the amount of storage required. The iMovie application has a CD-ROM output option that creates a file that's 20–30 times smaller than full-quality DV. However, it does this by printing every other frame (15 fps), providing $1/4$ the screen resolution (320 x 240), and, thankfully, leaving the stereo sound at CD quality (44.1kHz). This type of file will only play back on a computer that has a QuickTime player installed.

To create CD-ROM quality output in iMovie:

1. With the project open in iMovie, select File > Share from the menu bar. The output window will open.
2. Click the QuickTime icon.
3. In the Compress Movie For box, select CD-ROM (see Figure 9.3).
4. Click the Share button. The Save window will open.
5. Navigate to the folder on the hard drive where you want the movie file stored and click Save (see Figure 9.4). The compression process will start, and the window will close when file creation is complete.
6. Insert a blank disc into the drive burner. A window will open, prompting you to type a name for the disc and select an application. When you select Finder, a CD icon will appear on the desktop.
7. In the Finder, drag and drop the movie file onto the CD icon (see Figure 9.4).
8. Double-click the CD icon.
9. From the Finder menu bar, select File > Burn Disc > Burn. The Burn progress bar will open, and the process will be complete when it disappears (see Figure 9.5).

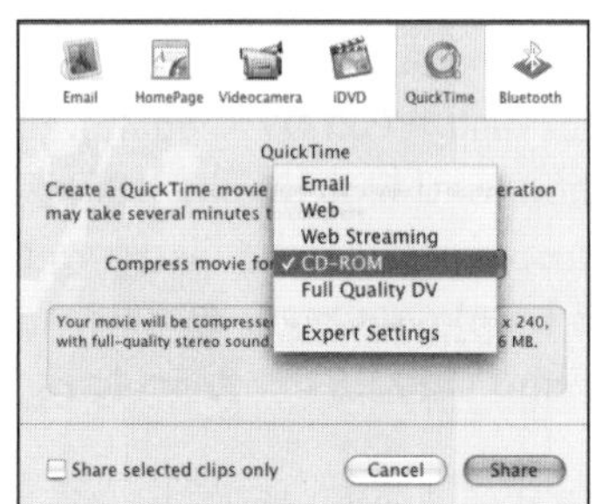

Figure 9.3

When you select File > Share > QuickTime, you'll find the option for CD-ROM output in the pop-up list.

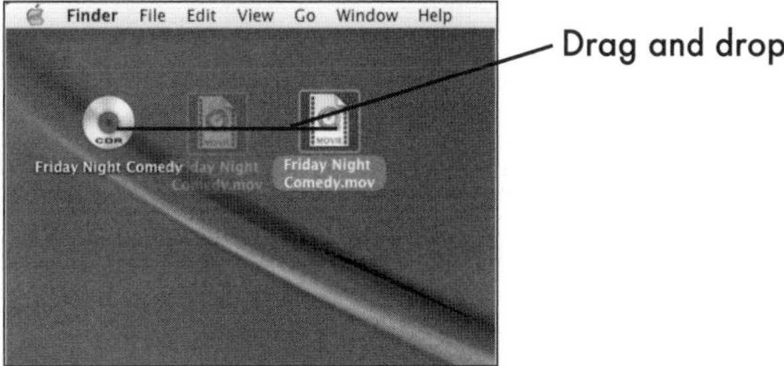

Figure 9.4

Use the Desktop as a temporary storage area for .MOV files you are about to burn to CD. That way you won't have to search through the hard drive directory looking for the file.

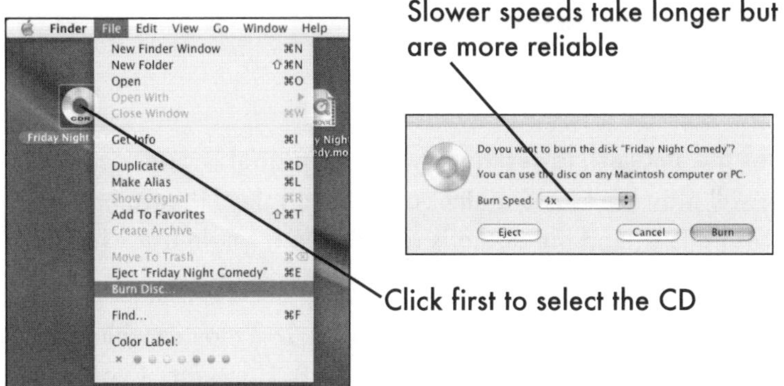

Figure 9.5

A blank disc inserted in the burner appears on the desktop as an icon. You can drag and drop any file on it, open it, and then select File > Burn Disc from the menu bar and start the operation by clicking the Burn button.

Creating a VCD

A special CD format called *Video CD (VCD)* can hold a little more than an hour of movie, which it achieves using *MPEG-1* compression. The resolution is about the same as QuickTime for CD-ROM. It's much less than full-quality DV. But the VCD format has the advantage of being compatible with many DVD players, as well as most computers.

To create a VCD, you will need an application like Roxio Toast Titanium. It has a plug-in for iMovie that permits you to output your movie directly to a disc in a conventional CD burner. With the plug-in installed, the File > Share procedure in iMovie is essentially the same as the one just described for QuickTime CD-ROM.

TIP

Most DVD drives are fast enough to play back a video directly from a CD. However, many CD drives aren't. If you load a CD into your computer and try to read it, the playback may be erratic. You'll see the video play for a while, stop for a moment while the drive catches up, and then resume. To avoid this problem, copy the entire video file to your hard drive first and then play back the file you created.

Creating Video Files for the Internet

When you select File > Share to output your project from iMovie, you actually have several choices for creating compressed QuickTime files. Full-quality DV is useful for archiving and mastering. CD-ROM is intended mainly for postcard-sized displays when playing back from a computer's local hard drive or over a high-speed network.

Even more compressed QuickTime options are:

- Email
- Web
- Web Streaming

Email. Of all the options, this one creates the smallest, lowest-quality files. The goal is compactness for sending as an email attachment that will play back as a matchbox-sized display. The frame rate is a rather jerky 10 fps, the resolution is 160 x 120, and the audio is reduced to a single track (mono). However, by this scheme, a three-minute movie can be squeezed into less than 2MB.

Web. Designed for posting on Web sites, this option produces 12 fps, 240 x 180 movies with medium-quality stereo sound. A three-minute movie compresses to about 4MB. However, if you post a video file to a Web site in this format, the user will have to download the entire file before it starts to play. Generally, people aren't that patient. The alternative is to use the Web Streaming option.

Web Streaming. This option delivers the same quality and compactness as Web, but adds compatibility with Internet servers that are specially designed to deliver video over lower-speed connections. Technically, the output process embeds *hints* in the QuickTime file that the QuickTime Streaming Server application can read. The hints are markers for starting and stopping the file transmission, doling it out in a series of *data bursts*, rather than as a continuous feed. If your Web hosting company supports streaming video (and many don't because it can overload their servers), they will probably require you to upload it in streaming format.

PRO TIP

There are actually quite a few more flavors of streaming Web files you can create with QuickTime. You've undoubtedly noticed streaming sites that offer three separate versions of videos—each *optimized* for a different network speed. If you select Expert Settings in the QuickTime Compress Movie For box, the options include optimized compressions for Modem—Audio Only, Modem, DSL/Cable (Low, Medium, or High speeds), or LAN (such as a T1 corporate network). Clicking the Options button lets you fine-tune the compression settings for frame rate, resolution, audio quality, and output file format. By manipulating the Expert Settings, you can even increase the output quality for a professional broadcast submission standard, such as DVCPRO50.

Authoring and Burning a DVD

As a video recording format, a DVD isn't like tape or like a CD-ROM—it's a different animal altogether. You can't just take a DV tape or movie file and copy it to DVD, as you can with a CD. (Actually, you can, but the result will be a *data DVD,* which will be playable only on a computer.)

The DVD format was designed about a decade ago as a kind of multimedia replacement for books. A DVD can store not only video, but also still pictures, digital music, and all kinds of audio files, as well as computer-generated documents and data files. What's more, a DVD can hold software programs that tell computerized players what to do with its content and how to react to choices users make. A computer-based DVD can even update its own content by accessing the Internet automatically, based on *hyperlinks* embedded in its programs.

Certainly, the full potential of the DVD medium hasn't been realized yet—and future generations of these devices are already being designed. There's no question—DVDs and their successor formats will play a major role in your life.

But futuristic speculation aside, as a media producer, you have to follow a special procedure to create a DVD that will play back reliably in both computers and set-top players.

A major difference between DVDs and tapes or CDs becomes apparent as soon as you insert one in a player. The movie doesn't start when you press Play. You see an on-screen menu instead. Each item on the menu represents a separate *chapter* on the DVD—and the term itself tells you that the designers of the DVD were thinking about the way books are organized.

In effect, each chapter is a separate movie. This book's companion DVD is organized that way—each chapter is a different short subject.

However, when all you want on your DVD is your lone movie project—the disc must still be divided into chapters. If you don't take pains to insert chapter *markers* in your movie then you'll end up with a one-chapter DVD.

TIP

You may have seen DVDs that play an entire movie just as soon as you insert them in the player. Achieving this behavior is actually somewhat more complicated technically than creating a menu with chapters. The disc must contain a program that's set to play automatically, to suppress the menu display, and to ignore any chapter markers that might exist in the movie.

Building the structure of a DVD, its clips, and its various optional behaviors is called *authoring* a DVD (notice it's another book publishing term). Although the authoring process can be quite complex, Apple has simplified it considerably by making iMovie work in close coordination with the iDVD application and by preselecting many of the more complicated choices for you.

PRO TIP

If your movie is no longer than 10 minutes or so, dividing it into chapters is probably unnecessary. The movie itself will be one chapter and one DVD menu item. But for longer movies, and especially for training videos, chapter organization can be very helpful to the user. So your first step in authoring a DVD should be to embed chapter markers in your movie. You do this while you're still working in iMovie. Ideally, chapter markers should come at act breaks. It will rarely make sense to embed a chapter marker in the middle of a scene—unless you've deliberately created a pause in the action for this purpose. To find act breaks, think about how television movies are interrupted for commercials. A perfect act break completes a scene, but leaves the audience eager to find out what happens next.

NOTE

DVDs typically use compressed video files in the *MPEG-2 variable bit rate (VBR)* format. Although the compression causes some loss of quality over the original DV recordings, it's usually not apparent to viewers.

To author a DVD using iMovie and iDVD :
(Skip Steps 1–5 if you don't want to insert chapter markers.)

1. With the project open in iMovie, click the iDVD button to open the iDVD Chapter Markers pane.
2. In the Timeline Viewer, move the playhead to the point at which you want to insert the marker.
3. Click the Add Chapter button.
4. A thumbnail of the first frame in the chapter will be inserted in the list. The title you gave the clip will appear in the Chapter Title text box. If you wish, type a new chapter title here (see Figure 9.6). (The iDVD application will pick up the title automatically as a menu selection.)

5. Repeat Steps 2–4 for each chapter that you want to appear in the DVD menu.
6. Click the Create iDVD Project button. The iDVD application window will open, overlaid on the iMovie window. An automatically generated DVD menu will appear. The title of your movie will be inserted as the main title in the menu. If you created chapter markers, you'll see two menu items: 1) Play Movie (which plays the entire movie without interruption) and 2) Scene Selections (which shows a submenu containing your chapter titles).
7. To select a different ready-made menu, click the Customize button. The Customize drawer will slide out to the left of the iDVD window, showing thumbnail selections of Themes. Scroll through the list and click the theme you prefer (see Figure 9.7). (Many of the themes have prebuilt animation and musical soundtracks. To modify how a Theme behaves, select the Settings button at the top of the Customize drawer, and change the options.)
8. To see the menu structure of your DVD, click the Map button. A chart of the menu and submenu with its scene selections will appear in the window (see Figure 9.8).
9. To see how your DVD will look to viewers, click the Preview button. The image of a remote control will appear. Click its controls to access the disc just as you would on a DVD player.
10. When you are satisfied with the options and menu structure you've created, insert a blank disc and click the Burn button. (The button will be dimmed if your Mac doesn't have a SuperDrive or if a blank disc isn't in it.)

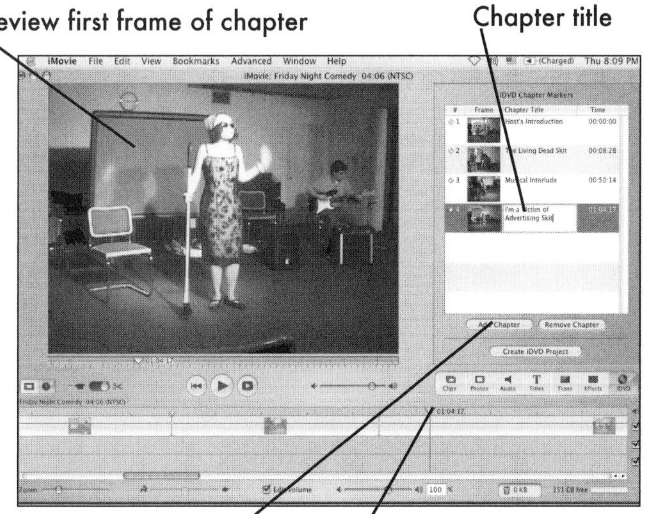

Figure 9.6

Chapter markers you insert at the playhead location in the timeline appear in a list in the iDVD pane. Rename them here with the titles you want displayed alongside the buttons in the DVD scene menu.

Figure 9.7

The Themes pane of the Customize drawer contains a variety of prebuilt animated DVD menus with musical soundtracks.

Figure 9.8

The DVD Map display shows the menu structure you've created. The AutoPlay module causes the main menu to be displayed. Clicking its Play Movie button will play the entire movie. Or clicking the Scene Selection button will display a menu of *branches* to individual chapters.

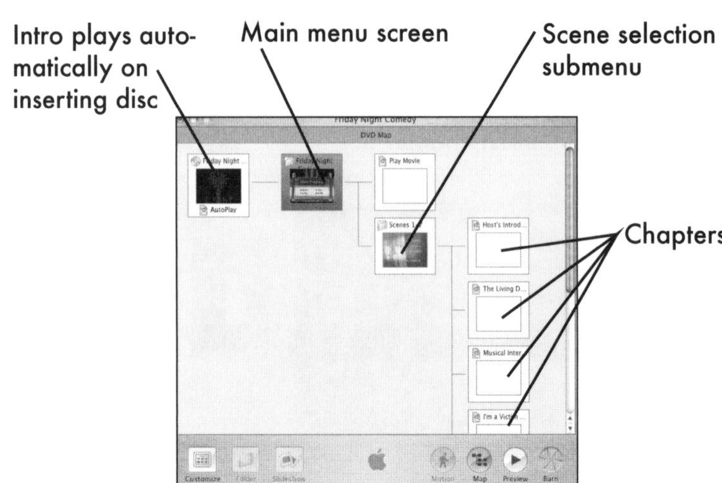

PRO TIP

Some of the prebuilt iDVD themes will appear with the text prompt "Drag Photos or Movie Here," which marks a *drop zone.* To insert media here that will be displayed on the menu, open the Media pane in the Customize drawer and drag media files from there into the drop zone (see Figure 9.9). Or drag files from the desktop or an open folder window in the Finder. When you drag a media file into the drop zone, you will see it surrounded by a dotted line. This indicates that the media will be displayed on the menu. If you drag and drop a media file into any other part of the DVD menu, a button will be created, permitting viewers to access or play the file by selecting that menu item.

Figure 9.9

Remember that a drop zone isn't a button. It's a place for a graphic display, which can be still or video, to illustrate a menu selection. If you drag a media file onto the menu and drop it outside a drop zone, a menu-item button linked to the file will be created instead.

Archiving Your Project

After you've output your movie to tape or disc, don't blow your project files off the hard drive just yet. While the .MOV file you create by printing to tape or saving to disk might be full-quality DV, it will serve you well as a duplication master, but it's not an editable version of your project. If you want to make changes later—adjusting scene in and out points, or incorporating ADR, for example—you'll have to load the original project files back into the editing program.

To assure that you can return to edit your project at some future date, you must archive the project and all its supporting files. An excellent and inexpensive storage medium is an external FireWire drive, as we've already mentioned. Another good high-capacity alternative is the online Internet storage available to you as an Apple computer user at www.mac.com. (A site that specializes in renting online storage is www.xdrive.com.)

The easiest and most reliable way to archive your project is to drag the project folder itself from the Movies directory and drop it on the open destination drive window in the Finder. That way, all your uploaded clips, audio files, digital stills, and other supporting files will go along for the ride. Opening the project folder and attempting to copy files individually or in groups risks breaking the data links among them. If that happens, it can be a real challenge to reconstruct the project (but it's not impossible). For that reason, we recommend backing up the entire folder in a single operation to a data storage area that's large enough to hold it. If the project is small, a single data DVD (4GB capacity) might work. But backing up files in groups to a series of CDs, while it's possible, might well cause unnecessary headaches later.

When the archiving is done, you're ready to delete the project file from your hard drive, fire up the word processor, and start writing your next script!

FROM THE DIRECTOR'S CHAIR

Speaking of screenwriting, formatting a script according to motion-picture standards can be a daunting task for a beginner. You can get so hung up in the placement of scene headings, character dialogue, and stage directions that you lose track of your story. Although you can learn to format a script in Microsoft Word or in AppleWorks, you don't need to work that hard. There's software specifically designed to help you format the script as you type. One program we particularly recommend is Final Draft, which is available for either Mac or Windows. We've included a demo copy on the DVD.

Because we provided an earlier version of Final Draft with some other books we wrote, we became acquainted with Frank Colin, Vice President of Product Development at Final Draft, Inc. Not long ago, Gerald met Frank at a trade show in Los Angeles, and they began talking. Frank was proud of the new version of another product they make called Final Draft AV. This program formats scripts differently, as two vertical columns, with video (shot descriptions) on the left and audio (narration and dialogue) on the right. *AV (audiovisual) format* is not as complicated as the motion-picture page, and it's preferred by professionals who make TV commercials and corporate videos.

Frank pointed out that, in India, AV is called *directors' format,* presumably because it's easier to scan down the left column, paying attention only to the video, to see the visual flow of the story. He also suggested that novice screenwriters who feel intimidated by motion-picture formatting should start out by using AV.

Conveniently for you as a screenwriter, and potentially profitably for Frank's company—Final Draft movie software can read Final Draft AV files and will convert them automatically into motion-picture format. After that, you need to do some tweaking, but the computer does a lot of the work.

No matter how you choose to do it, even if you just use a yellow pad and a pencil, put your original movie ideas into a script. Many Hollywood directors started as screenwriters. One reason they got the chance was because studio executives could see how they "directed on paper."

As an example of motion-picture formatting, the script of "Neo's Ring" is included on the DVD. You can also use it as a guide if you try to edit the raw clips we've provided for the park bench and chase scenes.

10 Going to the Next Level

If you're inclined to get serious about moviemaking, this chapter surveys the road ahead.

Having this information will help you think about career opportunities in the movie business. And, on a more practical level, it will help you appreciate what professional gear you might need and why, as well as how to get training and experience using it.

Learning How the Pros Work

A major difference between student and professional moviemaking lies in the way crews are organized. In general, professional crews have many more people than student and low-budget crews, and each of those people has a specialized function.

In fact, a big-budget movie crew could easily employ 100 people or more. We won't go into all the job descriptions here. We've listed the main ones in Table 10.1. This list of job categories is much the same as the production credits you'll see in a vertical crawl at the end of a movie.

Table 10.1 Below-the-Line Movie Crew for Full-Scale Production

Department	Job Title	Role
Production Staff	First Assistant Director (AD)	Scheduling, logistics, and cast/crew supervision
	Second AD	Cast supervision
	Script Supervisor	Continuity and script log
	Production Manager	Budgeting and hiring

(continued on next page)

Table 10.1 Below-the-Line Movie Crew for Full-Scale Production (continued)

Department	Job Title	Role
	Location Manager	Scouting and sets
	Production Designer	Visual design
	Catering	Meals
	Craft Services	Snacks and beverages
	Production Assistants (PA)	All-around help
Set Construction	Construction Supervisor	Boss of set builders
	Builders	Set carpentry
	Painters	Painting sets
Special Effects	Effects Supervisor	Explosions, weapons
	Technicians	Rigging of effects
Set Dressing	Decorator/Designer	Set appearance
	Set Dressers	Set decoration
Property	Prop Master	Managing props
	Prop Technicians	Handling props
Wardrobe	Costume Designer	Wardrobe appearance
	Dressers	Wardrobe assistance for actors
Makeup and Hairdressing	Lead Makeup Artist	Design of makeup effects
	Makeup/Hair Technicians	Makeup and hairdressing assistance for actors
Electrical Operations	Key Grip	Boss of grips
	Lead Gaffer	Boss of electricians
	Best Boy/First Assistant	Assistant to Lead Gaffer or Key Grip
	Rigging Gaffers	Installation of lines and cables

Department	Job Title	Role
	Generator Operator	Running portable electrical generator
	Lamp Operators	Maintaining movie lights
	Set Wiremen	Rigging assistant
	Grips	Moving equipment and setup
Camera Operations	Director of Photography (DP)	Camera and lighting supervisor
	Camera Operator	Hands-on cameraperson
	First Assistant Camera Operator	Focus puller
	Second Assistant Camera Operator	Camera and sound logs; custody of recording media
	Dolly Grip	Camera movement during takes
Sound Operations	Sound Mixer	Control of audio recording
	Sound Recorder	Audio recorder operator
	Boom Operator	Using boom pole during takes
	Rigging Technicians	Installation of audio cables on set
Transportation	Transportation Coordinator	Vehicle dispatcher
	Driver Captain	Vehicle fleet supervisor
	Drivers	Trucks and limos

Notice in the table that the jobs are grouped into separate departments. Just as in a business or a school, each department has its own reporting relationships. To make sure work gets done efficiently, each department has a supervisor and a chain of command.

Camera Operations

The creative hub of a production crew is the camera department. It typically has at least five highly skilled people:

- Director of photography (DP)
- Camera operator
- First assistant camera operator
- Second assistant camera operator
- Dolly grip

Director of Photography

Whether the movie is being shot on film or on video, the supervisor of the camera department is called the director of photography, or DP. This person is a cinematographer by training and is the director's main creative consultant on everything that will affect the images the audience will see on the screen.

Because he's responsible for both camerawork and lighting, the DP is actually in charge of electrical operations, as well. He tells the key grip where and how movie lights should be placed and rigged. Then the grips and gaffers go about the task of setting up for a shot.

Camera Operator

On a fully staffed camera crew, it's rare for the DP to go near the camera, except perhaps to look briefly through the viewfinder to check the framing of a shot. The hands-on camera operation is performed by the camera operator. She frames the shots, sets the exposure, and performs panning and tilting, if required, during takes.

First Assistant Camera Operator

One camera control the operator doesn't handle is focus. There's so much going on during a take, and precise control of focus is so crucial, that a separate technician stands beside the camera and operates its focus ring (see Figure 10.1). This person is the first assistant camera operator (or first camera assistant, for short), and another name for the same job is *focus puller*.

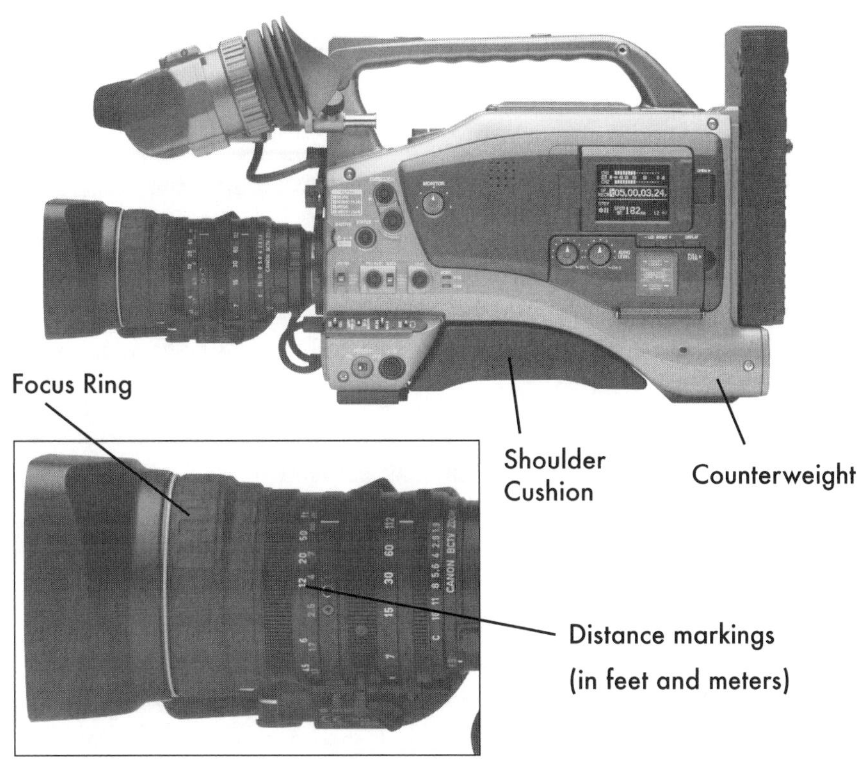

Figure 10.1

A cinema-style lens has a focus ring with distance markings by which the first assistant camera operator can make adjustments during a take without having to look through the viewfinder. For shooting news-style, a weight mounted at the back end of a camcorder helps counterbalance the heavy glass lens when the camera is held on the operator's shoulder. (Photo courtesy JVC Professional Products Company)

Second Assistant Camera Operator

Detailed recordkeeping is an important part of any professional shoot. The second assistant camera operator keeps the camera and sound log (refer back to Figure 5.15), noting the camera operator's comments about takes. She also labels the camcorder tapes (or film magazines) and any dual-system audio tapes. She is responsible for delivering completed log sheets and tapes to the editor. (On a film shoot, she also loads the camera film magazines and coordinates getting film to the lab for processing.)

Dolly Grip

As you'd expect, the dolly grip is the technician with his hands on the dolly, if there is one. He pushes the camera and its crew along the dolly track during a take. A related job is the crane operator, who raises and lowers the crane, if there is one, during a take. Both of these jobs are tougher than they look. The movement has to be just right—exactly what the director and DP want—and it must be smooth as glass.

Will You Shoot News-Style or Film-Style?

Shooting handheld with a camera crew of one is sometimes called shooting *news-style*. This style of shooting typically involves a television news cameraperson chasing fast-breaking action with a camcorder slung over his shoulder. News-style camera operators cover events as they happen, and they don't have much time to fiddle with camera controls. So some people call this less meticulous style running and gunning. Others call it shooting guerilla style.

A camera crew on a movie set shoots in carefully coordinated film-style. They set up each shot precisely, working with the grips to get the lighting just the way the DP wants it.

Matching the Camcorder to Your Shooting Style

Differences between news-style and *film-style* shooting show up in the design of different camera models. One way to spot a professional camcorder designed for film-style shooting is by its cinema-style lens (refer again to Figure 10.1). Film-style first assistants focus by distance, not by eye. Because a focus puller can't be looking through the viewfinder during a shot, she has to go by the distance markings on the focus ring of the lens. Working closely with the camera operator, she notes the correct focus setting during the rehearsal of the shot. However, even if the action takes a different improvised path, a professional focus puller will be able to follow it accurately—without ever having to look through the lens. Achieving this kind of control requires cameras equipped with lenses that have precise, repeatable mechanical adjustments and accurate distance markings.

Pro camcorders designed for news-style shooting typically have electronically controlled lenses that are sensitive to the speed of the operator's wrist movement. Since the camera operators don't have assistants, they prefer this type of lens because they can follow fast-breaking action easier while they're holding the camera and sighting through the viewfinder. News-style camera operators focus either by eye (while looking through the viewfinder) or by engaging the AF function briefly when fully zoomed in.

Another feature of a pro-model news camera used for news-style shooting is a weight at the back end that balances the heavy lens when you hold the camera on your shoulder (refer again to Figure 10.1).

Meet the Moviemaker's Power Tools

We've already mentioned that Final Cut Pro is a professional-level step up from iMovie. As you build your editing and postproduction skills, you'll begin to max out the capabilities of entry-level software such as iLife. When you find you need more extensive features in your tools, there are many good alternatives. But these programs are expensive. Here's where access to a school media lab can be a real advantage. They'll probably have many of the tools you need.

In recent years, software manufacturers have begun to offer video and audio postproduction applications as integrated suites. In a suite of applications, the programs have similar sets of controls, and they're designed to work together seamlessly. This arrangement is not only convenient, but it also reduces training time because you learn one set of menus and controls. If you've tried any of the iMovie features we described in Chapter 6, you've seen this kind of seamless integration at work. For example, when you select a music clip, iMovie opens iTunes automatically. When you select a photo, it opens iPhoto, and when you want to burn a DVD, it opens iDVD.

Two such video suites are offered by Apple and by Adobe. Apple's offerings for video and audio postproduction, which run exclusively on Macintosh computers, include the following:

- Final Cut Pro HD: video editing
- Motion: motion graphics
- Shake: compositing and visual effects
- Logic Pro: music composition and sound editing
- Soundtrack: loop-based music composition
- DVD Studio Pro: DVD authoring

We used Final Cut Pro to edit "Neo's Ring" and some of the other shorts on the DVD. And we used DVD Studio Pro to do the authoring, including the motion-effect menus and buttons.

If you want to use the full set of Adobe's video production applications, you'll need a Windows computer (although After Effects and Photoshop are available for the Mac). Adobe's integrated products for postproduction include the following:

- Premiere Pro: video editing
- After Effects: compositing and visual effects
- Audition: sound editing and loop-based music composition
- Photoshop CS: still photo editing and effects
- Encore DVD: DVD authoring

Of all the products listed here, Final Cut Pro and After Effects are the most popular. However, Avid's editing systems dominate in production companies, networks, and television stations. Avid software is manufactured by DigiDesign, which also makes ProTools, the most widely used professional audio editing software.

TIP

Professional-level editing software could cost you $1,000 or more. To ease your transition to the big leagues, the manufacturers have developed intermediate-level products. These are modestly priced, working versions of the higher-priced applications. Although they lack some features, you can edit video with them quite respectably. And most importantly, the menus and controls are the same. Obviously, they want to hook you on their way of doing things to hasten and ease your graduation to the full-featured product. These intermediate-level editing systems include Adobe Premiere Elements, Apple Final Cut Express, and Avid Free DV.

Avid Xpress DV and ProTools are available in either Mac or Windows versions. There's also a suite called Xpress PRO, which includes effects software. If you aspire to make editing your career, give serious consideration to learning Avid Xpress DV. Its menus and functions are designed to work the same as those in its larger corporate-level systems, Avid Media Composer and Avid Symphony.

What's Better Than DV? HDV Is Coming!

DV produces images that are roughly equivalent to 16mm film in quality. The video format more nearly like 35mm (theatrical) film is high definition (HD) video, which has four times as much detail as DV. In 2004, Sony announced it would market a camcorder in the new hybrid format that combines the image quality of HD with the economy of DV. It's called HDV. It records high-definition imagery on Mini DV cassettes. Technically, HDV doesn't have all the image detail of HD. It uses a type of MPEG-2 compression to fit all those pixels on a tiny cassette. Many other manufacturers have since announced that they will be introducing HDV camcorders and editing systems. The first HDV camcorder to appear on the market was the JVC GR-HD1 and then Sony introduced its HVR-Z1U.

Within the next few years, expect that most, if not all, prosumer camcorders will be able to record either HDV or DV at the flick of a switch. However, even with compressed files, HDV editing systems will require lots more processing power and storage capacity than DV does. Eventually, lower-priced consumer HDV camcorders will appear. For now, expect prosumer HDV camcorders to cost several thousand dollars. There's little doubt that, for its economy and high image quality, HDV will be the preferred format for low-budget feature filmmakers. More expensive HD gear will remain the choice for higher-budget productions.

Using HDV camcorders and editing systems won't be much different from DV, so you'll be able to use all the skills you've acquired.

For more information on the future of HDV surf to www.camcorderinfo.com.

Where to Get Training

You'll find it difficult, if not downright impossible, to develop professional level skills on your own. As you learn, you'll really benefit from the advice and guidance of an experienced instructor.

Trade schools, community colleges, and university extension programs offer semester-long, hands-on courses in directing, production, budgeting, cinematography, video editing, sound editing, and special effects. A typical course that goes beyond the basics usually takes about eight weeks. Call your local institution and request a course catalog, then pay a visit to check out the media lab. Fees vary considerably, and paying more doesn't necessarily mean you're getting better training. For example, a community college might charge just $35 per course plus lab fees. The same course as an evening class at a university could easily cost several hundred dollars.

If you want to gain experience with a particular software application, consult the manufacturer's Web site. There may be an online tutorial you can take. (Some colleges and universities are beginning to offer online instruction in programs they call *distance learning.*) To be successful in such a program, you need lots of motivation and self-discipline. And you won't have the advantage of having an experienced instructor looking over your shoulder.

> **TIP**
>
> If you are disciplined enough to train yourself, you can download demonstration versions of many editing and effects applications for free from the manufacturers' Web sites. The programs are disabled in some way, usually not permitting saving your project to disk or overlaying your images with the product logo. But you can learn and experiment to your heart's content. If you decide eventually to spend the money, your software installation is already done. Once you've paid online, the manufacturer will simply email you a code that unlocks the disabled features.

Software manufacturers and dealers offer intensive training courses, perhaps over a weekend. These tend to be expensive, and you don't get much practice in that short time. In our opinion, you'll gain more experience and get better instruction in a longer course.

You can learn a lot about the training resources available by surfing the Web. Here's a partial list to get you started:

- Adobe software training: www.adobe.com/products/premiere/training.html
- Apple software training: www.apple.com/software/pro/training
- Avid software training: www.avid.com/training/index.html
- Film schools and training programs: www.filmeducation.com, www.socapa.org

Going Commercial

Already bored with simply amusing your friends and family with your video productions? When you're ready to break into the mass media, here are some avenues:

Submit to film festivals. The competition is fierce, but it's worth a try. And most film festivals accept short subjects as well as features. You'll find a list of competitions at www.filmfestivals.com. And if you want help submitting your work, Without a Box, Inc. (www.withoutabox.com) will help you (for a fee).

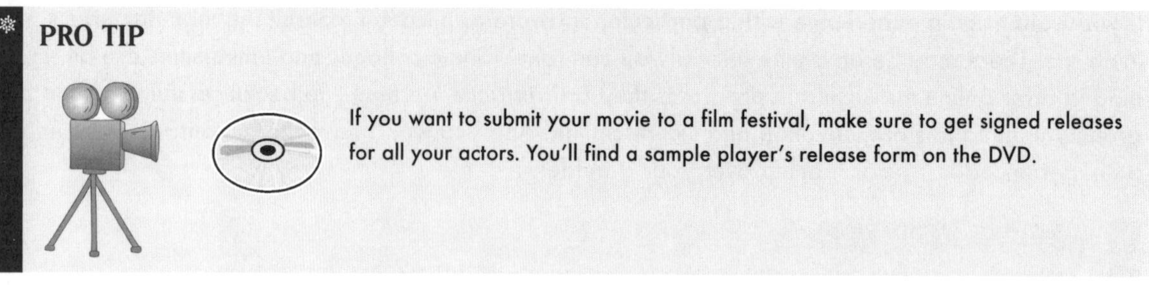

PRO TIP

If you want to submit your movie to a film festival, make sure to get signed releases for all your actors. You'll find a sample player's release form on the DVD.

Hustle your music videos. You can exhibit and sell your music videos in the electronic marketplace of the Web—right alongside the big bands. Two distribution sites that serve emerging artists are CD Baby (www.cdbaby.com) and MediaPal (www.mediapal.com). You can find more information on both services, as well as marketing tips, at www.musicbizacademy.com.

Exhibit your movie short on the Web. While it's possible to make money distributing original songs over the Web, online movie distribution is still in its infancy. Exhibiting your short subject on the Web might get you plenty of attention, but don't expect to get rich. Atom Films maintains a site where budding moviemakers can show their stuff: http://atomfilms.shockwave.com/af/home.

Get on public access TV. If you long to have your own TV show, it's easier than you think. You just can't expect to get paid. Call your local cable company to find out what training programs they offer for aspiring public access broadcasters. Types of programming offered on public access channels include talk shows, variety shows, and performance art.

Write a spec screenplay. One way to put your own story on the big screen is to put it on paper first and then peddle it to Hollywood producers. In general, no one in the industry will pay you to write your first successful screenplay. Instead, you'll write it on your own initiative, on speculation ("on spec"). Professional screenwriters have a strong union, the Writers Guild of America (www.wga.org), which forbids producers from contracting with a writer without paying for the work. But if it's your own story and you're working on your own—and not because a producer talked you into it—you're in good company. These days even the pros write spec scripts when they're between assignments. Just like you, they know that the best way of convincing the studios to fund their dream projects is to put them on paper. When you're ready to hustle your script, go to Inktip.com (www.inktip.com), which maintains an online marketplace for spec scripts. Your best shot at selling a script won't be to write a blockbuster. Limit the story to just a few characters and set it at a single location. If it's also a compelling story, producers of low-budget video movies will pay attention.

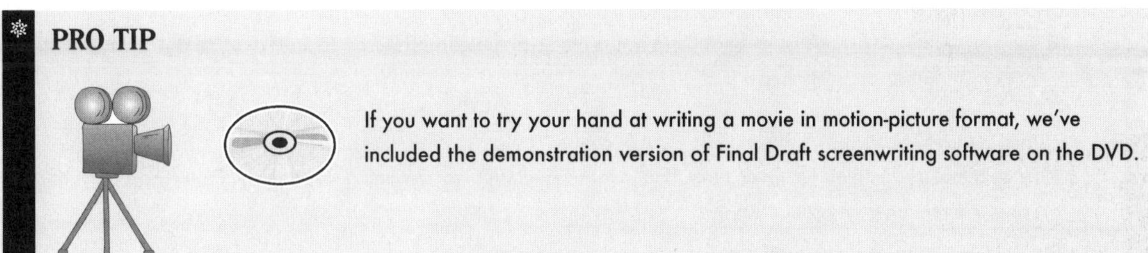

PRO TIP

If you want to try your hand at writing a movie in motion-picture format, we've included the demonstration version of Final Draft screenwriting software on the DVD.

Here's Your Big Send-Off

You now know enough to be truly dangerous.

If you've read through the book to this point, made and edited a short movie, and studied the techniques and examples on the DVD, you have much the same basic understanding and skills as the average film school graduate. You only lack hours of spirited discussion in student coffee lounges, vehement arguments over auteur theory (equating director and author of a movie), and a careful study of cinema history.

But you haven't spent a fortune on tuition, either.

Now, we're not saying don't go to film school or that film-school students are wasting their time. But, having mastered the basics of digital filmmaking, you don't need to wait for some prestigious institution to award you a degree. You know most of what it takes to go out and make serious movies. (Or wacky ones.)

And if you're not sure what to do next, here are a couple of suggestions. If you have an idea for a screenplay, count out 120 sheets of blank letter-sized paper. (That's just right for a feature-length script.) If you're itching to shoot a documentary or a music video, buy a blank DV cassette.

Put the stack of paper or the cassette someplace you can't help but see it every day.

Sooner or later, you'll get so frustrated that you'll have to put some words on the paper or some tracks on the cassette.

Make it sooner!

FROM THE DIRECTOR'S CHAIR

OR

HERE'S AN ASSIGNMENT

If neither a stack of empty pages nor a blank cassette inspires you to start your next project, we have another suggestion.

1. Pick a feature film you've never seen. Preferably, select an award-winning screenplay. (You'll find a list of past winners at www.oscars.org.)
2. Get your hands on a copy of the script. (Try Drew's Script-O-Rama at www.script-o-rama.com.)
3. Select a scene that runs three to five minutes.
4. Break it down, cast it, and shoot it in a day.
5. Still without looking at the movie, edit the scene.
6. Then, and only then, rent the movie DVD and see how the famous director handled the same scene.

Being able to compare your work with that of an A-list Hollywood director will teach you more than any film school can. And you'll have taken an important first step in discovering your own unique vision as a filmmaker.

Setting Up a Computer Editing System

We won't go into all the technical details involved in making your computer ready for video editing. Consult the helpful staff at your local computer store, get information from Apple's Web site and phone support, study one of the many books on iMovie, or seek out the overworked tech support person in your school's media lab. (Hint: Buy him a sandwich for his trouble!)

But we will offer some essential tips, many of which might be difficult to get unless you're talking to an experienced digital editor.

Computer Configuration

Make sure that your computer is configured according to the software manufacturer's specifications. For iMovie, you can find these at www.apple.com/support/imovie under the heading "iLife System Requirements." In particular, you'll want more than the minimum amount of computer memory. Apple says you need at least 256MB of physical RAM, but we'd recommend 512MB or more. (Read on to find out about hard-drive requirements, which can go well beyond what's listed.)

TIP

All newer Macs are configured to handle video. But, if you're outfitting a Windows-based system, there are more choices and more opportunities to get it wrong. A fairly safe bet is to get a so-called "multimedia PC," which is designed for video. For example, Sony Vaio PCs include the Vaio Suite, a software package much like iLife, which has a basic video editor.

Hard-Drive Requirements

If the total running time of all the clips you need to upload for a project is less than an hour, and your finished movie will run less than 10 minutes or so, don't sweat this part. An internal hard drive that can store at least 20GB will do nicely. After you've burned your finished movie to DVD or printed it to tape, back up the iMovie project file to CDs or an external hard drive, delete the project from your hard drive, and you're ready for the next one.

For longer video projects, always think of hard-drive capacity as needing two separate buckets—one for the program, the other for your data (video clips). When Apple says you need a minimum of 250MB for iMovie, that amount refers only to the first bucket and doesn't include *any* data storage space. (You actually need 4.3GB for the entire iLife suite, most of which is gobbled up by the GarageBand music application.)

Dealing with the second (data-storage) bucket is the one that frustrates many novice editors. In the first place, it really should be a separate storage area. Ideally, it should be on a separate drive, either a second hard drive installed inside your computer, or a plug-in external FireWire drive. (All recent Macs are equipped with FireWire ports.) Whether internal or external, its speed should be *7200 RPM* or greater. If you're using an external FireWire drive—as we recommend in Chapter 1—here's a tip you'll thank us for: Even if you're on a Mac, *order it formatted FAT32,* the default *Windows* standard. Why? Macs can read Windows FAT32 disks, but PCs can't read Mac-formatted disks. Whether you're a student or an indie (low-budget independent) filmmaker, chances are at some point you'll want to load your clips to a different computer, which might well be a Windows machine. This is good advice for students who might have to move from one computer to another in a school media lab, as well as for budding pros who need to take their projects to professional editing services.

TIP

If you need to use a Mac-formatted external drive with a Windows PC, download Mediafour MacDrive (www.macdrive.com). This software utility will enable the Windows operating system to "see" the drive. However, don't work directly with the drive for editing. The constant translation from Mac to PC can slow your computer down. Instead, copy the files to a PC-formatted drive first and create your new project folder there.

If you don't have a second hard drive, put the video data on a separate *partition,* a separate section of the same drive that the computer handles like a separate disk. *(Stop! Read the cautionary note in this appendix before you try to partition a disk.)* To find out how to partition your drive in Mac OS, in Finder, go to Help > Mac Help, type **partition** in the search box, and press Return. You should find a Help article titled "Partitioning a hard disk."

CAUTION

Partitioning a hard drive *completely and irreversibly erases* any programs or data already stored on the disk. So back up the entire disk first. Get technical assistance if you aren't used to doing this kind of thing, and be aware that you'll have to reinstall your application programs on the first partition.

Regardless of how you add a second drive, its capacity must be large enough to store at least all of the clips you shot for a single project, and then some. DV files eat up 13GB for every hour of uploaded video footage—or about 220MB per minute. Unless you're producing a feature film as your first project, an hour of video storage might seem like a lot. It's not. Remember what we said about shooting ratios in Chapter 5. Even a director who doesn't require many retakes will typically shoot about four times as much footage as the editor will eventually use. But especially as you're learning your craft, you could easily shoot 10:1 or more. In that case, editing a five-minute movie could require uploading 50 minutes of clips. You also need enough storage to hold your finished show and perhaps several versions of it. So if your project will eventually run five minutes, a 20GB hard drive—just for video data—is about as small as you can get away with. (These days, external FireWire hard drives cost about a dollar per gigabyte, and the new models start at 80GB.)

TIP

Some external hard-drive models (as well as some camcorders) support either of two types of data communication—FireWire or USB 2. Even if your computer has both types of ports, always use the FireWire for video data. When comparing products and features, remember that Apple FireWire, Sony iLINK, and IEEE 1394 are different names for the same type of DV data connection.

WINDOWS EDITING SOFTWARE

Unlike iMovie for Apple users, there isn't a single obvious software choice for Windows. There are many good products out there. If your computer came with video editing software, use it. Like word processing applications, the competing products all work much the same way, and most of the advice in this book still applies.

Besides the previously mentioned Sony Vaio Suite, video editing applications for the PC include AIST Movie DV, Avid Free DV, Digital Origin introDV, Microsoft Windows Movie Maker, Pinnacle Studio, Roxio Easy Media Creator, Sony Pictures Digital Vegas Movie Studio+DVD, and Ulead VideoStudio.

If you enjoyed using the demo version of Sonicfire Pro we've included on the DVD, you may be interested to know that the application is included at no extra charge when you purchase some editing applications, including Pinnacle Studio or Ulead VideoStudio.

If you have serious aspirations as a movie editor, consider that most of these entry-level products offer upgrades to professional-level software. For example, if you learn Avid Free DV (which is available for Mac or PC),

(continued on next page)

WINDOWS EDITING SOFTWARE (CONTINUED)

you'll feel right at home with the desktop and controls of its full-featured Avid Xpress product line. (Not all programs from a manufacturer share this similarity. Apple Final Cut Pro is very powerful, but it bears only a slight resemblance to iMovie.)

For basic editing, especially for your first projects, any of these applications will do the job. Differences lie mostly in what the software manufacturers call "look and feel." It's all a matter of what you get used to, and what you like. As you gain experience as an editor, you'll have stronger opinions about what you prefer in a more powerful program. When you start out as a filmmaker, it's better for you to do hands-on editing with any program rather than spend your time reading books or taking courses on how to use advanced editing software.

Whichever software product you select, be guided by the manufacturer's specifications when configuring hardware. And remember that you'll probably want more memory and disk-storage space than they recommend.

Again, PCs have to be configured just right to support video. For example, some recent model PCs don't have FireWire ports for connecting to your camcorder and external hard drive, so don't assume these features are built-in. Even then, you might invest in an add-on FireWire card for your PC, only to find that the computer's performance is too slow to support it.

In Chapter 1, we suggested you use an external FireWire drive to hold your clips. However, since many computers (including the iBook) have just one FireWire port, how can you capture clips and write them to the external drive at the same time?

Probably the most reliable solution is to purchase a FireWire hub, which costs about $50. One side of the hub plugs into the FireWire port on the computer. The other side has connections for multiple FireWire devices, such as camcorders and drives.

Without a hub, you can "daisy-chain" your FireWire connection. Most external FireWire drives have at least two FireWire jacks. Plug the external drive into the computer and then plug the camcorder into the second jack on the drive. The iMovie application will detect both the drive and the camcorder. When you start a new iMovie project, select a folder on the external drive. Your clips will then be uploaded from the camcorder to the external drive, where the entire project will be stored.

NOTE

Even if you use the computer's hard drive, you'll want to archive your project to an external disk or tape drive when you're done. Then you can delete the project from the computer disk so you're ready to start the next one. Be careful when copying video projects from one drive to another. Always copy the entire project folder—the starred file folder shown in the Movies folder. If you copy media files individually, you could break necessary links to the iMovie application support files, making it difficult to rebuild a workable version of your project.

References

Here's a convenient listing of the books, DVDs, movies, and Web sites mentioned in the book, as well as a few others you may find useful. If you don't find the information you want in these resources, visit our Reader Support pages at www.lapuerta.tv or send email to info@lapuerta.tv.

Books

Egri, Lajos, *The Art of Dramatic Writing* (New York: Touchstone/Simon and Schuster, 1960)

Gabler, Neal, *An Empire of Their Own: How the Jews Invented Hollywood* (New York: Doubleday Anchor, 1988)

Hunter, Lew, *Lew Hunter's Screenwriting 434* (New York: Perigee/Penguin Putnam, 1995)

Shaner, Pete and Gerald Everett Jones, *Real World Digital Video,* Second Edition (Berkeley: Peachpit Press, 2004)

Koppelman, Charles, *Behind the Seen: How Walter Murch Edited Cold Mountain Using Apple's Final Cut Pro and What This Means for Cinema* (Indianapolis: New Riders Press, 2004)

Rodriguez, Robert, *Rebel Without a Crew: Or How a 23-Year-Old Filmmaker with $7,000 Became a Hollywood Player* (New York: Plume/E. P. Dutton, 1996)

DVD Collections

Directors, The: The Essential DVD Collection (Los Angeles: Fox Lorber, 2001)

Wilson, Michael Henry (dir.), Personal Journey with Martin Scorsese Through American Movies, A (Burbank: Miramax, 1995)

Movies

28 Days Later, directed by Danny Boyle (2003)

Apocalypse Now, directed by Francis Ford Coppola (1979)

Bowling for Columbine, directed by Michael Moore (2002)

Civil War, The, TV mini-series, directed by Ken Burns (1990)

Close Call for Boston Blackie, A, directed by Lew Landers (1946)

Cold Mountain, directed by Anthony Minghella (2003)

English Patient, The, directed by Anthony Minghella (1996)

Fahrenheit 9/11, directed by Michael Moore (2004)

Gangs of New York, directed by Martin Scorsese (2002)

Gladiator, directed by Ridley Scott (2000)

Hamlet, directed by Kenneth Branagh (starring Branagh, 1996)

Hamlet, directed by Franco Zeffirelli (starring Mel Gibson, 1990)

Hamlet, directed by Laurence Olivier (starring Olivier, 1948)

Harry Potter and the Sorcerer's Stone, directed by Chris Columbus (2001)

Jaws, directed by Steven Spielberg (1975)

Lethal Weapon, directed by Richard Donner (1987)

Lord of the Rings: The Fellowship of the Ring, The, directed by Peter Jackson (2001)

Love Story, directed by Arthur Hiller (1970)

MacGyver, TV series, created by Lee David Zlotoff (1985–1992)

Matrix, The, directed by Andy Wachowski and Larry Wachowski (1999)

Men in Black II, directed by Barry Sonnenfeld (2002)

Pretty Woman, directed by Garry Marshall (1990)

Princess Diaries, The, directed by Garry Marshall (2001)

Roger & Me, directed by Michael Moore (1989)

Star Wars: Episode II—Attack of the Clones, directed by George Lucas (2002)

Web Sites

Academy of Motion Picture Arts and Sciences www.oscars.org

Adobe software training www.adobe.com/products/premiere/training.html

American Film Institute (AFI) www.afi.com

Apple software training www.apple.com/software/pro/training

Atom Films (e-distributor) atomfilms.shockwave.com/af/home

Avid software training www.avid.com/training/index.html

B&H Photo (gear and supplies) www.bhphotovideo.com

BeachTek (audio adapters) www.beachtek.com

Camcorderinfo.com (camera technology) www.camcorderinfo.com

CD Baby (online music distribution) www.cdbaby.com

Craigslist (classified ads for used gear) www.craigslist.org

Drew's Script-o-Rama, www.script-o-ram.com

Famous Frames, Inc. (storyboard artists) www.famousframes.com

Film Festivals (listing) www.filmfestivals.com

Film Music Magazine www.filmmusicmag.com

Film Education.com (film school directory) www.filmeducation.com

Filmmaker.com (forms and tips) www.filmmaker.com

Final Draft, Inc. www.finaldraft.com

Gee Three (iMovie plug-ins) www.geethree.com

Internet Movie Database www.imdb.com

Independent Feature Project www.ifp.org

International Documentary Association (IDA) www.documentary.org

.Mac (online storage) www.mac.com

Media Access Project (free-speech issues) www.mediaaccess.org

Media Pal (online media distribution) www.mediapal.com

Music Biz Academy.com (online music distribution) www.musicbizacademy.com

Netflix (DVDs) www.netflix.com

School of Cinema and Performing Arts www.socapa.org

Screen Actors Guild www.sag.org

Shure, Inc. (audio gear) www.shure.com

SmartSound, Inc. (Sonicfire Pro) www.smartsound.com

Sound Hunter (sound effects) www.soundhunter.com

Storyboard Quick! (software) www.storyboardartist.com

Studio 1 (audio gear) www.studio1productions.com

U.S. Library of Congress (copyright information and forms) www.loc.gov/copyright

Without a Box, Inc. (film festival submission service) www.withoutabox.com

Writers Guild of America www.wga.org

InkTip (writer-to-producer online mart) www.inktip.com

X Drive (online storage) www.xdrive.com

Glossary

A

above-the-line—Motion-picture budget category that includes high-priced creative talent, including director, writer, and starring actors.

amplification—Process in audio equipment that boosts the volume, or level, of the signal.

aperture—Variable opening in a camera that controls exposure; iris.

aspect ratio—Width of a film or video frame divided by its height. The aspect ratio of standard TV (SDTV) is 4:3. High-def (HDTV) uses the widescreen 16:9 format.

audio perspective—Apparent distance of the subject from the listener or microphone, as perceived by the audience.

audiovisual (AV) format—Two-column page formatting for movie scripts that puts video (shot descriptions and action) on the left, audio (dialogue, music, and sound effects) on the right; director's format.

automated dialogue replacement (ADR)—Rerecording of synchronous-sound dialogue during postproduction; dubbing; looping.

automatic scene detection—Feature of editing software that automatically creates a separate video clip file for each take during the continuous uploading of a camcorder cassette recording.

B

backlight—In a classic three-point lighting scheme, a light source coming from in back of the subject that serves to separate it from the background and add depth to the shot.

backtiming—Sound editor's technique of timing backward in a music clip from the desired cue to determine the starting point.

below-the-line—Motion-picture budget category that includes non-star cast and crew.

bin—In an editing system, holding area for clips that haven't yet been inserted into the assembly or timeline.

block—In loop-based music composition software, a modular music clip; in acting, to plot actor's movements on a stage or playing area during a scene.

blown-out—Area of a video frame that is totally overexposed, or 100 percent white.

bounce—To light a subject by reflecting light off a surface, such as a wall, ceiling, or reflector.

breakdown—Decomposition of a movie script into its elements, such as actors, locations, and props.

breaker panel—Electrical control box that prevents overloading of circuits by breaking the connection to the power source.

C

C-47—Gaffer's term for a common wooden clothespin. (Movie lights get hot enough to melt the plastic kind.)

C-stand—Multipurpose piece of hardware used by movie grips to hold silks, flags, boards, and other devices on the set.

call sheet—First assistant director's list of cast and crew assignments and instructions for each shooting day.

camera and sound log—Written record of the takes, by timecode, on each DV cassette and audio tape recorded on the set; daily editor's log.

camera angle—Position of the camera in relation to the subject: low, neutral, or high.

camera movement—Any of several ways of moving the camera during a shot, such as panning or tilting.

chapter—Content subdivision on a DVD; menu item.

charge-coupled device (CCD)—Image-sensing chip in a camcorder.

checkerboarding—Separating dialogue clips for each actor onto different audio tracks for editing. Also, separation (extraction) of any tracks, whether audio or video, for editing.

chroma key—Compositing technique that substitutes the pixels from a second image for every instance of the key color in the original image.

cleaning—Sound-editing process of reducing noise in audio clips.

cliffhanger—Movie act break that leaves the audience hanging, curious to find out what happens next.

color balance—Adjustment of lighting or camcorder settings to achieve realistic-looking color overall in an image.

color cast—Undesirable tint in a video image.

combination—In stunt fighting, a short sequence of punches shot during a single take.

compositing—Video postproduction process that combines one or more images with another.

compression—Processing of data by computer to describe it with fewer bits to save storage space and transmission time.

conflict—Essential element that lends tension and interest to a dramatic story, such as a fight or an argument.

continuity—Logical flow of visual imagery that tells a story.

coverage—Adequate selection of shots an editor needs to assemble a screen story.

craft services—On a movie set, a department that provides snacks and beverages.

crane—Large lever-action device for raising or lowering the camera and its operator during a take.

crop—In video editing, to trim a clip by resetting its in and out points.

cross dissolve—Video editing term for a movie dissolve, which creates a time-lapse transition between scenes.

cue card—Printed copy of actors' lines held beside the camera as a way of prompting them during a take.

cueing—In editing, determining the exact point at which an effect, such as music or sound effect, will be inserted; in directing, signaling for an action to start.

cutaway—An edit that diverts attention from the preceding shot or that refocuses audience attention with a different shot.

cutter—Hollywood term for a film editor.

D

daisy chain—To connect digital devices to a computer by plugging one into another in a series, or chain, ending in a single input rather than by connecting them separately.

day-for-night—Shooting a night scene during the day by placing a dark filter over the camera lens.

daylight—Blue-tinted light cast by the sun.

depth of field–Distance over which a particular camera lens remains in focus.

desaturated–Lacking intense color; washed out.

diffusion–Scattering of light to make it softer by means of a silk or other translucent material.

digital matte–Image used to create a choma-key effect.

digital video (DV)–Recording format for capturing standard-definition television on magnetic tape.

digital zoom–Magnification of an image electronically (by manipulating pixels) rather than with a lens.

director's cut–Edited version of a movie that has been approved by the director.

director's format–Audiovisual (AV) script format.

dirty single–Actor's closeup, or single, in which part of the profile of another actor in the scene is included in the frame.

distance–Measurement in feet between the camera lens and the subject.

distortion–Amplification of an audio signal to a level at which it ceases to sound pure, or faithful, to the source.

dolly–Movable camera mount that glides along a track.

dolly counter-zoom–Shot that dollies in while zooming out, or vice versa, such that the framing of the subject doesn't change.

double tracking–Rerecording that permits a vocalist to accompany herself.

downbeat–First beat of a musical measure.

drama–A story that involves conflict between people over something valuable that they each want.

drop zone–In a DVD menu, an area of the image that may contain a photo or a movie clip.

dropped frame–Video error caused by skipping of one or more frames during a DV upload, usually caused by the computer not being fast enough to keep up with the video frame rate.

dual system sound–On a movie set, recording of dialogue on a separate audio tape device rather than in the camcorder.

dub–To replace dialogue in postproduction; to make a copy of an analog audiotape or videotape.

duration–Running time of a video or audio clip; length of time from the in point to the out point of a clip.

dynamic mic–Type of microphone that senses sound by the movement of a metal diaphragm within a magnetic field.

E

effect—Part of a movie experience not recorded on the set but added later in postproduction; visual effect; sound effect.

engine of comedy—In a movie plot, an ongoing clash of personalities that generates recurring humor.

establishing shot—Image that introduces the audience to a new location or that orients them to the scene that follows.

extract audio—In video editing, to separate the audio portion of a video clip and place it on a separate track in the timeline.

eye line—Imaginary line that shows where an actor appears to be looking, whether into the camera lens or at another actor or object in the shot.

eyelight—When lighting a closeup, a small spotlight aimed at the actor's eye to add sparkle and personality.

F

f-stop—Numeric index of camcorder aperture size, typically ranging from f1.6 (widest opening) to f/16 (narrowest opening).

fade in—Visual effect, usually at the opening of a movie, by which the first scene appears gradually out of darkness.

fade out—Visual effect, usually at the end of a movie, by which the last scene disappears gradually into darkness.

fill—In classic three-point lighting, an overall light that fills in shadow areas caused by the key light.

film look—Technical choices and effects added to video to make it look like a projected film image.

FireWire—Apple product name for IEEE 1394 high-speed data link for transferring DV; Sony iLINK.

flag—Opaque material, such as a sheet of black felt mounted on a metal frame, used to block a light source from hitting the subject.

focal length—Characteristic of a camera lens indicating the distance from it at which a subject can be in focus. Focal length can affect the perception of a scene because it's related to field of view (how much of the scene appears within the frame). More of the scene will be visible in a wide shot, much less in a telephoto shot. A normal shot sees approximately what the unaided human eye would see.

focus—Degree of sharpness of an image.

Foley walker—Postproduction audio technician who performs live sound effects, such as walking and hitting; Foley artist.

frames per second (fps)—Rate of frame capture or display: 30 fps for video (North American standard) and 24 fps for motion-picture film.

framing—Adjustment of camcorder that determines the boundaries of the image and how much of the subject appears in the shot.

G

gaffer—Electrician on a movie crew.

gaffer's tape—Movie crews' term for cloth adhesive tape (much like duct tape).

grip—Movie crewmember who moves things, such as camera or lights.

guide track—In editing, a temporary audio track used as a reference for synchronizing dialogue, music, or sound effects to the video.

H

handle—In editing, extra running time before the in point or after the out point of a clip, used to provide time for fades and dissolves.

hard light—Light source that shines with a glare and produces sharp-edged shadows.

head—Starting point of a clip or a recording; electrical device within a camcorder that puts signals on magnetic tape.

high angle—Position of camera above the subject.

hint—Digital marker in a streaming video file by which Web servers can divide it into segments for transmission.

hyperlink—In a computer text document, encoded text that indicates the location of a file or digital object on a network, permitting the user to access the object by clicking on the text.

I

image stabilization—Digital or mechanical means in a camcorder that minimizes the effect of jarring during a shot.

in point—In editing, timecode at which a clip begins.

in-betweening–In digital postproduction, process that generates the action or motion that occurs between two specified key frames.

insert–An extreme closeup of a significant object, such as a newspaper headline, intercut with a scene.

intercut–To insert a shot within a scene that comes before and after it; or, to cut back and forth between two scenes.

interlaced–A scheme of subdividing a video frame into two fields of alternating scan lines.

interpolation–In a camcorder or other digital device, to calculate an intermediate value, such as determining a shade of gray that lies between white and black.

iris–See aperture.

J

jitter–Jerky screen image produced by movie projectors when running film with worn sprocket holes.

jump cut–An edit that transports the audience suddenly to another location or that joins shots that don't have matching action or continuity.

K

Ken Burns effect–Transition effect for digital stills in iMovie that applies variable pan-and-scan or pan-and-zoom, named for the famous documentary filmmaker.

key frame–In digital editing and postproduction, an image that specifies the starting point or the ending point of an effect.

key grip–On a movie crew, the top lighting technician who works closely with the lead gaffer.

key light–In classic three-point lighting, the primary light source, used to highlight the subject.

kicker–A source in addition to three-point lighting that gives an extra highlight to the subject. It's angled on the subject from behind or above and typically is even brighter than the key light.

L

lap dissolve–In editing, a particularly slow dissolve, indicating a leisurely or lengthy transition.

lavaliere (lav)–Tiny microphone designed to be worn in the subject's clothing or hair.

LCD screen–Display screen that folds out of a camcorder; liquid crystal display.

Letterbox—Widescreen aspect ratio, such as the 16:9 used for high-definition television (HDTV).

lighting theory—Study of effects of various light sources on video and film images.

locked audio—Audio recording, such as dialogue, that's in sync with video, such as lip movements.

locked picture—Approved final cut of a movie that's ready for music scoring and to which no further changes will be permitted.

loop—Prerecorded music clip, such as a drum track; to perform ADR.

low angle—Position of camera below the subject.

luminance key—Using a white, black, or gray area instead of a color as the key for a digital matte.

M

mark—On a movie set, to indicate the actor's required position on the floor with strips of tape; spike.

marker—In DVD authoring, a point on the timeline that indicates the start of a chapter.

master scene—A recording of an entire scene from beginning to end, used by the editor as a guide for intercutting other shots.

matching action—Continuity of subjects' motion and screen direction from one shot to the next in an edited sequence so that the result looks like a single, continuous motion.

mic—Short for microphone.

mit out sound (MOS)—Old Hollywood term for shooting silently, supposedly derived from the commands of German émigré directors. (*Mit* means "with" in German.)

mix—In sound editing, to overlay one audio track with another.

motion-picture format—Screenplay page format preferred by movie studios, partly because it helps producers do breakdowns.

motivate—To make the audience think the lighting in a scene occurs from a source they can see, such as window or a lamp, in the shot.

MP3—One of the common digital file formats for music.

MPEG-1—Video compression scheme, typically used for VCDs, that uses a fixed bit rate.

MPEG-2—Video compression scheme, typically used for DVDs, that uses variable bit rate, depending on the amount of detail in the picture.

multiple camera—The practice of shooting a scene from several viewpoints using several cameras at the same time.

mute—Reduce audio level to zero; silence.

N

neutral—Camera angle on the same level with the subject.

no good (NG)—Notation in a camera log marking a bad take that needn't be uploaded or used; not OK.

O

objective—In acting, the result a character wants to achieve in a scene.

off mic—Low-level audio resulting when an actor turns away from the microphone.

optical zoom—In a camcorder, magnification of an image by means of the lens, rather than electronically.

optimize—In digital processing, to tailor the size and quality of a file, such as a video clip, to a distribution medium, such as broadcast television or the Web.

out point—In editing, timecode at which a clip ends.

overlay—To superimpose one audio clip on another (mix) or a video title on a background.

P

pacing—Speed and timing of events in a movie.

pan—To pivot the camera horizontally during a shot, usually by swiveling it to the right or left on a tripod.

peak—In sound editing, the highest point, or maximum level, on an audio waveform.

phantom power—External voltage required for certain types of microphones.

photocell—In electronics, a silicon chip that reacts to light by emitting electrical signals.

playhead—In editing, the point on the timeline at which the next edit or effect will be inserted.

playlist—List of music clips in the order in which they will be played back.

plot—In a screen story, the characters' sequence of actions.

point of view (POV)—Movie effect by which the audience sees what one of the characters is supposed to be seeing.

presence—Sound of a quiet movie set; room tone.

prosumer—Referring to production gear that is professional in some features but offered at a consumer-level price.

public access programming—Government requirement on cable companies to provide air time inexpensively to the general public on a nondiscriminatory basis.

R

radial—In editing, a circular transition effect; circular wipe.

release form—Signed legal document permitting the filmmaker to use recordings of a person's image or voice.

render—In video editing, to generate finished-quality imagery for output.

reverse angle—To turn the camera to look back in the other direction (almost 180 degrees), as when shifting from one over-the-shoulder shot on an actor to focus on the other actor.

rig—Gaffer's term for arranging and connecting equipment on the set.

room tone—Sound of a quiet movie set; presence.

rough cut—Editor's early version of an assembled movie.

S

safe action area—Rectangular region within a video frame in which action should take place to avoid being cut off at edges by television receivers.

safe title area—Rectangular region within a video frame in which titles should appear to avoid being cut off at edges by television receivers.

scanning mode—Scheme of capturing a video frame either in a single pass (progressive scanning) or by means of two fields with alternating sets of scan lines (interlaced scanning).

scene—Portion of a script that takes place at a single location in one continuous time period, usually composed of a series of related shots, representing a significant step in the plot.

score—Original music composition for a movie soundtrack.

scratch track—Temporary music track built from prerecorded clips used during editing and test screenings until the original score is completed.

screen direction—Description of the subject's movement in relation to the frame—left, right, neutral, up, or down.

screen story—A dramatic story suitable for a movie, told visually.

sequence—An assembled series of related shots or scenes.

setup—Particular placement of camera and lights on a movie set.

shiny board—Reflective surface used to redirect light (usually sunlight) on a movie set.

shortie—Handheld dynamic microphone used by vocalists and interviewers.

shot design—Director's planned visual composition for a take, involving such choices as lens, lighting, framing, camera angle, and so on.

shot list—Director's breakdown of all shots required for a specific setup.

shotgun mic—Highly directional boom microphone.

silk—Translucent material used to soften light.

single—Closeup.

single camera—Film-style shooting involving one camera used in a series of setups.

sneak in—In sound editing, to fade up gradually.

soft—Out of focus; blurred.

soft light—Diffuse light that does not cast sharp shadows.

spike—To mark actors' positions on the set with tape; mark.

split edit—In editing, cutting video and audio at slightly different times.

splitter cable—Wire that divides a single output into two separate lines.

stage blood—Liquid makeup made to simulate bleeding from wounds.

stinger—Gaffer's term for an electrical extension cord.

stopped down—Reduced exposure level; increased f-stop setting.

story line—Main plot of a screenplay, usually the sequence of the main character's actions.

story sequence—Order of scenes as they appear in the script, as opposed to the different order in which they might be shot.

storyboard–Graphic depiction of a screen story as a series of still frames. It's a kind of graphic novel or comic-strip version of the story.

streaming–Video clip optimized for broadcast as a series of data bursts over a network.

string-out–Editor's preliminary assembly of a movie.

super–To overlay titles on an image; superimpose.

surround sound–Dolby Laboratories technology for reproducing three-dimensional audio.

S-Video–Analog video in which luminance (Y) and chrominance (C) signals are transmitted on separate lines; Y/C video.

sync–Matched timing of video and audio; synchronization.

T

tail–End of a video or audio clip.

take–On a movie set, one attempt to capture a shot.

test roll–Videotape recording shot to evaluate lighting and color choices, camera settings, or other technical concerns.

three-point lighting–Classic Hollywood lighting scheme employing key light, fill light, and backlight.

thumbnail–Small-sized preview image.

tilt–To swivel a camera up or down during a take.

time bending–To speed up or slow down the action to alter the audience's perception of time.

time fuse–Screen story technique involving jeopardy or a threat that must be averted before a deadline.

timecode–Numeric index used by camcorders and video recorders to mark running time; code composed of hours, minutes, seconds, and frames: HH:MM:SS:FF.

timeline–In editing software, horizontal scale that indicates running time.

track–In editing software, a horizontal segment of the timeline reserved for video or for audio; in a DV cassette, the recording path for each channel (video or audio) on the tape.

trim–In video editing, to mark the in and out points of a clip; crop.

truck–Camera movement during a take that follows alongside a moving subject or parallel to the subject.

tungsten—Type of incandescent lighting from lamps with wire filaments that has a characteristic orange color cast.

TV safe area—Rectangular region of a video frame that contains the safe action and safe title areas.

twirl—Spiraling transition effect.

two-shot—Framing of two actors in conversation, usually in a medium shot.

U

upload—To transfer a recorded clip into a computer.

V

variable bit rate (VBR)—MPEG encoding scheme by which the data rate varies according to the complexity of the video picture—slower to capture more detail, faster to capture less.

vertical crawl—Motion effect for movie titles and credits.

Video CD (VCD)—Videodisc recording scheme that puts MPEG-1 video recordings on CDs.

voiceover (VO)—Unseen narration.

volume level—Loudness of an audio clip.

W

waveform—Graphic representation of an audio clip as sound waves.

white balance—Camcorder or postproduction adjustment that sets all colors in the image in relation to pure white.

wild—Recording of sound effect without picture.

windscreen—Foam-rubber guard for microphones that reduces wind noise.

wipe—Transition effect that appears to slide one image over another.

Z

zebra bars—Camcorder feature that displays stripes within overexposed areas in the viewfinder.

zoom—To magnify an image, either digitally or optically.

Index

D

F

G

H

Q

R

U

V

W

X

Z

COURSE TECHNOLOGY

Professional ■ Trade ■ Reference

Write, direct, produce, shoot, edit, distribute, tour with, and sell your own no-budget DIGITAL movie!

We're entering a new era. Mini-DV filmmaking is the new folk, the new punk rock, the new medium where anyone can tell his story. *$30 Film School* is an alternative to spending four years and a hundred thousand dollars to learn the trade. It is influenced by punk rock's Do-It-Yourself spirit of just learning the basics and then jumping up on a stage and making a point, and by the American work ethic back when it was pure, before it became all about corporations crushing the little guy. Throw in the hacker idea that information wants to be free (or at least very cheap) and you've got our deal. Inside you'll find many interviews from insightful independent filmmakers and artists, as well as a host of practical advice, knowledge, and resources.

$30 Film School

ISBN: 1-59200-067-3 ■ $30.00